Revolutionary Moments

Textual Moments in the History of Political Thought

Series Editors
J. C. Davis, Emeritus Professor of History, University of East Anglia, UK
John Morrow, Professor of Political Studies, University of Auckland, New Zealand

*Textual Moments* provides accessible, short readings of key texts in selected fields of political thought, encouraging close reading informed by cutting-edge scholarship. The unique short essay format of the series ensures that volumes cover a range of texts in roughly chronological order. The essays in each volume aim to open up a reading of the text and its significance in the political discourse in question and in the history of political thought more widely. Key moments in the textual history of a particular genre of political discourse are made accessible, appealing and instructive to students, scholars and general readers.

Available in the Series
*Utopian Moments: Reading Utopian Texts*
Edited by Miguel Avilés and J. C. Davis
*Censorship Moments: Reading Texts in the History of Censorship and Freedom of Expression*
Edited by Geoff Kemp

Forthcoming
*Patriarchal Moments: Reading Texts on Patriarchalism*
Edited by Cesare Cuttica and Gaby Mahlberg

*Feminist Moments: Reading Feminist Texts*
Edited by Katherine Smits and Susan Bruce

*Liberal Moments: Reading Liberal Texts*
Edited by Alan S. Kahan and Ewa Atanassow

# Revolutionary Moments

## Reading Revolutionary Texts

Edited by
Rachel Hammersley

Bloomsbury Academic
An imprint of Bloomsbury Publishing Plc

B L O O M S B U R Y
LONDON • NEW DELHI • NEW YORK • SYDNEY

**Bloomsbury Academic**
An imprint of Bloomsbury Publishing Plc

| | |
|---|---|
| 50 Bedford Square | 1385 Broadway |
| London | New York |
| WC1B 3DP | NY 10018 |
| UK | USA |

www.bloomsbury.com

**BLOOMSBURY and the Diana logo are trademarks of Bloomsbury Publishing Plc**

First published 2015

© Rachel Hammersley and Contributors, 2015

Rachel Hammersley and the Contributors have asserted their right under the Copyright, Designs and Patents Act, 1988, to be identified as Authors of this work.

This work is published subject to a Creative Commons Attribution Non-commercial No Derivatives Licence. You may share this work for non-commercial purposes only, provided you give attribution to the copyright holder and the publisher. For permission to publish commercial versions please contact Bloomsbury Academic.

No responsibility for loss caused to any individual or organization acting on or refraining from action as a result of the material in this publication can be accepted by Bloomsbury or the author.

**British Library Cataloguing-in-Publication Data**
A catalogue record for this book is available from the British Library.

ISBN: HB: 978-1-4725-1720-3
PB: 978-1-4725-1721-0
ePDF: 978-1-4725-1723-4
ePub: 978-1-4725-1722-7

**Library of Congress Cataloging-in-Publication Data**
Revolutionary moments : reading revolutionary texts / edited by Rachel Hammersley.
pages cm. – (Textual moments in the history of political thought)
ISBN 978-1-4725-1720-3 (hardback) – ISBN 978-1-4725-1721-0 (pbk.) – ISBN 978-1-4411-0023-8 (ePDF) – ISBN 978-1-4411-2382-4 (ePub) 1. Revolutions–History–Sources. I. Hammersley, Rachel, 1974-
JC491.R489 2015
321.09'4–dc23
2015004232

Series: Textual Moments in the History of Political Thought

Typeset by Deanta Global Publishing Services, Chennai, India

*To the memory of John Gurney (1960–2014)*

# Contents

| | |
|---|---|
| Contributors | ix |
| Series Editors' Foreword | xiii |
| Acknowledgements | xvi |

| | | |
|---|---|---|
| | Introduction  *Rachel Hammersley* | 1 |
| 1 | From Native Rights to Natural Equality: *The Agreement of the People* (1647)  *Rachel Foxley* | 11 |
| 2 | James Harrington, *The Commonwealth of Oceana* and a Revolution in the Language of Politics  *Rachel Hammersley* | 19 |
| 3 | Revolution Principles  *Mark Knights* | 27 |
| 4 | A *'révolution ménagée'*: Mably's *Des droits et des devoirs du citoyen*  *Johnson Kent Wright* | 37 |
| 5 | Rousseau and Revolutions  *Richard Whatmore* | 45 |
| 6 | Exclusion at the Founding: The Declaration of Independence  *Robert G. Parkinson* | 53 |
| 7 | Securing Liberty: The *Federalist Papers*  *T. G. Rodgers* | 61 |
| 8 | Revolution, Reform and the Political Thought of Emmanuel-Joseph Sieyès  *Michael Sonenscher* | 69 |
| 9 | The Declaration of the Rights of Man and of the Citizen, August 1789: A Revolutionary Document  *Lynn Hunt* | 77 |
| 10 | Paine's *Rights of Man* and the Religiosity of Rights Doctrines  *Gregory Claeys* | 85 |
| 11 | Virtue and Terror: Maximilien Robespierre on the Principles of the French Revolution  *Marisa Linton* | 93 |

| | | |
|---|---|---|
| 12 | The Haitian Declaration of Independence: Recognition, Freedom and Anti-French Sentiment *Julia Gaffield* | 101 |
| 13 | A Lesson in Revolution: Karl Marx and Friedrich Engels, *The Communist Manifesto* *Julian Wright* | 109 |
| 14 | From National Backwardness to Revolutionary Leadership: Alexander Herzen's Book *On the Development of Revolutionary Ideas in Russia* *Derek Offord* | 117 |
| 15 | George Plekhanov and the Marxist Turn in Russia *Christopher Read* | 125 |
| 16 | Ordinary Miracles: Lenin's Call for Revolutionary Ambition *Lars T. Lih* | 133 |
| 17 | Revolution and Evolution: Kropotkin's Anarchism *George Crowder* | 141 |
| 18 | Revolutionary Cultivation: Liu Shaoqi's *How to Be a Good Communist* (1939) and the Rejection of Confucian Tradition *Jonathan J. Howlett* | 151 |
| 19 | Between Socialist Futures: Mao Zedong on the 'Ten Major Relationships' *Daniel Leese* | 159 |
| 20 | Frantz Fanon's *The Wretched of the Earth*: Embodying Anti-Colonial Action *Xavier Guégan* | 167 |
| 21 | Social Imperialism and Mao's Three Worlds: Deng Xiaoping's Speech at the UN General Assembly, 1974 *Jennifer Altehenger* | 175 |

| | |
|---|---|
| Notes | 183 |
| Index | 203 |

# Contributors

**Jennifer E. Altehenger** is a lecturer in Contemporary Chinese History at King's College London, UK. She has published essays and reviews in *Twentieth-Century China*, *Frontiers of History in China* and *Times Higher Education*, and is currently working on a book manuscript that examines the dissemination of legal knowledge via propaganda and mass campaigns in the People's Republic of China.

**Gregory Claeys** is professor of history at Royal Holloway, University of London, UK. He is the author of eight books and editor of some fifty volumes. Most of these focus on the history of radical, socialist and anti-imperialist movements from c. 1790–1920. His current research focuses upon utopianism.

**George Crowder** is a professor in the School of Social and Policy Studies, Flinders University, Adelaide, Australia. He is the author of *Classical Anarchism* (1991), *Liberalism and Value Pluralism* (2002), *Isaiah Berlin: Liberty and Pluralism* (2004) and *Theories of Multiculturalism* (2013).

**Rachel Foxley** is an associate professor in Early Modern British History at the University of Reading, UK. She is the author of *The Levellers: Radical Political Thought in the English Revolution* (2013) and of several chapters and articles on radical and republican thought in the English Revolution, including 'Problems of sovereignty in Leveller writings', *History of Political Thought* 24, no. 4 (2007).

**Julia Gaffield** is assistant professor of history at Georgia State University, USA. Her research focuses on the early independence period in Haiti and analyses Haiti's connections with the broader Atlantic World during the period of non-recognition. She is currently working on a manuscript entitled *Haitian Connections in the Atlantic World: Recognition after Revolution* (Chapel Hill: The University of North Carolina Press, 2015).

**Xavier Guégan** is a senior lecturer in Colonial and Postcolonial History at the University of Winchester, UK. He is the author of *The Imperial Aesthetic: Photography, Samuel Bourne and the Indian Peoples in the Post-Mutiny Era* (forthcoming) and 'Transmissible Sites: Monuments, Memorials and their visibility on the metropole and periphery (French Algeria and British India)' in Müller and Geppert's *Sites of Imperial Memory: Commemorating Dominion in the 19th and 20th Centuries* (2015). He is also the co-editor, with M. Farr, of *The British Abroad since the Eighteenth Century*, Vol. 1: *Travellers and Tourists* and Vol. 2: *Experiencing Imperialism* (2013).

**Rachel Hammersley** is a senior lecturer in Intellectual History at Newcastle University, UK. She is the author of *French Revolutionaries and English Republicans: The Cordeliers Club, 1790-1794* (2005) and *The English Republican Tradition and Eighteenth-Century France: Between the Ancients and the Moderns* (2010). She has also written a number of articles dealing with the ideas of revolution, republicanism and democracy in seventeenth- and eighteenth-century Britain, France and America.

**Jonathan J. Howlett** is a lecturer in Modern Asian History at the University of York, UK. His research focuses on the elimination of the Western presence from China after 1949 and the manifold ways in which this change was experienced by ordinary people. A monograph on this subject is forthcoming. Articles on related topics have been published in *Modern Asian Studies* and the *European Journal of East Asian History*. He is also the co-editor of a soon-to-be-published volume titled *Britain and China: Empire, Finance and War*.

**Lynn Hunt** is Distinguished Research Professor at the University of California, Los Angeles, USA. Among her publications are *Inventing Human Rights* (2007); with Jack Censer, *Liberty, Equality, Fraternity: Exploring the French Revolution* (2001); and with Suzanne Desan and William Nelson (eds), *The French Revolution in Global Perspective* (2013).

**Mark Knights** is professor of history at the University of Warwick, UK. He has published a number of works about later Stuart political culture, including *The Devil in Disguise: Deception, Delusion and Fanaticism in the Early English Enlightenment* (2011), which contains a chapter about the Sacheverell trial. He is also the editor of *Faction Displayed: Reconsidering the Impeachment of Dr*

*Henry Sacheverell* (2012). He is currently working on a book about corruption in Britain and its colonies from the reformation to reform.

**Daniel Leese** is associate professor of modern Chinese history and politics at the University of Freiburg, Germany. He is the author of *Mao Cult: Rhetoric and Ritual in China's Cultural Revolution* (2011) and the editor of *Brill's Encyclopedia of China* (2009).

**Lars T. Lih** is an adjunct professor at the Schulich School of Music, McGill University, Canada, and writes about Russian and socialist history. His publications include *Bread and Authority in Russia, 1914–1921* (1990), *Lenin Rediscovered* (2006) and *Lenin* (2011). At present, he is engaged in research on Bolshevik politics in 1917.

**Marisa Linton** is reader in history at Kingston University, UK. She has written extensively on the French Revolution and its ideological origins. She is the author of *Choosing Terror: Virtue, Friendship and Authenticity in the French Revolution* (2013) and *The Politics of Virtue in Enlightenment France* (2001); and she is the co-editor of *Conspiracy in the French Revolution* (2007).

**Derek Offord** is research professor in Russian at the University of Bristol, UK. He is a specialist in pre-revolutionary Russian history and culture and has published books on the Russian revolutionary movement, early Russian liberalism, Russian travel writing and the broader history of Russian thought, as well as two books on contemporary Russian grammar and usage. He is currently leading a multidisciplinary project, funded by the AHRC, on the history of the French language in Russia. Within the framework of this project he has co-authored and co-edited (with Gesine Argent and Vladislav Rjéoutski) a book on European francophonie, a cluster of articles on foreign-language use in eighteenth-century Russia and two volumes forthcoming with Edinburgh University Press on the interplay of French and Russian in Imperial Russia.

**Robert G. Parkinson** is assistant professor of history at SUNY-Binghamton University, USA. He is a former postdoctoral fellow at the Omohundro Institute for Early American History and Culture. His book, *The Common Cause: The Foundations of Race and Nation in the American Revolution*, is forthcoming with the University of North Carolina Press.

**Christopher Read** is professor of modern European history at the University of Warwick, UK. He has written widely on the intellectual, political and social history of Russia from 1881 to 1930. His works include *Lenin: a Revolutionary Life* (2006) and *War and Revolution in Russia 1914-1922* (2013). He is currently writing a biography of Stalin scheduled to appear in 2015.

**Thomas Rodgers** is a lecturer in American History at the University of Portsmouth, UK. His current research investigates the concept of coercion in the process of state formation during the American Revolution.

**Michael Sonenscher** is a fellow of King's College, Cambridge, UK. He is the author of several books on eighteenth-century French political thought, including *Sans-Culottes: An Eighteenth-Century Emblem in the French Revolution* (2008). He is presently writing a book entitled *The Ancients, the Moderns and the Political Ideologies of Modernity*.

**Richard Whatmore** is professor of modern history at the University of St Andrews, UK, and director of the St Andrews Institute of Intellectual History. He is the author of *Republicanism and the French Revolution* (2000) and *Against War and Empire* (2012).

**Johnson Kent Wright** is professor of history at Arizona State University, USA, former editor of the journal *French Historical Studies* and author of *A Classical Republican in Eighteenth-Century France: the Political Thought of Mably* (1997). He has also written a number of articles dealing with Montesquieu, Rousseau and the historiography of the Enlightenment.

**Julian Wright** is an intellectual historian, concerned with the problem of time in political culture. He is exploring the theme of revolutionary and post-revolutionary culture in France through a study of the French socialist movement, currently under contract with Oxford University Press: *Time Present and Time Future: Socialism and Modernity in France*.

# Series Editors' Foreword

At the heart of the serious study of the history of political thought, as expressed through both canonical and non-canonical works of all kinds, has been the question (to which we all too readily assume an answer), 'How shall I read this text?' Answers have varied greatly over time. Once the political works of the past – especially those of Classical Greece and Rome – were read with an eye to their immediate application to the present. And, until comparatively recently, the canonical works of political philosophy were selected and read as expressions of perennial, abiding truths about politics, social morality and justice. The problem was that this made little or no concession to historically changing contexts, that the 'truths' we identified were all too often *our* truths. A marxisant sociology of knowledge struggled to break free from the 'eternal verities' of political thought by exploring the ways in which past societies shaped their own forms of political expression in distinctive yet commonly grounded conceptions of their own image. The problem remained that the perception of what shaped past societies was all too often driven by the demands of a current political agenda. In both cases, present concerns shaped the narrative history of political thought off which the reading of texts fed. The last half century has seen another powerful and influential attempt to break free from a present-centred history of political thought by locating texts as speech acts or moves within a contemporary context of linguistic usage. Here the frequently perceived problem has been (a by-no-means inevitable) narrowing of focus to canonical texts, while the study of other forms of political expression in images, speech, performance and gesture – in all forms of political culture – has burgeoned independently.

    We have, then, a variety of ways of approaching past texts and the interplay of text and context. The series 'Textual Moments in the History of Political Thought' (in which the present volume is the third to be published) is designed to encourage fresh readings of thematically selected texts. Each chapter identifies a key textual moment or passage and exposes it to a reading by an acknowledged expert. The aim is fresh insight, accessibility and the encouragement to read in a more informed way for oneself.

Our attitudes to revolution, as the overthrow of the status quo and the demolition of continuities, have changed rapidly – almost generationally – over time. At times, and for some of the thinkers discussed here, revolution has been seen as the essential means of liberating people from corrupt, effete, oppressive or unjust political cultures and systems of rule. At others, and to others, it has seemed all too prone to unpredictability, to run out of control, consuming its progenitors and either destroying all vestiges of stability or generating inflexible, monolithic and oppressive state structures. Seen for the perspective of a closer reading of revolutionary texts, the process of developing a revolutionary 'tradition' looks much more like a highly contested one. We have perhaps been all too prone to the assumption that 'revolution' as a concept has been a constant, unchanging entity. The texts under consideration here present a very different view: one that begins with the acknowledgement that the classic revolutionary texts are not timeless documents but specific to time and place, written to address particular problems in particular circumstances. Accordingly, we need to read them with sensitivity to context and alert to the changing conceptual meaning of the idea of revolution.

The project of thinking through the revolutionary transformation of society and politics necessarily leads on to a range of supplementary questions. Is it sufficient for the revolutionary to legitimate the overthrow of the status quo or is some blueprint of a new order essential? Can the mobilization of forces sufficient to empower the revolution be achieved without giving rhetorical hostages to fortune? Does the revolution require elite leadership and guidance, the existence of a revolutionary vanguard, or can it be achieved by the spontaneous action of the masses? To what extent does the revolution require the elaboration and instilling of new ways of thinking, a new political culture, even a new language of politics? And does the stabilization or management of the revolution require the kind of authority which might put in jeopardy the principles on which the revolution was inaugurated?

These questions, among others, are raised in the texts under discussion here. Rachel Hammersley has assembled an international team of experts to guide our approach to reading them. Time and again we are reminded of the fact that in order to more fully grasp the textual moments which each of these works represent we must enter its immediate and sometimes polemical context. We must engage with the specific circumstances in which it was conceived and of which, to some extent, it remains an expression. Seen from a distance, these essays, with some deviations, might look like an alternative way of charting the history of the Great Revolution – from the English, to the American, to the French and then the Russian and Chinese revolutions. Read more closely we see that they take us to the heart of debates, not only about the revolutionary tradition, but also within that tradition itself. They take us to the heart of the revolutionary moment.

John Morrow
J. C. Davis

# Acknowledgements

Producing an edited collection can be a demanding and difficult process. Thankfully, in this case it has been a pleasure more or less from start to finish. This is largely due to the knowledge, professionalism and geniality of the contributors, the series editors (J. C. Davis and John Morrow) and the editorial team at Bloomsbury Academic, to all of whom I am deeply grateful. Particular thanks should go to J. C. Davis for inviting me to participate in this project at the beginning and for being supportive all the way through, particularly towards the end when support was especially needed. I am also grateful to my colleague at Newcastle University, David Saunders, for his help early on.

The final stages of this project were marred by the illness and subsequent death of my husband and fellow historian, John Gurney. John was due to contribute a chapter to the volume, but his illness made this impossible. Nevertheless he did read and provide comments on my contributions to the volume, and as a result of our shared interest in revolutions his ideas have long been a continuing source of inspiration to me. It seems fitting that this book should be dedicated to his memory.

# Introduction

Rachel Hammersley

'Revolution' is a concept that occupies a key position within the political culture of the modern world. Born out of the struggles in the Netherlands and England in the sixteenth and seventeenth centuries, the modern concept of revolution grew to maturity in the eighteenth century, being shaped and coloured by events in North America and Europe. Indeed, the revolution in France formed the basis of an archetype. The concept continued to be deployed and developed in the nineteenth century, being strongly influenced by the events of 1848 and by the development of socialist and anarchist ideas. A fresh spate of revolutions at the beginning of the twentieth century gave new fuel and direction to the concept. The Russian Revolution, in particular, provided another influential model and greatly boosted the importance of Marxism (both as a political doctrine and as a tool of historical analysis). Indeed, revolution came to be so closely linked to Marxism that, with the decline of the latter in the late twentieth century, observers could be forgiven for predicting the concomitant demise of the concept of revolution itself. Yet, just like the early years of the twentieth century, so those of the twenty-first have witnessed a new burst of revolutionary activity with the Occupy movements in New York, London and a number of other cities across the globe; the Arab Spring; and even a series of events that have been explicitly labelled as revolutions including: the Rose Revolution in Georgia (2003); the Orange Revolution in Ukraine (2004); the Tulip Revolution in Kyrgystan (2005) and the Green Revolution in Iran (2009).

This recent resurgence of revolutionary activity demonstrates the continuing relevance of the concept of revolution to the contemporary world, thereby reinforcing the importance of a proper understanding of the theory and practice of revolutions. Moreover, by extending both the chronological and geographical reach of the concept, these recent examples underline the fact that revolution is a remarkably flexible idea that has been adapted to a wide variety of contexts. There is, therefore, particular justification for adopting an avowedly historical approach to the study of revolutions; one that pays attention to contextual nuances and differences, as well as to similarities, and also to the connections between different revolutions and revolutionaries.

While revolution as a collective phenomenon has most commonly been approached from a theoretical social science perspective, the idea of adopting a more empirical, historical approach is not new. In 1979 such a transformation was proclaimed by Theda Skocpol in her ground-breaking, but controversial, book *States and Social Revolutions*.[1] Skocpol's structural and state-focused perspective was designed as a corrective to previous sociological accounts and her 'comparative historical analysis' was intended to offer explanations of revolutions that were both 'historically grounded and generalizable beyond unique cases'.[2] However, as well as provoking criticisms from both social scientists and historians, Skocpol's structural approach meant that she paid little attention to the important role that ideas play within revolutionary movements. Furthermore, despite a recent resurgence of interest in intellectual history, which has even resulted in the production of a number of intellectual histories of individual revolutions, most historically focused works comparing revolutions published since 1979 have also neglected the role of ideas.[3]

This volume takes a rather different approach. In the spirit of the series to which it belongs, the emphasis is on addressing the history of revolutions by focusing on key texts – the ideas they presented and the role they played – rather than focusing primarily on providing narrative accounts of particular revolutions. The contributors were asked to select a short extract from an important revolutionary text and to use it as a springboard to offer a fresh interpretation of the text and the ideas of its author or authors. The earliest text to be analysed here dates from 1647 and the latest one from 1974. While the term revolution only took on its modern meaning in the late seventeenth century, that definition owed much to the events of the mid-century English Revolution and consequently it is an appropriate starting point. Within this time frame, particular attention has been given to those revolutions and revolutionary thinkers that did most to give shape and direction to the concept of revolution. At the same time, the range of texts examined is deliberately broad. The volume encompasses revolutionary documents (such as the Declaration of Independence and the Declaration of the Rights of Man and of the Citizen); speeches and pamphlets written by revolutionary activists in the heat of revolution or with a view to influencing events (e.g. Emmanuel-Joseph Sieyès's *What is the Third Estate?*, Lenin's *What Is to Be Done?* and Deng Xiaoping's 'Three Worlds' speech to the UN); and more reflective or philosophical works by leading political thinkers and theorists who have strongly influenced revolutions (for instance, Jean-Jacques Rousseau's

*Social Contract*; Alexander Herzen's *The Development of Revolutionary Ideas in Russia*; and Peter Kropotkin's *Modern Science and Anarchism*). Together, therefore, the chapters offer an overview of the ways in which the concept of revolution has changed and developed since the seventeenth century and explore its adaptation to fit different circumstances and its development by particular individuals.

Interestingly, the perspective offered by this textual approach is rather different from the focus on definitions, models and theories that tends to arise from conventional narrative accounts of multiple revolutions. First, a textual approach draws into focus the close relationship between the enacting of revolutionary events and the development (and even transformation) of political language and key political concepts. Second, this approach highlights the extent to which later revolutionaries were influenced by earlier revolutionary events, models and ideas. Finally, it turns the spotlight on key issues that were debated by leading revolutionary theorists and practitioners, some of which were only important at particular moments in time but others of which have been of perennial concern to revolutionaries from the seventeenth to the twentieth century.

Before exploring each of these three areas in a little more detail, it is perhaps appropriate to point to a further methodological issue raised by these contributions. No doubt influenced by the Cambridge School of political thought, there is widespread emphasis here on the need to read the documents and texts in their historical context and an acknowledgement that later interpretations have often distorted the aims and intentions of the authors and distanced us from the ways in which the texts would have been understood by their immediate audiences. Moreover, several authors – particularly Robert G. Parkinson and Julia Gaffield, who deal with the American and Haitian declarations of independence respectively – emphasize the fact that certain documents were written for multiple audiences and that reading them with an eye to only one of these can distort our understanding. Similarly, several commentators, including Parkinson and Lars Lih, in his essay on Lenin's *What Is to Be Done?*, emphasize that the interpretation of a text can differ depending on which particular passages are focused on.

The textual approach adopted here highlights the frequency and importance of linguistic transformation as a common accompaniment to revolutionary action. Rachel Foxley, in her chapter on *The Agreement of the People*, argues that while the Levellers did not see themselves as revolutionaries, we might identify them as such on the grounds that their understanding of key concepts such as rights and equality challenged traditional views and pointed in new directions. Moreover, Leveller understandings of both these terms were taken up and developed by later revolutionaries. As I argue in my chapter on *The Commonwealth of Oceana*, James Harrington was very deliberate and self-conscious in making his own linguistic transformations – indeed, I suggest that we might see him as seeking to produce a revolutionary political language to match the revolutionary circumstances through which he was living. Similarly, Tom Rodgers, in his account of *The Federalist Papers*, suggests that the transformation of language was part of the revolutionary process for James Madison, Alexander Hamilton and John Jay, with conventional understandings of liberty and authority changing as a result of the American experience. Moreover, this kind of linguistic transformation was not restricted to the early years of revolutionary thought. Lih demonstrates how Lenin very deliberately took terms that were used by his opponents and transformed them, adapting them to his own purposes and ends. Similarly, Jonathan J. Howlett demonstrates that Liu Shaoqi's use of Confucian rhetoric in *How to Be a Good Communist* was a deliberate rhetorical ploy, and a means of promoting the Marxist–Leninist message, rather than an endorsement of Confucian ideology itself.

In line with this emphasis on revolutionary language, a number of the thinkers discussed here can be seen as contributing towards the transformation of certain key revolutionary concepts. Equality is one revolutionary idea that comes in for considerable examination in the chapters that follow, particularly during the seventeenth and eighteenth centuries. Several thinkers during this period seem to shift the concept of equality in new directions. This is true of the Levellers, but also of Harrington and of Sieyès (in Michael Sonenscher's account), both of whom are presented as enacting a shift away from hereditary rule as an acceptable system and towards greater emphasis on meritocracy, social mobility and election. At the same time, both Parkinson and Hunt make the point that the promise of equality enshrined in key constitutional documents was sometimes qualified and often not honoured in practice.

Rights is another revolutionary concept that provoked much debate and has undergone various transformations. The shift from historic rights to natural rights was hinted at by the Levellers and became more entrenched during the course of the eighteenth century. In Kent Wright's essay on the Abbé Mably, for example, he refers to Mably's merging of republicanism with natural rights doctrine. However, the shift was by no means uncomplicated. As Richard Whatmore indicates, in his essay on *The Social Contract*, Rousseau followed Thomas Hobbes in seeing rights as derived not from nature but from convention. And even by the end of the eighteenth century the shift from rights as embodied in existing laws, traditions and customs to universal and abstract human rights was not complete. While this shift is announced in theory in the Declaration of the Rights of Man, Hunt argues that in practice the French never quite moved away from the earlier understanding, and Gaffield demonstrates, through the Haitian example, that revolutions and revolutionary documents do not always work to protect individual rights. Similarly, Greg Claeys challenges our view of Thomas Paine as a thoroughly modern thinker by demonstrating the extent to which his understanding of rights in *The Rights of Man* was embedded in an older religious language.

Finally, the texts examined here reveal fundamental transformations in the understanding of the very notion of revolution itself. With regard to the seventeenth and eighteenth centuries, the key question is whether innovation was central to revolution. This issue is explored by Foxley in her account of the Levellers and by Parkinson in his examination of the Declaration of Independence. In both cases there is a sense of the actors doing something innovatory or revolutionary, but not really wanting to admit to doing so and therefore appealing back to an earlier golden age or to existing privileges to justify their actions. Claeys's account of Paine's debt to older, more traditional ideas is again relevant here. The key shift in this debate seems to have taken place in the late eighteenth and early nineteenth centuries. Marisa Linton presents Maximilian Robespierre's understanding of revolution as based precisely on the idea of forging a new path and not having to rely on historical precedent (e.g., his use of ruthless tactics is justified on this basis). A similar view is also offered in Julian Wright's account of *The Communist Manifesto*. Marx and Engels are presented as being 'revolutionary' precisely because their ideas are at odds with their age and yet this also means that they were at odds with other supposedly 'revolutionary' attitudes of the time.

This sense of there being multiple understandings of revolution circulating by the mid-nineteenth century is also worthy of note. In the seventeenth and eighteenth centuries the understanding of revolution was largely political, though, as Mark Knights makes clear in his chapter on Sacheverell, 1688 can also be seen as having been revolutionary not just in political terms but also in other areas including finance and culture. The French Revolution and the development of socialist and Marxist ideas in the nineteenth century brought a new shift towards an emphasis on social and economic transformations, but as Christopher Read and Lih show in their examinations of the writings of George Plekanov and Lenin, respectively, the political notion did not go away and its importance was reasserted by various revolutionary writers. Moreover, at the same time as Marx and Engels were seeking to offer a more precise and narrow understanding of revolution, Alexander Herzen, as Derek Offord makes clear, was shunning the idea of a narrow political, social or economic account and arguing in favour of a much broader ideological understanding of the term. By the twentieth century a further element is added to the mix with both Frantz Fanon and Mao emphasizing the importance of cultural transformation for the idea of revolution, as the essays by Xavier Guégan and Daniel Leese make clear.

While this book is not explicitly structured around revolutionary influences, the textual approach means that these sorts of connection are given more prominence than in conventional narrative accounts. This approach offers an ideal way into thinking about how different revolutionary thinkers and actors in the past have understood the concept of revolution, but it also highlights the extent to which earlier models and ideas were drawn upon by later revolutionaries.

A large number of the thinkers discussed in the chapters that follow were clearly aware of earlier revolutionary events and sought to learn from them. This is true right across the chronological period covered by the book. Kent Wright demonstrates the importance to the Abbé Mably of the earlier revolutions that had occurred in the Dutch Republic and in England and Mably dramatizes his intention to draw directly on previous experience by using a British Commonwealthman as one of his main characters. The French Revolution of 1789 is clearly an important precedent for a broad swathe of later revolutionaries, including Marx and Engels, Herzen, Kropotkin and even Fanon, while the Russian Revolution was an important model for Chinese revolutionaries (as Howlett and Leese make clear). Revolutionary documents also became important templates for later revolutionaries (Gaffield, for example, notes the importance of the American Declaration of Independence as a model for the later Haitian version). However, it is important to remember that influence was not always positive. As George Crowder indicates, Kropotkin's interest in 1789, 1848 and 1871 was primarily driven by his belief that their failure could be attributed to the revolutionaries' excessive reliance on the state, a point which he then used to justify his alternative anarchist understanding of revolution. Moreover, links between revolutions could also be made by counter-revolutionaries. Sacheverell, as Knights makes clear, drew a direct link between 1640 and 1688 and used the memory of the former to tarnish the reputation of the latter. In addition, several revolutionaries were influenced not simply by past revolutions but also by those through which they lived themselves. For example, Wright demonstrates how the revolutionary theories of Marx and Engels changed as a result of their own lived experience of 1848. There is further complexity too as regards the place of the English Revolution in all this. It was, of course, not described as a revolution by contemporaries, and historians ever since have debated the applicability of the term 'revolution' to the period. And yet, as Foxley argues, it did contribute to the development of certain ideas, institutions and principles that were central to later revolutions. Foxley is careful not to imply that this was the result of the direct influence of Leveller ideas on later revolutionaries. Rather she makes the more interesting suggestion that, given the parallels, later thinkers looking back at the English Revolution, and especially at the Levellers and the *Agreement of the People*, were inclined to view them through the prism of subsequent events. This suggests that the influence of later revolutions on the historiography of earlier ones may be as important as the influence that one revolutionary moment exerts on another.

It was not only revolutionary models that influenced revolutionaries. The ideas of earlier thinkers could also provide an important source of inspiration. Mably explicitly set out the idea of a political revolution and the form it would take several decades before the French Revolution broke out, not only predicting but also endorsing the opening stages of that revolution when it occurred. Similarly, Offord demonstrates how Herzen helped to lay the foundations for Russian populism and for Russia's independent path to socialism, and Lih stresses the crucial importance of Plekhanov's ideas for Lenin. And, of course, Marxist ideas were of crucial importance to the revolutionary events in Russia, and Marxist–Leninist ideas for China. However, the relationship between revolutionary theory and revolutionary action was often complex. For example, Whatmore notes that although French revolutionaries drew directly on the ideas of Rousseau, he had not favoured revolutionary solutions and anyway regarded France as not at all suitable for the adoption of his ideas. Similarly, in the case of both Russia and China, there was much debate among revolutionaries about the extent to which they could or should follow Marxist theory or how far they should take an independent route more appropriate to their own particular circumstances.

As well as highlighting the importance of linguistic transformation to the history of revolution and drawing attention to what various revolutionaries learnt from each other, the texts analysed here also suggest certain perennial issues that seem to preoccupy revolutionaries in different times and places. The first of these is the tension between ambitions and theories, on the one hand, and practical reality, on the other. Parkinson, Hunt and Gaffield all present the revolutionary documents that they have studied as making bold promises that cannot necessarily be fulfilled in practice and as containing within them inherent paradoxes and tensions that create problems for years to come. This was not just a feature of constitutional documents. Wright, for example, notes the ambiguity at the heart of Marx and Engels' seminal text.

Another perennial issue that seems to trouble the revolutionary writers discussed here is the question of whether revolution needs to be imposed and directed from above or whether it should be allowed to spring up from below and what the balance should be between leaders and the masses during its subsequent course. Several earlier thinkers – including Harrington, Mably and the Federalists – seem to see leadership and considerable control from above as essential, and Rousseau and Sieyès used the distinction between sovereignty and government as a means of structuring the balance between leaders and citizens and demarcating the functions of each. By contrast, Kropotkin offers the most extreme argument in favour of a spontaneous uprising, insisting that a revolution should not be led from above. Similarly, the importance of popular uprising is also emphasized by both Mao and Fanon. It is difficult to unpick the exact relationship between underlying forces and human agency in the thought of Marx and Engels, but revolutionaries inspired by Marx, starting with Plekhanov and Lenin, emphasized the need for a party and the crucial role of the intelligentsia in organizing and leading it. Other thinkers across the timeframe explored here express a related concern with how to ensure a certain kind of behaviour on the part of both the leaders (Robespierre) and the population (Liu Shaoqi and Mao).

More than anything else, adopting a textual approach to multiple revolutions demonstrates the complex, multilayered and, most importantly, constantly changing nature of the concept of revolution between the seventeenth and the twentieth centuries. Not only has the meaning and understanding of the term revolution itself been adapted and developed, narrowed and expanded, during the course of these centuries, but so also have a host of other related political concepts and ideas. Yet, the evidence provided here also implies that it would be wrong to suggest that the changing nature of the concept should lead us to conclude that it has no meaning or to suggest that, for example, Mably's understanding of revolution has so little in common with Mao's understanding that the same term should not be applied to them both. It is clear that revolutionary thinkers from as early as the eighteenth century were very conscious of past revolutionary events and ideas and that they drew on them (albeit in complex ways) in their own writings. There is therefore a clear sense if not of a revolutionary tradition then at least of a revolutionary conversation or series of conversations that have been taking place since at least the seventeenth century, and the writers discussed here have certainly been major contributors to that conversation. Moreover, it is also clear that while individuals and circumstances have changed since the seventeenth century at least some of the issues facing revolutionaries remain exactly the same. The remarkable persistence of concerns about the relationship between revolutionary leadership and spontaneous revolutionary action by the people is perhaps the most obvious example. Given this, and the fact that the twenty-first century has already seen a number of 'revolutionary' uprisings, it seems likely that revolution as a concept will remain relevant for many years to come, though of course when it comes to predicting in exactly what ways the concept of revolution will develop over the course of the twenty-first century it seems wise to invoke what was long believed to be Zhou Enlai's response when asked about the impact of the French Revolution, namely that it is 'too early to say'.[4]

# 1

# From Native Rights to Natural Equality: *The Agreement of the People* (1647)

Rachel Foxley

… [S]*ince therefore our former oppressions, and scarce yet ended troubles have beene occasioned, either by want of frequent Nationall meetings in Councell, or by rendring those meetings ineffectuall: We are fully agreed and resolved, to provide that hereafter our Representatives be neither left to an uncertainty for the time, nor made uselesse to the ends for which they are intended: In order whereunto we declare,*

*I.*

*That the People of England being at this day very unequally distributed by Counties, Cities, & Burroughs, for the election of their Deputies in Parliament, ought to be more indifferently proportioned, according to the number of the Inhabitants: …*

*III.*

*That the People do of course chuse themselves a Parliament once in two yeares …*

*IV.*

*That the power of this, and all future Representatives of this Nation, is inferiour only to theirs who chuse them, and doth extend, without the consent or concurrence of any other person or persons; to the enacting, altering, and repealing of Lawes; to the erecting and abolishing of Offices and Courts; to the appointing, removing, and calling to account Magistrates, and Officers of all degrees; to the making War and peace; to the treating with forraigne States: And generally, to whatsoever is not expresly, or impliedly reserved by the represented to themselves.*

*Which are as followeth,*

*1. That matters of Religion, and the wayes of Gods Worship, are not at all intrusted by us to any humane power, because therein wee cannot remit or exceed a tittle of what our Consciences dictate to be the mind of God, without wilfull sinne: neverthelesse the publike way of instructing the Nation (so it be not compulsive) is referred to their discretion.*[1]

The *Agreement of the People for a firm and present peace upon grounds of common right and freedom* did not proclaim itself a revolutionary text. The proposers of the 1647 *Agreement* were responding to the 'oppressions' of Charles I's government and the bloodshed of the English civil war, which had ended with Charles's defeat by his own parliament the year before this text was written. These upheavals, according to the *Agreement*, were caused by a failure to maintain an existing system of 'national meetings in council', and similar troubles could be prevented in future by the restoration of this system. Although contemporaries did come to see the mid-seventeenth-century crisis as a time of 'confusions and revolutions of government' – at least after the king had been executed in 1649 – they did not embrace deliberately revolutionary programmes, and one word which sometimes came close to modern senses of the word revolution – 'innovation' – remained pejorative even in the vocabulary of the Levellers when they put forward their final version of the *Agreement of the People* in 1649. But in spite of its authors' protestations, this document has had revolutionary resonances for readers from the nineteenth century onwards, as aspects both of its content and its form reminded them of key documents produced in the course of the eighteenth-century American and French Revolutions.[2] To many seventeenth-century contemporaries too the 1647 *Agreement of the People* and its subsequent versions seemed to threaten a profound change in the political order.[3] It is easy for us to see the *Agreement* as a programme for change, as an expression of novel assumptions about people and politics and as a revolutionary device to bring about change; but the *Agreement* was rooted in the modes of thought about politics available in the mid-seventeenth century, which included thought about the nation's past. Those resources could generate revolutionary visions of the future, but they often did so by reimagining and reinterpreting the past and the present.

The draft *Agreement* read on 28 October 1647 in the General Council of the Army served as one foundation for the Putney Debates, in which grandees, officers and some rank and file members of parliament's New Model Army debated the terms of settlement for the nation with the participation of a couple of civilian radicals. The parliamentarians had defeated the king in the civil war, but now the New Model had banded together to resist disbandment orders from parliament, creating a novel General Council of the Army which included 'agitators' representing rank-and-file soldiers and junior officers. Radicals within the army had in turn pulled away from the agenda of their leaders, converging to some extent with the concerns of the group of civilian radicals in London who were soon to be christened 'Levellers', although the extent of any collaboration is much disputed.[4] The *Agreement* of 1647 is thus a document which reflects the serial displacements of power and energy often found in revolutions, as oppositional coalitions fragment and different forces seize the initiative. It was a position paper produced for debate under specific and tense circumstances, but it was also printed and 'offered to the joynt concurrence of all the free Commons of England' (title page). It was one peace proposal among many in the 1640s, but it was unusual in not just claiming but actively seeking the real agreement of the people of the nation as a precondition for peace. It failed in 1647, but the notion of settlement by an 'Agreement of the People' had been established as one which could potentially bind army and civilian radicals together and offer a legitimating process for a final resolution of England's troubles. Its centrality for the civilian Levellers can be questioned but a second *Agreement* was debated in the prelude to regicide in December 1648 (resulting in slightly different versions endorsed by the army and the Levellers), and on 1 May 1649 the Leveller leaders issued a third *Agreement of the People* designed to rally opponents of the post-regicide regime around a vision of a more legitimate and more radical alternative.

The *Agreement* of 1647 marked a revolutionary moment in its (partly tacit) abolition of the political assumptions of the old regime, if not the social structures which went with them. No longer was power to be organized around a conception of the three estates (however malleable that had been in practice) or the coordination of powers between king, Lords and Commons. It was to be two more years before the newly purged House of Commons awarded itself legislative sovereignty in order to put the king on trial without the consent of the House of Lords, but here in the autumn of 1647 we have a proposed constitutional settlement in which an unwary student could easily miss the only references to the king and Lords which are present: 'That the power of this, and all future Representatives of this Nation ... doth extend, without the consent or concurrence of any other person or persons; to the enacting, altering, and repealing of Lawes'. Not only have the arrangements for the election and meeting of the Representative been discussed without any reference to a king or non-elected upper House, but the legislative sovereignty of the elected Representative – a reformed version of the House of Commons – is asserted against the potential veto of any other person or persons, that is, a king or a House of Lords. Whether or not king and Lords are to survive, they are not to partake of the traditional 'marks of sovereignty', legislative and executive, annexed to the Representative under clause IV. What is more, the Representative itself is not just the House of Commons of old: geographical representation is to be 'more indifferently proportioned, according to the number of the Inhabitants' – an apparently innocuous stipulation which might be taken to mean the rectification of historical anomalies caused by depopulation of boroughs, but which was rightly (and hostilely) read by Henry Ireton in the Putney Debates as a demand for a radical extension of the franchise among adult males. The form, composition and workings of the institutions of government would all have been radically transformed by the implementation of the *Agreement*.

This transformation reflected a fundamental rethinking of political principles, although one which took its pivotal vocabulary and some of its starting points from contemporary discourse. The language used to gloss the transition from the old parliament to new Representative is notably slippery: 'Parliament' is only used to refer to the past body but is used as if it referred only to the elected House and not the House of Lords; 'Nationall meetings in Councell', also used of the past, neatly abstracts from form to function and paves the way for a new body which might better represent the nation. The House of Commons is nowhere mentioned: the representative character (however imperfect) of the old Commons facilitates the move to a new 'Representative', which actually replaces the whole parliament. 'Representation' was one of the pivotal concepts which legitimated the claims made in the *Agreement*: Leveller writers and other parliamentarians had begun to question the idea that the parliament, because it represented the whole nation, could not be challenged, instead making representation a test which parliament had to pass: an unrepresentative parliament could be challenged. The only place where modern students of politics are still likely to encounter the older notion of representation as preventing rather than enabling challenge from the ruled is in Hobbes's argument for an absolute sovereign, but at the time Hobbes's view ran in parallel with some similarly absolutist parliamentarian arguments. The radicals' revision of the concept of representation fed into the connected ideas of an expanded franchise and an ultimate popular sovereignty which set limits to governmental power.

The limitation of power was, of course, a natural parliamentarian response to the perceived abuses of Charles I's prerogative powers before the wars; this could have been achieved by formalizing the role of parliament and privy council to hold the king in check. However, by effectively abolishing the king, and any council (including the House of Lords itself) dependent on the king's prerogative, the radicals closed off the option of putting a check on power by distributing it between several institutions of government. In declaring the supremacy of a unicameral body, they had landed themselves with the potential for a new tyranny, a danger they were very alive to, given the behaviour of the Long Parliament which had been sitting since 1640. The *Agreement* accordingly enacted a new type of division of powers: 'That the power of this, and all future Representatives of this Nation, is inferiour only to theirs who chuse them.' Whatever the origins of the *Agreement* in army circles, this stipulation reflected the way in which the imprisoned civilian Leveller leaders John Lilburne and Richard Overton had begun to 'appeal to the people' over the heads of the current parliament in 1647. The *Agreement* offers a more orderly way in which popular sovereignty could place limits on parliamentary power: what Lilburne and Overton were appealing to the people to *do* was never quite clear, but without an institutional framework for action, the possibilities ranged from petitioning to violence. In the *Agreement*, by contrast, popular sovereignty retained specific areas of operation: in certain matters, starting with religion, the people would retain their power rather than handing over any 'compulsive' authority to their representatives. Even apart from these crucial 'reserves', though, the assertion of the subordinate nature of the Representative's power had implications. When a second *Agreement of the People* was being negotiated at the end of 1648, one of the sticking-points for the Leveller leader John Lilburne was the army men's desire to give the Representative the 'highest and finall Judgement, concerning all Naturall or Civill things', apart from those reserved.[5] By contrast, in the radicals' versions of the *Agreements* (the first, the third and Lilburne's version of the second, entitled *Foundations of Freedom*), power remained with the people unless otherwise stated, and the matters reserved were of secular as well as religious import. Spelling out the bounds of institutionally exercised governmental power might obviate the need for action by the people in future or, if the worst came to the worst, make clear when popular action was justified. With biennial elections specified (the preferred option for the civilian Levellers was annual elections), there would also be regular opportunities for the people's sovereignty to be exercised and erring representatives removed.

The *Agreement* did not overtly express its aspirations in universal terms; it talked of the people of England and the nation's representatives, and even tacitly located its own authors as only one party in the civil war, regretting that 'so many of our Country-men … opposed us in this quarrel' (1). However, behind its demands lay principles which at least pulled in the direction of universalism. The authors of the *Agreement* summed up their demands and prescriptions with a resonant phrase: '*These things we declare to be our* native Rights' (5).

This claim to rights, and the assertion that such rights simply exist as part of the moral universe and are waiting to be claimed, is reminiscent of the later invocation of the 'rights of man' in the French Revolution. But here the 'rights' are 'native' – due to the authors and subscribers of the *Agreement* by birth – probably by English birth rather than as a universal human inheritance. The birthright invoked is probably that of the English law and the fundamental or ancient constitution which '*our Ancestors*' (5) sought to defend or recover after the Norman Conquest. However, that law and constitution were themselves interpreted by radicals in the light of universal principles, and the rights of the law and the natural rights of human beings could – and should – converge.

One fundamental principle which is foundational to the *Agreement* is a principle of equality. The scope and implications of this are not spelt out, but one of the 'reserves' against governmental power states 'That in all Laws made, or to be made, every person may be bound alike, and that no Tenure, Estate, Charter, Degree, Birth, or place, do confer any exemption from the ordinary Course of Legall proceedings, whereunto others are subjected' (5). This is a statement of *legal* equality; but it must rest on a belief that there is a relevant equality of *worth* between all those who are subject to the nation's laws. This presumably also informed the demands for a widened franchise, even though the franchise itself had some limits (including its restriction to adult males, which was spelt out in subsequent versions of the *Agreement*). The grounds of the right to vote were never definitively settled by army or civilian radicals, but at one end of the scale the relationship between obedience and consent implied an almost universal franchise, as did the sketchy but generous criterion embedded in Rainborough's comment during the franchise debate at Putney that 'the poorest hee that is in England hath a life to live as the greatest hee', although the gendered assumption here is telling.[6] Contemporaries leapt to the conclusion – denied by the radicals themselves – that such claims for political equality involved a desire to see economic 'levelling'. The radicals simply argued that a fundamental type of human equality, coupled perhaps with a minimal degree of social and economic independence which women were assumed not to have, grounded a basic *political* equality. These claims were not elaborated enough to be read as grand claims of human equality grounding universal human rights, but at times the Levellers emphasized the consequences of a fundamental human equality: all human beings since Adam and Eve 'are, and were by nature all equall and alike in power, digni[t]y, authority, and majesty, none of them having (by nature) any authority, dominion or majesteriall power, one over or above another'.[7] Similarly, the claims of conscience, both in secular and in specifically religious matters, were enshrined in fundamental law by the *Agreement*, suggesting a deep spiritual and moral equality between adults. Such claims to equality – plural, overlapping and ill-defined though they might be – were what lay behind the *Agreement*'s toppling of the old political regime in favour of a system founded on popular sovereignty.

That notion of ultimate popular sovereignty underlay the final and most revolutionary aspect of the *Agreement*: its own standing as a foundational constitutional document which, once legitimated by popular subscription, would be unalterable by future parliaments. In spite of the modest wording of the 1647 *Agreement*, its ambition to provide a definitive settlement was already a contentious issue at the Putney Debates; the second *Agreement* at the turn of 1648–9 made citizenship dependent on subscription to it and the third *Agreement* made any attempt to overthrow it treasonable. For modern readers, these features may hint at the 'social contract' later expounded by Rousseau and at the theory of fundamental law underlying the Constitution of the United States.[8] In the context of the 1640s, though, the claim being made in these documents was not so much that the people had the power to create a new political order out of nothing, but that the people were able to recognize and ratify the fundamental laws which could already be discerned operating in the 'ancient constitution' of (pre-Norman) England and which were in tune with the laws of nature.[9] For that reason, perhaps, there was no provision even for the people themselves to alter or replace the *Agreement* in the future. The *Agreements of the People* were revolutionary re-imaginings of the nature and basis of politics and the ancient constitution; but for their authors, it was still tyrannical rulers rather than reforming people who could be expected to 'innovate in Government'.[10]

# Further Reading

Baker, P. and Vernon, E., *The Agreements of the People, the Levellers and the Constitutional Crisis of the English Revolution* (Basingstoke: Palgrave Macmillan, 2012).

Foxley, R., *The Levellers: Radical Political Thought in the English Revolution* (Manchester: Manchester University Press, 2013).

Mendle, M., *The Putney Debates of 1647: The Army, the Levellers, and the English State* (Cambridge: Cambridge University Press, 2001).

Vernon, E. and Baker, P., 'What Was the First Agreement of the People?', *Historical Journal* 53 (2010): 39–60.

2

# James Harrington, *The Commonwealth of Oceana* and a Revolution in the Language of Politics

Rachel Hammersley

*Government, according to the ancients and their learned disciple Machiavel, the only politician of later ages, is of three kinds: the government of one man, or of the better sort, or of the whole people; which by their more learned names are called monarchy, aristocracy, and democracy. These they hold, through their proneness to degenerate, to be all evil. For whereas they that govern should govern according to reason, if they govern according unto passion, they do that which they should not do.*

…

*The corruption then of monarchy is called tyranny; that of aristocracy, oligarchy; and that of democracy, anarchy. But legislators, having found these three governments at the best to be naught, have invented another consisting of a mixture of them all, which only is good. This is the doctrine of the ancients.*

…

*To go mine own way, and yet to follow the ancients, the principles of government are twofold: internal, or the goods of the mind, and external, or the goods of fortune. The goods of the mind are natural or acquired virtues, as wisdom, prudence, and courage, etc. The goods of fortune are riches. … The principles of government then are in the goods of the mind, or in the goods of fortune. To the goods of the mind answers authority; to the goods of fortune, power or empire.*[1]

James Harrington lived through the English Revolution of the mid-seventeenth century and wrote almost all of his works during the 1650s. However, his revolutionary credentials relate less to his involvement in the events of that important decade than to the transformation he executed on early modern political thought in his magnum opus, *The Commonwealth of Oceana* (1656). That work was written in the middle of the Interregnum and at a time when Oliver Cromwell was struggling to find a workable means of 'healing and settling' the nation. What it offered was an alternative vision for a future English republic.

That Harrington was doing something new, even revolutionary, in *Oceana* has been acknowledged by various commentators. Though their interpretations of his writings differed, both Zera Fink and J. G. A. Pocock placed Harrington at the heart of their accounts of seventeenth-century English republicanism, and Pocock in particular presented Harrington's ideas as marking a turning point within the republican tradition.[2] Harrington's distinctiveness was, at least in part, the result of his application of republican constitution-building (previously associated with city states) to a large nation-state. In this respect, as Jonathan Scott has emphasized, Harrington was different even from most other English republicans of the period, whose emphasis was on the importance of reviving republican values (such as liberty and virtue) and embedding them within the system, rather than on constitution-building itself.[3] Harrington's attempt to build a republican constitution in a large state led him to develop his distinctive theory concerning the crucial relationship between land ownership and political power. His innovation on this point was already being acknowledged in the late seventeenth century. For example, in *An Essay upon the Constitution of the Roman Government*, written around 1699, Walter Moyle asserted:

> Thus it appears that Land is the true Center of Power, and that the Ballance of Dominion changes with the Ballance of Property; as the Needle in the Compass shifts its Points just as the great Magnet in the Earth changes its Place. This is an eternal Truth, and confirm'd by the Experience of all Ages and Governments; and so fully demonstrated by the Great HARRINGTON in his OCEANA, that'tis as difficult to find out new Arguments for it, as to resist the Cogency of the old.[4]

This chapter will focus on another example of Harrington 'go[ing] his own way'. It will examine the way in which he transformed the ancient notion of mixed government by subtly redefining its key components.

In the passage cited at the beginning of this chapter Harrington alludes to the conventional typology of government, originally set out by Aristotle in the *Politics*, which identifies three basic types of government – monarchy, aristocracy and polity – and then their equivalent corrupt forms – tyranny, oligarchy and democracy. Harrington also refers to the theory, usually associated with Polybius, according to which the tendency of each good form to degenerate into its corrupt equivalent could be avoided by establishing a mixed system of government involving elements of each of the good forms. Harrington's ideal constitution as set out in *Oceana* constituted his own distinctive version of a mixed system, but he also introduced subtle, but significant, changes in how the three basic forms of government – monarchy, aristocracy and democracy (which by this time had replaced 'polity' as the good form) – were understood.

There has been a tendency among historians in recent years to see seventeenth-century English republicanism as inherently anti-monarchical.[5] Consequently, as a leading English republican, Harrington has conventionally been seen as fundamentally opposed to monarchical government. Yet Harrington's personal relations with Charles I have always sat uneasily with this interpretation. Harrington was, by all accounts, a loyal and affectionate servant of Charles I when he was employed by parliament as gentleman of the king's bedchamber from 1647. His grief at the regicide was attested by his acquaintance John Aubrey who 'oftentimes heard him speake of Charles I with the greatest zeale and passion imaginable'.[6]

A close reading of Harrington's works reinforces the ambiguity of his attitude to monarchical government. Ultimately Harrington insisted that it was the balance of property within a state that determined its ideal form of government. Thus he was even willing to acknowledge the superiority of monarchy under certain circumstances: 'Kings, no question, where the balance is monarchical, are of divine right, and if they be good the greatest blessings that the government so standing can be capable of.'[7] Moreover, even though he presented a republic as the best government for mid-seventeenth-century England he did not see that form as necessarily excluding the possibility of a single magistrate at the apex of the government. Indeed this is precisely the role that Lord Archon ends up occupying in *Oceana*. Though initially employed as a legislator who abdicated once the constitution was established, in the account offered in 'The Corollary' he is soon persuaded (following a democratic process) to resume his post in order to deal with the immediate dangers of foreign invasion and internal divisions and he then acts as a figurehead and statesman for the commonwealth for more than forty years (245 and 251–7). This fact should not come as a surprise given Harrington's sympathy with and respect for the Venetian system in which the Doge performed a similar role. Of course, Harrington's figurehead differed from a traditional monarch in several crucial respects. In the first place, he did not assume his position on the basis of hereditary right, but rather had earned it by his outstanding actions. Second, Lord Archon's powers were carefully defined and severely limited. Nevertheless, not only was Harrington willing to accept the validity of monarchy under certain circumstances, but even within his ideal model he was less concerned with proscribing single-person rule than with ensuring that those holding powerful office were there on the basis of merit, had clearly defined powers and could be called to account if necessary, rather like a modern-day president.

These features were also echoed in Harrington's treatment of 'aristocracy'. There can be no denying that the aristocratic element had a fundamental role to play in Harrington's political system; in many respects the aristocracy is the most powerful group within *Oceana*. The 'horse' (those who earn at least £100 per year in lands, goods or money) completely control the senate, and this means that they alone have the right to debate legislative matters. In this sense, Harrington's republic is aristocratic in organization. Once again, this fits with Harrington's respect for the Venetian Republic as well as being typical of his time.

Yet, simply describing Harrington's republic as 'aristocratic' does not do justice to either the complexity or the innovatory character of his thinking. In reality, Harrington's definition of the term 'aristocracy' was very different from the way in which the concept was understood in seventeenth-century Venice and from the convention of the day. In the first place, Harrington explicitly talked in terms of a 'natural aristocracy'. He argued that in any group of men there would always be approximately one-third wiser than the rest and primed to lead:

> Wherefore this can be no other than a natural aristocracy diffused by God throughout the whole body of mankind to this end and purpose, and therefore such as the people have not only a natural but a positive obligation to make use of as their guides. (23)

It was crucial to Harrington that the right of this minority to rule was based neither on heredity, 'nor in regard of the greatness of their estates only' 'but by election for their excellent parts, which tendeth unto the advancement of the influence of their virtue or authority that leads the people' (23). Harrington was thus advocating an aristocracy of merit rather than one based either on birth or purely on wealth. Of course, a certain degree of wealth was required for inclusion within the 'horse', and was perhaps also a precondition of the study and travel that would bring political wisdom and therefore merit, but the fact that the criteria are couched in terms of various forms of wealth (not just landed property) meant that there was considerable room for social mobility, particularly when accompanied by Harrington's agrarian law which was designed to prevent the concentration of vast swathes of land in the hands of a small number of families. In the context of the time, Harrington's emphasis on social mobility was highly innovative. In addition to this, Harrington was insistent on the need for rotation of office in order to avoid a narrow oligarchy from gaining and holding power. The senate, the Prerogative Tribe and most offices at both a local and national level were subject to this rotation. In the assemblies this required one-third of members to stand down each year so that individual members would only serve for three years in a row and would then be compelled to spend at least three years out of office before being eligible for re-election. Thus Harrington's model spread power more widely than in the Venetian system, where rotation was applied to the senate only and citizenship was restricted to descendants of the original citizens.

Harrington's transformation of the terminology is perhaps most striking in the case of 'democracy'. In the first place, Harrington was one of the first thinkers to use this term positively.[8] Not only did he use 'democracy' (rather than 'polity') in his account of the Aristotelian typology to describe the uncorrupted rule of the many, but also he used the term interchangeably with 'commonwealth' to describe the particular system of government that he favoured. His first use of the term in this way appears in *Oceana*. Following the twentieth order, which sets out the procedures by which matters are proposed and debated within the senate, Harrington has Lord Archon deliver a speech to the Council of Legislators in which he explores the nature and function of the nobility and senate in various historical commonwealths. In the midst of his discussion of the Lacedaemonian Senate he claimed to have hit upon a 'riddle, which I have heretofore found troublesome to unfold', namely, 'why, Athens and Lacedaemon consisting each of the senate and the people, the one should be held a democracy and the other an aristocracy' (143). The main difference between them, as Harrington noted, was that in the former, the people could both debate and vote on legislation, whereas in the latter, they had no right of debate but could simply accept or reject the proposals introduced by the senate. Harrington continued:

> But for my part, where the people have the election of the senate, not bound unto a distinct order, and the result, which is the sovereign power, I hold them to have that share in the government (the senate being not for life) whereof, with the safety of the commonwealth, they are capable in nature, and such a government for that cause to be democracy. (143)

Thus Harrington was redefining 'democracy' as a form of government in which the senate was elected and the popular assembly had (at least) the right of veto over what it proposed. Harrington further developed this understanding of the term in *The Prerogative of Popular Government* (1658). And between July and December 1659 he used it in a series of pamphlets to refer to his preferred form of government. For example, in *Aphorisms Political* he insisted: 'That democracy, or equal government by the people, consist[ing] of an assembly of the people and a senate, is that whereby art is altogether directed, limited and necessitated by the nature of her materials.'[9] This use of the term was also employed around the same time in the titles of two pamphlets that were produced by Harrington's associates: *A Proposition in Order to the Proposing of a Commonwealth or Democracy* and *A Model of a Democratical Government*. As I have argued elsewhere, Harrington's reappropriation of the term in this way was undoubtedly determined by his conflict with the so-called 'godly republicans'. By describing his own model as 'democratic' his intention was to dismiss theirs as 'oligarchic'.[10]

Moreover, there was also substance behind the terminological changes that Harrington introduced. In the first place, he has no explicit property qualification for citizenship. The only requirement is that citizens must not be servants but rather must 'live of themselves', though he does implicitly exclude women.[11] Citizens start to participate in politics only when they turn thirty, but before that they exercise their citizenship (and prepare for their political role) by serving in the army. Secondly, while poorer citizens (defined as those earning less than £100 per year) do have fewer opportunities for political participation than their richer neighbours, there are several tasks that they are able to perform. As well as being involved in elections locally, they are eligible for election to the assemblies at each level, including (as long as they are married) the Prerogative Tribe; they can hold various local offices; and they also have the opportunity to initiate legislation through the Academy of Provosts. Thus even though Harrington's system is explicitly designed to give more power to the natural aristocracy and to restrict the political participation of poorer citizens, citizenship in *Oceana* is still both considerably more inclusive and involves a wider range of powers than was typical of the time. Finally, Harrington's emphasis on inclusivity meant that he was even willing to include former royalists and delinquents as active citizens within the political nation.

As has been demonstrated, despite advocating mixed government, Harrington subtly redefined the key terms 'monarchy', 'aristocracy' and 'democracy'.[12] These redefinitions were significant in themselves, but taken together they constitute a more fundamental shift. Harrington's system was, at heart, meritocratic rather than being based on the more conventional hereditary principle. This emphasis was reflected in his attitude to both monarchy and aristocracy and was reinforced by his acceptance (and even encouragement) of the principle of social mobility. While his belief in meritocracy resulted in restrictions on who could engage in political participation at a higher level, his basic understanding of citizenship was broad and inclusive. Interestingly, this commitment to meritocracy and inclusive citizenship was not based on a positive view of human nature. Rather Harrington shared Thomas Hobbes's pessimism on this front, fearing that no one is immune from being swayed by their own personal interests. His solution was to rely on a carefully constructed constitutional system in which rotation of office would prevent any individual from holding office for too long and in which the interests of the democratic element could be used to control and restrain those with greater power.

In enacting this transformation Harrington really was 'go[ing] his own way'. His re-evaluation of the ancient understanding of mixed government and the key political concepts associated with it reinforce the notion that he was not simply a 'classical republican' in the conventional sense.[13] This is also reflected in his utilization not just of ancient republican models but also of those of the early modern world, most notably Venice. Yet, as has been demonstrated here, while the Venetian Republic was a crucial inspiration for him, his own constitution departed from that model in a number of important respects.

It was suggested at the beginning of this chapter that Harrington's 'revolutionary' credentials are derived from his transformation of political thought rather than his involvement in political affairs. Yet the two are not wholly unconnected. Harrington was, of course, one of the earliest commentators to suggest that the events of the 1640s and 1650s were the outcome of a long-term process and constituted a major political transformation. And it was for precisely this reason that he set about transforming the conventional political vocabulary. A transformation or revolution in politics, government and society of the kind that Harrington had witnessed necessitated a concomitant revolution in political thought and language. Enacting the latter was a key purpose of *The Commonwealth of Oceana*.

## Further Reading

*The Political Works of James Harrington*, ed. J. G. A. Pocock (Cambridge: Cambridge University Press, 1977).

Hammersley, R., 'Rethinking the Political Thought of James Harrington: Royalism, Republicanism and Democracy', *History of European Ideas* 39, no. 3 (2013): 354–70.

Rahe, P. A., *Against Throne and Altar: Machiavelli and Political Theory Under the English Republic* (Cambridge: Cambridge University Press, 2008).

Scott, J., *Commonwealth Principles* (Cambridge: Cambridge University Press, 2004).

# 3

# Revolution Principles

## Mark Knights

*The Grand Security of our Government, and the very Pillar upon which it stands, is founded upon the steady Belief of the Subject's Obligation to an Absolute, and Unconditional Obedience to the Supreme Power, in All Things Lawful, and the utter Illegality of Resistance upon any Pretence whatsoever. But this Fundamental Doctrine, notwithstanding its Divine Sanction in the Express Command of God in Scripture, and without which, it is impossible any Government of any Kind, or Denomination in the World should subsist with Safety, and which has been so long the Honourable, and Distinguishing Characteristic of Our Church, is now, it seems, quite Exploded and Ridicul'd out of Countenance, as an Unfashionable, Superannuated, nay (which is more wonderful) as a Dangerous Tenet, utterly Inconsistent with the Right, Liberty and Property, of the PEOPLE; who, as our New Preachers, and New Politicians teach us, (I suppose by a New and Unheard-of Gospel, as well as Laws) have in Contradiction to Both, the Power Invested in Them, the Fountain and Original, of it, to Cancel their Allegiance at pleasure, and call their Sovereign to account for High Treason against his Supream Subjects forsooth; nay to Dethrone and Murther Him for a Criminal, as they did the Royal Martyr by a Judiciary Sentence. And what is almost Incredible, presume to make their Court to their Prince, by maintaining such Anti-monarchical Schemes. But, God be Thanked! neither the Constitution of our Church or State, is so far Alter'd, but that by the Laws of Both, still in Force, and which I hope for ever will be) these Damnable Positions, let'em come either from Rome, or Geneva, from the Pulpit, or the Press, are condemn'd for Rebellion, and High Treason. Our Adversaries think they effectually stop our Mouths, and have Us Sure and Unanswerable on this Point, when they urge the Revolution of this Day in their Defence. But certainly They are the Greatest Enemies of That, and His Late Majesty, and the most Ungrateful for the Deliverance, who endeavour to cast such Black, and Odious Colours upon Both.*[1]

This sermon was preached on 5 November 1709, a highly charged day in the Protestant calendar, marking not only the Catholic gunpowder conspiracy of 1605 but also the landing of William of Orange at Torbay in 1688, the start of what became known as 'the Glorious Revolution'. In 1688 William's father-in-law, the Catholic James II, had fled his kingdom and in 1689 William and Mary had been crowned joint monarchs in a transfer of the Crown that did extreme violence to notions of irresistible divine right monarchy. Indeed 1688 has recently been given added significance by the work of Steve Pincus who argues that it was the 'first modern revolution'.[2] Preaching twenty years after 1688, Dr Henry Sacheverell was prosecuted in Parliament because his sermon had seemed to question the legality of 1688 and linked it conceptually to the other seventeenth-century revolution of the 1640s, arguing, as we see in this extract, that they shared a common ideology. His impeachment put 'revolution principles', as they had come to be known in Anne's reign, on trial. It provoked a vast printed debate (with about a thousand items it was one of the largest in the eighteenth century); contributed to the Tory party landslide in the elections of 1710; and resonated throughout the eighteenth century. In 1790, in the wake of the French Revolution, Edmund Burke returned to the Whig speeches at Sacheverell's trial, in order to clarify what the Whig party stood for, a party which Burke claimed had, in 1709-10, disowned the type of abstract natural rights that he warned would bring disaster in France. Sacheverell's sermon thus linked the two revolutions of the seventeenth century with the revolutionary era of the late eighteenth century.

Sacheverell was not a distinguished cleric and his hopes of becoming a bishop never materialized; he was found guilty of the impeachment charges. Yet the very mild penalty imposed on him – a ban from preaching for three years – represented a pyrrhic victory which he celebrated with an extraordinary 'progress' through the Midlands in 1710, during which he was mobbed and feted by enthusiastic supporters. His critics, the Whigs, had hoped for a show trial that would buttress their position; but Sacheverell successfully articulated and galvanized hostility to the principles underlying both the mid-seventeenth- and later-seventeenth-century revolutions.

The debate centred on three main 'revolution principles': the right of resistance; the right to freedom of worship; and the right to freedom of speech.

Underlying both the Puritan Revolution of the 1640s and the Revolution of 1688 lays a right to resist a monarch who had become a tyrant. Such a right had already been explored in the sixteenth century by French Protestants, the Huguenots, who had waged war against persecuting Catholic kings. In the passage quoted, Sacheverell was fiercely attacking Britain's own adoption of resistance theory. He had a number of targets. One was what he saw as the unholy conjuncture of Rome and Geneva, Catholicism and Calvinism, both of which upheld resistance against religious apostates and tyrants. A second was the Whig invocation of the need to protect 'Liberty and Property' at the expense, as he saw it, of religion. William's invading ship had the banner of Liberty and Property flying from its mast, and in the hands of a theorist such as John Locke, these concepts were welded, in his *Two Treatises* of 1690, into a powerful set of arguments that justified a right of resistance when liberty and property had been invaded. Sacheverell noted that alongside Liberty and Property, the Whigs also appealed to a notion of inviolable law and to the 'People' – for Locke there was a law of entrusted power that reverted to the people, the original source of all human authority, when its legal terms were breached by a tyrannous sovereign. Law was also important for other revolutionaries in both the mid- and later seventeenth centuries who nurtured a belief in an ancient constitution, a set of privileges and rights that had been won over centuries and which defended the subject against the encroaching power of a monarch. Liberty, Property, the People and the Law were thus the bedrock concepts of a new way of thinking about the nature of authority and the right of the people to resist illegal attacks on them. For a few, such rights were natural and fundamental to the contract which had created society; for more, perhaps, these rights were legal privileges that had been hard fought for over many generations. Against all this, Sacheverell clung to a notion of authority that derived from scripture and monarchical power. Such authority could not be legitimately resisted, he argued, since to do so would be to resist God; and it was a tenet of the Church of England that resistance was unlawful. In this rival version, then, church and king stood and fell together. Without an absolute and unconditional obedience, Sacheverell asserted (and many High Church Tories agreed), all authority was unstable.

The second 'revolution principle' was freedom of worship. Less apparent in the extract, but pervading Sacheverell's sermon, he voiced a vehement hostility to dissenters: those (mostly Calvinist) Protestants who either refused to worship within the Church of England, preferring to set up their own communities of gathered believers, or those who wanted to see reform of the Church of England, to remove remnants of popery that had not been fully purged by the reformation. There is a hint of Sacheverell's view in the passage where he yokes together Rome and Geneva as being in an unholy alliance against the Church of England – both Papists and Calvinists, he suggested, wanted to destroy the Church of England. Both wanted toleration from worshipping within the established church, so were natural allies. The issue of freedom of worship for such tender consciences had split the nation apart in the mid-seventeenth-century revolution (called 'wars of religion' by some commentators) and again in the later seventeenth century, when the restored monarchy had first persecuted and then tolerated the church's critics. The revolution of 1688 had resulted in the passage of the 1689 Toleration Act, which enshrined in law the principle of freedom of worship for most (Catholics, atheists and those who did not believe in the Trinity were specifically excepted). Sacheverell's sermon was so inflammatory because he suggested that the Toleration Act had been a pernicious mistake. Toleration, he insisted, nurtured 'Monsters and Vipers in our Bosom' who not only undermined the church but also took advantage of toleration to advance their political ambitions – often by hypocritically 'occasionally conforming' to the Church of England (taking the sacrament that for the rest of the year they refused) merely to qualify themselves for office under the terms of the Test and Corporation Acts, which had been passed in Charles II's reign to protect the Church of England against papists and dissenters. Thus the 'revolution principle' of liberty of conscience, Sacheverell suggested, unleashed religious unorthodoxy in the form of atheism, deism and anti-trinitarianism but it also undermined the constitution. Freedom of worship did persist, despite Sacheverell, but the relationship between church and state remained a bugbear until at least the 1820s.

The third revolution principle was the freedom of speech and of the press. The revolution of the 1640s had in part been ushered in by the collapse of the government's control over the press in November 1641 and the resulting rush of print from the presses had been revolutionary in articulating 'public opinion'. Similarly, in the wake of the Glorious Revolution, the laws requiring print to be licensed before publication were allowed to lapse in 1695, creating another flood of print and the consolidation of a newspaper and periodical market. Sacheverell claimed that the press was another means by which dangerous religious and political opinions were disseminated; and he also positioned his own trial as an attempt to censor him into silence (the extract refers to attempts to 'stop the mouths' of those like him). His sermon was condemned to be burnt by the common hangman. One image thus portrayed him with a padlocked mouth. Yet during his trial, Sacheverell had invoked, with approval, a decree of the University of Oxford in 1683 which had proscribed a set of ideological tenets drawn from Milton, Hobbes and other mid-century radicals. Moreover, Sacheverell's sermon was itself a publishing sensation, with almost 100,000 copies sold. Indeed, his trial helped consolidate an emerging visual revolution in political culture, as printed images became a routine part of the contests. This had begun in earnest during the similarly febrile atmosphere in the aftermath of the Popish Plot in 1678, but it reached new heights with the Sacheverell affair: portraits of the doctor were everywhere, and the contest over revolution principles was summed up in emblematic engravings and woodcuts. Sacheverell was depicted as a hero in some; an ally of the devil in others. Pre-publication censorship was not restored in 1710, and liberty of the press became a prized post-revolutionary norm, though in the 1790s the government again sought to clamp down on the press in the wake of the French Revolution.

The passage includes Sacheverell's outrage at the 'Murther' of Charles I on 30 January 1649, a day that in 1662 was declared an annual national day of mourning when sermon after sermon was delivered to castigate the nation for the regicide. Charles had been tried for initiating the second civil war and condemned to death by a court that he refused to recognize. His trial represented for Sacheverell the unjust perversion of the power of the people being placed over the power of the sovereign and Charles was thus a 'Martyr' for church and state. Sacheverell too saw himself as a martyr for his opposition to 'revolution principles'. Numerous copies were made of an image in which he held a portrait of Charles I, a self-conscious attempt to use the memory of one revolution to blacken the legitimacy of another. Indeed, Stuart imagery continued to be used in a variety of items – fans, handkerchiefs, glassware, pottery, ribbons – well into the eighteenth century to poke fun at the Whig heirs of 1688. Revolution was a commercial as well as an ideological commodity.

Sacheverell's sermon had also attacked those who were indifferent to religion but wedded to advancing their own self-interest, those who took advantage of the emerging fiscal-military state that the war against France that was declared in 1689 (itself a revolution in foreign policy) strengthened.[3] This was a state capable of raising unheard of amounts of taxation (following precedents along those lines in the 1640s revolution) and mobilizing unprecedentedly large armed forces, fighting not just naval war but also continental ground war. This opened up vast opportunities: not only to supply and man the army and navy but also to lend money to the crown in what became known as the 'financial revolution' that included the creation of the Bank of England in 1694 and the national debt. Sacheverell thus attacked the 'False Brethren' who 'mean nothing but getting money and preferment' at the expense of traditional values. They followed 'meer Interest and Ambition', 'the little Sordid Lucre of a Place or Preferment', ready to betray church and state if it was to their advantage. Sacheverell was tapping here into the ways in which the financial revolution was changing society – ushering in a set of commercial values that seemed to him (and to others, such

32  Revolutionary Moments

To preach up Truth, some say tis not a time | But since y⁰ Truth offends, I'll vex you more
False Brethren allwaies think y⁰ Truth a Crime | And shew y⁰ face of Truth you've wrong'd before

**Figure 3.1** Sacheverell holding a portrait of Charles I. © Trustees of the British Museum.

as Jonathan Swift) to be undermining the traditional social structures. Monied men seemed to be winning out. Indeed, Steve Pincus has recently called 1688 the 'first modern revolution' in part because it saw the triumph of a new model of 'political economy' – a rejection of the French, authoritarian form of government that equated power and land and the adoption of a Dutch model of consensual government in which labour and manufacture were key.[4]

For other commentators, 1688 marked a cultural revolution: with religious and constitutional liberty came politeness, a way of interacting with others that was perfectly suited to the post-revolutionary world of free discussion and debate and to the economic benefits that allowed men and women to consume new global commodities, such as tea, coffee and sugar, which could be consumed at the private tea-table or in the public coffee house.[5] Coffee had been introduced during the first seventeenth-century revolution – a coffee house was established in Oxford in 1650 – and the fashion caught on: by the time Sacheverell delivered his sermon, London was teeming with coffee houses. The German sociologist Jürgen Habermas thought that this conjunction of a free press, a bourgeois financial revolution and new cultural spaces in which a 'public' could operate signalled the emergence of a 'public sphere'.[6] Yet politeness was an ideal as much as a code of behaviour; and it was one that Sacheverell breached. He was a noisy firebrand who hectored his opponents with 'heat, passion, violence and scurrilous language'. His abusive, railing tone – clearly evident in the passage but even riper in other parts of the sermon – was almost the opposite of polite. Indeed, contemporaries talked of this time as the 'rage of party' – a moment when partisan passions, loyalties to the two parties of Whig and Tory that had emerged in the 1680s, had become so heightened that scuffles broke out in coffee houses and there were even some Whig drinking dens – 'mug houses' – from which violent gangs emerged to beat up Tory rivals. Vigorous and at times vicious partisanship resulted in personal attacks, in print as well as in person; in biting satires; in impassioned language; and in electioneering that frequently descended into mud-slinging and lies (the revolution of 1688 had enabled the passage of an act in 1694 that guaranteed a general election at least once every three years, keeping the nation in a state of almost perpetual electoral fever). Indeed, it can be argued that the culture of politeness was in part a reaction to the excessive passions of the partisan. Although in his sermon Sacheverell attacked 'moderation' as a lukewarm affection for the church and state, it was a quality which was prized by the polite as one that would moderate the heat of division. The cleric saw moderation as a danger; but there were plenty who thought there needed to be far more of it. And while Sacheverell railed at the dissenters as 'fanatics', he too appeared to be fanatical in his zeal (the 'Arch-Phanatick' according to one critic), an 'enthusiast' who criticized puritan enthusiasm. In the vehemence of his attack on revolution principles, Sacheverell was fuelling a cultural revolution that prized moderation, cool and rational debate and a polite way of interacting with others.

Such politeness was aimed at women as well as men. Joseph Addison's *Spectator*, which was perhaps the epitome of polite advice, specifically aimed to reach their tea-tables and give them, he said, more to talk about than their dress. Some women were leading as well as consuming this literature. Delarivier Manley, for example, was one of the first women to earn her living by her writing, a critic of the Whigs not quite in the Sacheverell mould but still sharply critical. Indeed, the revolution of 1688 sparked a reconsideration of the role of women. Mary Astell thus used Whig arguments against James II's tyranny to suggest that men privately tyrannized women, and Judith Drake even compared the plight of women to the 'Negroes in our Western Plantations'.[7] Others discerned something of a sexual revolution – toleration of religion not only leading to irreligion and atheism, as Sacheverell said, but also to libertinism. Taking off the restraints of morality and authority unleashed immorality and vice.[8] Thus 1688 provoked a 'moral revolution' – a campaign to prosecute prostitutes and to bear down on immoral behaviour. It was perhaps for this reason, as well as the flocks of adoring women who allegedly greeted his progress, that Sacheverell was satirized in visual prints with prostitutes. Hogarth even included a portrait of Sacheverell on the wall of the town miss in his series of *The Harlot's Progress* (1732).

1688 is sometimes dismissed as little more than a coup, a replacement of one monarch by his son-in-law without effecting real change. Seen through the eyes of Sacheverell, however, and seen as linked to the earlier mid-century revolution of the 1640s as he did, 1688 takes on a different complexion. For Sacheverell, and those like him, the two revolutions were profoundly disruptive and innovating: they not only introduced new principles of a right to resist, freedom of worship and freedom of the press but also provoked economic and cultural change that threatened the established order of things, introducing revolutions in foreign policy, in finance, in the armed forces, in morality and in politeness. Indeed, in many ways the revolutions of the 1640s and 1688 were still going on when Sacheverell delivered his sermon in 1709: the same issues were at stake as had troubled the nation for the previous three generations. In that sense, Sacheverell's sermon reminds us that revolutions need not be particularly quick affairs, however much the flare of events might make us think otherwise: the fallout from a revolution could provoke later revolutionary moments and the legacy of division might burn for a considerable time. Of course, with hindsight it is possible to discern that 1688 became a conservative rather than a radical revolution: partisan rivalries ossified into Whig oligarchy; adherence to property as well as liberty foreclosed any possibility of a social revolution; politeness opened up and embraced gaps between the wealthy elite and the poor and impolite masses. Yet it is also worth remembering that in 1788 celebrations of the centenary of the revolution were quite widespread and that people did look back in the later eighteenth century to 1688 as some sort of moment of change and rupture. The word 'revolution' was beginning to acquire something like its modern meaning.

## Further Reading

Cowan, B., *The State Trial of Doctor Henry Sacheverell* (Oxford: Wiley-Blackwell, 2012).

Harris, T., *Revolution: The Great Crisis of the British Monarchy, 1685-1720* (London: Penguin, 2007).

Holmes, G., *The Trial of Doctor Sacheverell* (London: Eyre Methuen, 1973).

Hoppit, J., *Land of liberty? England 1680-1727* (Oxford: Oxford University Press, 2000).

Knights, M., *The Devil in Disguise: Deception, Delusion and Fanaticism in the Early English Enlightenment* (Oxford: Oxford University Press, 2011).

Knights, M. (ed.), *Faction Displayed: Reconsidering the Impeachment of Dr Henry Sacheverell* (Oxford: Wiley-Blackwell, 2012).

# 4

# A '*révolution ménagée*': Mably's *Des droits et des devoirs du citoyen*

Johnson Kent Wright

*The faculty of reason bestowed on us by nature, the liberty in which she placed us, and the invincible desire for happiness she has fixed in our souls, are three titles to which all men may appeal in the face of the unjust government under which they live. I conclude therefore that a citizen is neither a conspirator nor a disturber of the peace, if he proposes to his compatriots a wiser form of government than that which they have adopted freely, or which events, passions, or circumstances have fashioned imperceptibly. … I believe that revolutions are still possible: a good citizen must continue to hope, and is indeed obligated, according to his position, powers, and talents, to work towards rendering these revolutions useful to his country. … I have told you my secret, added Milord with a smile, and perhaps, as an Englishman, I should not have revealed to you the sole conceivable remedy for your misfortunes. I have studied your government, your customs, your prejudices, your doctrines, and I defy you to tell me any other way to give your nation the spirit, character, and virtues that are necessary to it, and which will lead, gradually, to the destruction of despotism. By what other means can you avoid the shameful decline with which you are already menaced and to which your neighbouring nephew will certainly fall prey? Choose between a revolution and slavery: there is no middle ground. … By contrast, a revolution, prepared and followed through in the way that I have recommended to you, will be all the more advantageous, in that a love of order and law, and not that of a licentious liberty, will be its guiding principle. I mistrust any liberty that requires soldiers to establish itself; if they suppress the tyrant, it is rare indeed that they do not also usurp the tyranny – Cromwell will always have his admirers. But the wisdom of your magistrates will indeed spread to all orders of the state and will dispose men to act with courage, but also with prudence and method.*[1]

*Des droits et des devoirs du citoyen* is in many ways the most remarkable work of the abbé Gabriel Bonnot de Mably, whose career as a writer extended from the start of the War of the Austrian Succession to virtually the eve of the French Revolution. Comprising eight letters, dated 12–21 August 1758, it records a series of conversations between an Englishman, 'Milord Stanhope', and an anonymous French narrator, as the two stroll through the royal gardens at Marly. The actual date of its composition remains uncertain. There is no surviving reference to its existence on Mably's part before 1776; the dialogue was first published, posthumously, more than a decade later. But there is no internal evidence for any date later than 1758, and it is perfectly plausible that its author's well-attested circumspection had long kept *Des droits et des devoirs du citoyen* from print. If so, the reasons for Mably's caution are clear enough. For not only does the dialogue set forth a detailed scenario for toppling the Bourbon monarchy – an astonishingly clairvoyant anticipation of the actual course of events of 1787–9 – it also justifies the plan it recommends in incendiary terms, to the point of sanctioning 'civil war' itself. As the passages above make clear, central to both justification and plan was a specific conception of political 'revolution' – an idea waiting in the wings, as it were, a moment before stepping onto the stage of modern history.

The author of *Des droits et des devoirs du citoyen* was born in Grenoble in 1709, into the provincial *noblesse de robe*. An older brother became a magistrate in Lyon, where in 1740 he briefly hired a very young Jean-Jacques Rousseau as tutor in his household. Mably and his younger brother, who became the philosopher Condillac, secured modest sinecures within the ecclesiastical establishment, as precisely the sort of irreligious abbés excoriated by Voltaire. Mably in fact made his debut as a political thinker as a moderate royalist, very much in the mould of Voltaire. Around mid-century, however, he reversed course entirely, for reasons that remain obscure – although a season labouring in the bureaucracy of Foreign Affairs at Versailles seems to have played a role. By the early 1750s, he had published the works announcing his conversion to republicanism: twin observations on Ancient Greece and Rome, praising the constitutions of Sparta and the Roman Republic as the 'masterpieces' of human political design. If actually written in the late 1750s, *Des droits et des devoirs du citoyen* is likely to have been Mably's first philosophical dialogue, the literary form to which he then returned a dozen more times over the next thirty years. Not that he abandoned philosophical history: the *chef-d'oeuvre* of Mably's maturity was his three-volume *Observations sur l'histoire de France*, which traced the inexorable advance of 'despotism' in his native land. By the time it was completed, however,

Mably's earlier optimism about the prospects for overturning the Bourbon monarchy had vanished. The 'Maupeou' coup against the parlements, the end of the 'Age of Liberty' in Sweden, the First Partition of Poland, all suggested that, far from retreating, autocracy was advancing across Europe. The one bright spot was American independence. One of Mably's last works was a comparative study of the state constitutions. But at his death in 1785, the outlook for even the fledgling republics of North America looked bleak.

Scarcely two years later, the Bourbon monarchy began its slide into revolution. In the circumstances, it is hardly surprising that *Des droits et des devoirs du citoyen* met with widespread acclaim when it was finally published late in 1788. Part of its success was doubtless owing to the dialogue form itself, which permitted Mably to make effective use of date, scene and characterization alike. The catastrophe of the Seven Years' War forms the largely tacit, but unmistakable, backdrop to the dialogue – by autumn 1758 the scale of French defeat was evident enough. The gardens of Marly, on the edge of Versailles, made famous by Saint-Simon's description but now in full decline, make an apposite setting for searching conversations with a distinguished English visitor. Who was 'Milord Stanhope'? One possibility is that the reference is to Philip Dormer Stanhope, Fourth Earl of Chesterfield (1694–1773), author of the celebrated letters. Likelier still, however, is Philip Stanhope, Second Earl of Stanhope (1714–86), a more obscure figure but famed for his skill in mathematics and Greek and for the radical Whig principles he instilled in his son, Charles Stanhope, later a fervent admirer of the French Revolution; Mably alludes to both father and son in his correspondence. But whatever the precise referent, there is no doubt about the generic identity of Mably's Stanhope – here, the very model of a radical Commonwealthman, who bestows an eye-opening political education on his initially reluctant French acquaintance in two broad steps.

The first four letters of *Des droits et des devoirs du citoyen* are devoted largely to the question of political obligation and rights of resistance. The starting point is a confrontation between the two wings of modern natural rights theory, pitting Grotius, Hobbes and Pufendorf, the conservatives to whom the Frenchman appeals, against Stanhope's Locke, who is portrayed as justifying, not just a right to 'revolution', but also the duty of the citizen 'to work towards rendering these revolutions useful to his country'. Having clinched the argument, Stanhope moves on to destinations far more radical than anything in Locke. These include a ringing statement of inalienable popular sovereignty ('The people, to whom sovereign power originally belongs, the sole author of political government and bestower of power on magistrates, always retains the right to interpret its contract, or rather its gifts, to modify its clauses, or to cancel them and establish an entirely new order of things', 76); expressions of warm appreciation for class struggle and civil war ('What benefits did not result from the eternal quarrels of the patricians and plebeians in the Roman Republic? If the people had preferred repose to everything else, they would have become enslaved to the nobility and the name of the Romans unknown to us today. ... Civil war is sometimes a great good', 59); and finally, a surprising icing on the cake, an avowal that 'private property is the principle source of all the misfortunes that afflict humanity' (103). The fourth letter of *Des droits et des devoirs du citoyen* indeed ends with a brief utopian reverie à la More, with Stanhope conjuring up an island republic founded on the *communauté des biens*.

This intermezzo concluded, Stanhope then turns in the second half of the dialogue to his plan for what is explicitly termed a French 'revolution'. The basic model is supplied by the Dutch Revolt, the English Civil War and the Revolution of 1688–9 – with the proviso that none represented a fully successful overthrow of absolute monarchy. The first and third, Stanhope argues, were marred by aiming too low, the second by self-defeating overreach. Even so, the Frenchman objects, dealing with the creeping hereditization of the Stadtholdership or the excessive prerogative power of the English Crown today was one thing: 'But matters are different in nations that have a legislative monarch armed with all the powers of the state, whose presence and activity is felt everywhere, by means of officials who are instruments of his will and who believe they can extend their own power by removing any limit to that of their master' (116). How exactly was Bourbon absolutism to be overthrown? In response, Stanhope sets forth a strategic plan, consisting of three interlinked steps. The first, he argues, has actually already been accomplished, in and through the confrontation between court and parlements that had unfolded over the past decade – the successful assertion of the right of the parlements, as a whole, to represent the French 'nation' in its dealings with its king. What was still in reach of the parlements – though just barely: the moment was fading fast – was to take a second, decisive step and use the right of representation just reclaimed in order to demand a convocation of the moribund Estates-General. Once the latter had met, thirdly and finally, the estates had to make it its 'fixed and determined object' to give itself a new form and a rigorous periodicity, such as to effect a permanent transfer of legislative sovereignty: 'Thus, before dispersing, the Estates must necessarily have announced a fundamental law, a PRAGMATIC SANCTION, by which it is ordered that the representatives of the nation, armed with all of its powers, will assemble every three years without meeting any impediment, and without the need of some particular act for their convocation' (175). As to any further actions the remodelled Estates-General might take, Stanhope declines to speculate beyond urging caution. Certainly, a rigorous separation between legislative and executive power must be established, ensuring the supremacy of the former. But executive authority should be retained by a hereditary monarch, for the time being; nor should the estates make any moves to strip the nobility of its privileges, at least in the short term.

Such then was Mably's Commonwealthman's scenario for a French Revolution *'ménagée par la voie que je vous ai indiquée'*, rendered above as 'a revolution, prepared and followed through in the way that I have recommended'. There is no exact equivalent in English for the verb *'ménager'*: 'managed', 'organized', 'arranged', 'overseen' or 'guided' would be plausible alternatives. What is not in doubt is the aspiration to exert wilful control over the process by which a change of political regimes would be effected in France, by contrast with what Mably regarded as the haphazard and incomplete character of the Dutch Revolt and English Revolutions. Assuming the mask of an English sage, Mably called for what might be termed a Whig Revolution *évoluée* – to be made all the more glorious by achieving a more conclusive and irreversible transfer of sovereignty from monarch to representative assembly than the English had managed in 1689, while also avoiding the violence that had helped to defeat the earlier attempt at a Commonwealth. If the prerogative powers of the English Crown, in defiance of orthodox separation-of-powers theory, represented Scylla, the corresponding Charybdis, the citation above makes clear, was military dictatorship. It is hardly necessary to point out the degree of Mably's prescience in both respects. Thirty years before the fact, he had correctly grasped the potential for revolutionary leverage possessed by the parlements. Mably's own optimism did not survive the Maupeou 'coup' and its aftermath, which he wrongly thought had permanently robbed the parlements of this capacity. Nor did he grasp the wider dynamics of inter-state and imperial completion in this epoch – the fact that revolution in the New World was capable of detonating an even greater upheaval in the Old. But once the 'pre-Revolution' was underway, it turned out that Mably had predicted its course with uncanny precision. Just as 'Milord Stanhope' had suggested, parlementary resistance, backed by both elite and popular support, led directly to a convocation of the Estates-General for the first time in a century and a half; and the estates, once convened, proceeded with equal dispatch to a revolutionary remodelling of the French state. At the same time, the various objections that Mably ascribed to Stanhope's French interlocutor, invoking the Dutch Revolt or the English Civil War to warn of the risks of popular violence or

Cromwellian dictatorship, demonstrate the other side of his foresight. It was one thing to launch a revolution '*ménagée par la voie*' recommended by Stanhope, another to steer it to a successful conclusion.

But *Des droits et des devoirs du citoyen* represents more than just an accurate prediction of how the Bourbon monarchy would meet its end. Mably's grasp of the likely shape of a French Revolution owed everything to the way in which his thought stood at the crossroads of traditions of political thought that had hitherto tended to develop at some distance from one another. At the end of the 1960s, in his widely influential set of lectures, *Utopia and Reform in the Enlightenment*, the great historian of eighteenth-century thought Franco Venturi suggested that the 'republican ferment' that gripped France at mid-century – a first premonition of the ideological upheaval to come – was the result of the French embrace of the English Commonwealth tradition, the distilled essence of the revolutionary republicanisms of the previous century.[2] It has taken a long time for scholars to act on Venturi's suggestion. But we at last have a commanding history of the reception of Commonwealth ideas in France in Rachel Hammersley's *The English Republican Tradition and Eighteenth-Century France: Between the Ancients and the Moderns*, which rightly gives pride of place to Mably and to *Des droits et devoirs du citoyen*.[3] Indeed, the dialogue form permitted Mably to re-enact, in classically compact mimetic fashion, the very process of reception and domestication of foreign thought that Venturi hinted at and that Hammersley has analysed in depth. In it, a Commonwealthman in person treats a Frenchman to a set of tutorials, at the end of which he can declare, wrily, 'Why, you have become a republican as proud and zealous as any I know in England' (501). Yet *Des droits et des devoirs du citoyen* is very far from representing merely a faithful reproduction of Commonwealth themes. Its very title, clearly intended to echo the title that Barbeyrac gave to his translation of Pufendorf's *De officio hominis et civis* – *Les devoirs de l'homme et du citoyen*, as well as to amend it with the addition of a pivotal term, is a reminder that Mably's was a hybrid republicanism, founded on an appeal to a theory of inalienable natural rights. This kind of compound was destined, of course, to become the ideological common coin of the cycle of 'Atlantic' revolutions, from Thomas Paine's *Common Sense* onwards. But here it appears in a clear and compact statement, nearly two decades before Paine – even slightly in advance, to all appearances, of the more idiosyncratic variant on offer in *Du contrat social*, which in any case owed rather more to Hobbes than it did to Locke.[4] At the same time, there was a second unusual element in Mably's amalgam, marginal to the main concerns of *Des droits et des devoirs du citoyen* but one with a grand future ahead of it. This is the gesture in the direction of the utopian tradition and, specifically, to the *communauté des biens* at the very centre of the dialogue. As the names of Thomas More or Henry Neville indicate, the distance between the republican and the utopian traditions had never been infinite. But with Mably, the gap had suddenly narrowed considerably, bringing the idea of the abolition of private property into at least close proximity with that of political revolution. Babeuvism was only a short step away.[5]

The fate of the *Conjuration des Egaux* is a reminder that Mably's synthesis of themes from the natural rights, republican and utopian traditions was an unstable compound. The momentary fusion between classical republicanism and utopianism in Babeuf and his followers was not destined to survive the age of revolutions. The same age, however, made the amalgamation of republicanism with natural rights theory into a permanent fixture of the thought-world of modern politics. At all events, *Des droits et des devoirs du citoyen* points us, like no other political text among its contemporaries, to one of the great mysteries of the fifty-year period of the 'Atlantic' revolutions – its sheer ideological radicalism, by comparison both with what came before and what came after. This was a general feature of the American, French, Caribbean and Latin American Revolutions, which saw virtually the entire repertoire of modern political ideas emerge in recognizable form. Within the set, however, the French Revolution plainly stands apart. As its classical costume makes clear, Jacobinism was obviously not without roots in an earlier Atlantic republican tradition. Yet it just as clearly represented a major breach with that tradition, shifting it decisively in a 'levelling' direction. There were paler equivalents elsewhere in the Atlantic World – but Jacobinism alone became the *fons et origo* of the modern revolutionary tradition. It goes without saying that a full explanation of the radical turn taken by French republicanism cannot confine itself to the realm of ideology but has to be sought in a wider account of the political and social character of the Revolution. Still, it is scarcely surprising that in his *Sans-Culottes*, the most searching analysis we have of the ideological *origines lointaines* of French revolutionary republicanism, Michael Sonenscher should pay specific tribute to Mably as a more fitting precursor to Jacobinism than even Rousseau.[6] It is possible that the abbé himself would not have been surprised. Mably enjoyed a reputation in his lifetime for skill at political prediction, later claiming that he had foreseen the coming of the American Revolution as early as 1764. Paying tribute to him in 1790, the abbé Barthélémy, author of the *Voyage du jeune Anacharsis en Grèce*, recalled that Mably frequently invoked the adage of Leibniz: 'the present age is pregnant with the future' – a fitting epigraph to *Des droits et des devoirs du citoyen* and the hope it expresses for a *'révolution ménagée'*.

## Further Reading

Baker, K. M., 'A Script for a French Revolution: the Political Consciousness of the abbé Mably', in *Inventing the French Revolution: Essays on French Political Culture in the Eighteenth Century* (Cambridge: Cambridge University Press, 1990), pp. 88–106.

Hammersley, R., *The English Republican Tradition and Eighteenth-Century France: Between the Ancients and the Moderns* (Manchester: Manchester University Press, 2010), pp. 86–98 in particular.

Sonenscher, M., *Sans-Culottes: An Eighteenth-Century Emblem in the French Revolution* (Princeton: Princeton University Press, 2008), pp. 372–408 in particular.

Wright, J. K., *A Classical Republican in Eighteenth-Century France: The Political Thought of Mably* (Stanford: Stanford University Press, 1997).

# 5

# Rousseau and Revolutions

## Richard Whatmore

*Man is born free, and everywhere he is in chains. One believes himself the others' master, and yet is more a slave than they. How did this change come about? I do not know. What can make it legitimate? I believe I can solve this question.*

*If I considered only force, and the effect that follows from it, I would say; as long as a People is compelled to obey, and does obey, it does well; as soon as it can shake off the yoke, and does shake it off, it does even better; for in recovering its freedom by the same right as the right by which it was robbed of it, either the people is well founded to take it back, or it was deprived of it without foundation. But the social order is a sacred right which provides the basis for all the others. Yet this right does not come from nature; it is therefore founded on conventions. The problem is to know what these conventions are. Before coming to that, I must establish what I have just set forth.*[1]

Jean-Jacques Rousseau's commencement of the *Social Contract* is among the most memorable in the history of political writing. As a statement with revolutionary implications it would be hard to better 'Man is born free, and everywhere he is in chains'. This is certainly how many have read and have been inspired by Rousseau. Rousseau has been variously associated with the most radical creeds of the Enlightenment, has been described as a luminary of the Counter Enlightenment, has been blamed for the French Revolution and has been called the arch-advocate of democratic politics and at the same time a precursor of twentieth-century totalitarianism. One of the reasons for Rousseau's unquestionable capacity to inspire devotees is the vibrancy of his prose. Perhaps this is also the reason why his ideas are so regularly misunderstood and more often than not associated with political causes that Rousseau himself would have rejected. What everyone can agree on is the influence of Rousseau's politics. As Etienne Dumont once put it, people associated the eighteenth century with Voltaire, but in literature and in ideas he was a pygmy by comparison with Rousseau. People were, Dumont said, living through 'the age of Rousseau' from the late eighteenth and into the nineteenth century.[2] Working out what this meant, for those who understood Rousseau as well as those who followed a shadow, is the goal of this chapter.

The *Social Contract* was published in 1762 from a manuscript that Rousseau had been working on since at least the mid-1750s. As he noted in the foreword, his 'small treatise' was part of 'a longer work undertaken many years ago without consulting my strength and long since abandoned'. The *Social Contract* was therefore a fragment 'the least unworthy of being submitted to the public'. The greater work, tantalizingly, Rousseau said 'no longer exists' (40). The fact that the *Social Contract* was unfinished is of the greatest significance. It did not affect its popularity. By the time Rousseau published the book he was already famous across Europe as an author. He had been born in the tiny city republic of Geneva in 1711 and his mother died in childbirth; he was brought up by his watchmaker father and apprenticed to an engraver as a youth. At the age of sixteen Rousseau rebelled against his father and his Protestant faith by running away from Geneva and converting to Catholicism on reaching nearby Savoy. He found work over the following years as a servant and as a secretary, as a copyist of musical scores and as a tutor. He travelled and came of age at Paris in the 1740s, where he became a close friend of the polymath Denis Diderot and wrote a number of entries, mainly on music, for the latter's *Encyclopédie*. Rousseau's fame as an author, however, came overnight, when he was given the prize of the Dijon Academy for his response to their essay competition asking whether the arts and sciences had been responsible for societal progress. In 1750 Rousseau answered no, and his critique of contemporary manners and mores was recognized to be more profound and more extreme than that of any other observer.

The eighteenth century was a time of crisis during which everyone anticipated change. It was a time of war and economic difficulty, of uncertainty about religion and above all about the future of politics. In consequence, Jeremiahs abounded. But Rousseau's was the voice that condemned everything and gave a grim picture of the way people behaved and of the likely consequences of their fraudulent and unnatural lives. His next essay, now called the *Second Discourse*, addressed the question of the origins and consequences of inequality. This time, in 1755, Rousseau did not win a prize. But he did create a following across Europe. He was recognized by some to be a cynic. Others were concerned about his unorthodox religious stance. The quality of his writing and the depth of his ideas could not be challenged. Rousseau argued that the original humans had lived a life close to nature. They were solitary animals who came together fleetingly only for sex. Their passions, other than the urge to procreate, were self-preservation and pity, the feeling that brought them into contact with other human beings in deprived or dangerous situations. Sociability was not implanted by nature. Nor was it imposed by God. Pity created the first societies. They maintained themselves because of a fourth passion, that of perfectibility, or the constant desire for self-improvement, to better the human condition. Basic societies, where people lived close to nature, either roaming around or in small units, living either in villages or in caves, were where people were at their happiest in history.

The great disaster for early humans was the unleashing of the unnatural passions, the greatest of which was what Rousseau called '*amour propre*' or egotism. Natural self-love, '*amour de soi-même*', entailed self-preservation and was altogether compatible with the natural passions. But egotism was different and the source of pride, envy, hatred, bitterness and war. Rousseau's most radical claim was that egotism emerged when property became a permanent part of social living. Erecting a fence and stating 'this land is mine' was a symbol of gargantuan and ultimately deadly social change. Rousseau remained convinced that the best way for modern humans to become happy was to return to nature. This was far from easy. Language and culture were altogether corrupted. Rousseau was famously accused of wanting people to abandon society and go and live in the woods. His enemy Voltaire said after reading the *Second Discourse* that Rousseau wanted people to walk on all fours.[3] Rousseau was consequently accused of being the author of a dreadful paradox. All humans were corrupted and there was nothing that they could do about it. Rousseau claimed that his actual message was subtle. It was never going to be possible to go back in time. Nor was it possible to abolish property. Going to live in the woods or imitating the animals that Rousseau lauded (especially horses and orangutans) was pointless. It was impossible to abandon existing ways of living or to reject centuries of human history. The question was whether modern humans could adapt their ways of life so that they were closer to the natural and gradually change human history so that a return was made to forms of life that made people happy?

As noted above, Rousseau was accused of not giving people any choice other than accepting contemporary corruption, after the publication of the *Second Discourse*. The *Social Contract* was his response and the goal of the book was to describe the kinds of politics that were legitimate in the sense that they would bring humans closer to nature. It has to be remembered that Rousseau also published a far more successful book in 1762 than the *Social Contract*; entitled *Emile, or On Education*, the intention of this novel was to describe how an individual could be educated to be happy, in other words to live a natural life. *Emile* was a publishing sensation, and profound social change, concerning how to be a parent, has been ascribed to it. The contents of the book will not be considered here, although there is a lot of overlap in terms of the argument of the *Social Contract* in the fifth book of *Emile*. The point is that in each book Rousseau was trying to respond to the criticism that he was purely a cynic. His approach was to identify the worst, in the sense of most unnatural, human practices and to condemn them. At the same time, he identified natural, or in Rousseau's language 'legitimate', modes of behaviour that could be considered most natural to humans gathered together in society.

With regard to politics, Rousseau's argument was complex to say the least. This is evident from the first sentences of the *Social Contract* (copied above). Rousseau stated that modern humans had been enslaved without realizing it. Rousseau did not know how 'this change [had] come about'. But he was certain he could identify the kinds of corruption that led the contemporary rejection of natural life to be legitimized. The first step was to reject any argument from strength alone. The dictum that might was right was everywhere denounced by Rousseau. Those who lived by it were the most deluded of people. The right of the strongest was straightforwardly unnatural. The 'social order' was a 'sacred right that is the basis of all other rights'. Rousseau might have been expected at this point to assert an argument from nature in order to refute the right of the strong. Instead he did the opposite. One of the reasons the *Social Contract* is such a complex and fascinating book is because Rousseau followed the author whom readers may have considered to be his nemesis, Thomas Hobbes, and stated that 'right does not come from nature'. Social rules and political laws could not be founded on nature because the first humans were not social beings. Rather, the 'principles of political right' were to be 'founded on conventions'. Rousseau was seeking what conventions could be found to make contemporary people most happy. Rousseau's practical politics were as radical as his philosophical principles.

Perhaps the most radical statement of any Rousseau made was that states, if they were going to be ruled in the interests of the people who formed them, had to be small. Rousseau was always and straightforwardly antagonistic towards large states. Above every other he detested France, believing that it was the most corrupted country, being the most civilized in the world, and with the worst capital city in Paris, a true source of evil and iniquity. When it was suggested that Rousseau might contemplate the reform of France his response was the same: it was not possible in large states and never possible in corrupt states. France was beyond the pale. This is important for those who have drawn a line between Rousseau's work and the French Revolution.[4] The basic fact is that Rousseau would always have opposed revolution or rebellion in France, and especially any reform project that anticipated maintaining France as a large state, as all of the revolutionaries did in 1789. Rousseau was acutely aware that small states were in crisis during his lifetime. Their traditional survival strategies, from economic specialization to confederation, diplomacy and the balance of power, were insufficient before the vast resources and ambition of the centralized monarchies. Rousseau blamed commerce.

Commerce was the force that was transforming the eighteenth-century world. David Hume had written in his essay 'Of Civil Liberty' that commerce had become 'a reason of state'.[5] What he meant was that all states sought ever-greater commerce. It allowed them to project tax revenue into the future and to borrow accordingly to create huge armies supported by military technologies capable of destroying the walls of any small city and of laying waste to large areas as they battled their rivals across states and continents. Bernard Mandeville, in his famous prose poem 'The Fable of the Bees' (1705, revised 1711), wrote that commerce ought to be lauded for the wealth that came with it. The price was the growth of luxury and above all the loss of the traditional virtues, because commerce was inspired by greed and selfishness and any state that clung to ideals of self-sacrifice and dedication to the public good would quickly become poor and wretched.[6] Rousseau adopted Mandeville's view of commercial society in his description of contemporary Europe. The difference was that he disparaged the result, arguing that the loss of virtue and the growth of luxury were destroying the world. His claim was that bankers and merchants were ruling the world, with monarchs and politicians their lackeys. Something had to be done.

Rousseau's solution in the *Social Contract* was to envisage a state that was run for the people and thereby avoided the excesses of commercial society. The key was to allow the people a voice without allowing them to constitute a government. Rousseau argued that this vision could be realized by distinguishing between sovereignty and government. In the third book of the *Social Contract* he argued that the people as a whole should be sovereign. What he meant was that they should consider laws and give their consent to them gathered together in an assembly. They should never, however, put the laws into practice or propose them. This was the job of the government, the executive that ruled the small state on a day-to-day basis. The government should ideally be aristocratic, which meant for Rousseau, in Platonic register, an ideal of the rule of the worldly and the wise. Harmony was anticipated between government and people through the general will that would emerge from the laws passed by the assembly. Acknowledging the quality of their polity and the resulting legitimacy of general laws that applied to every person in the state, a common culture would emerge that for Rousseau would stand for all that was moral, virtuous and healthy. Rousseau asserted his best-known paradox in consequence. The general will, because it could be trusted neither to entail persecution or corruption, had to be adhered to by every citizen, who had of course had the chance to determine its content in the assembly. It was legitimate therefore to ensure that everyone abided by the general will. In short, it was entirely proper for people to be 'forced to be free'.

Many commentators on Rousseau during his lifetime and after have been certain that his ideal state was Geneva.[7] Genevan government embodied the distinction between sovereignty and government (having a small council of twenty-five that ran the state and a large assembly of 1,500 persons who gathered twice a year to accept or reject laws). Rousseau returned to Geneva in 1755 and was given permission by the Consistory of Pastors to return to the faith of Calvin. He praised Geneva above other places in the preface to the *Second Discourse*. The *Social Contract* was written in the aftermath of Rousseau's return. But Rousseau was never happy with the state of Geneva. He felt that it was overly commercial and corrupted by wealth. He was also certain that while many pastors were virtuous, and became his close friends and disciples, the church as a whole was not doing enough to stem the torrent of moral and political corruption within Geneva and beyond. Rousseau's ideal was actually the Alpine cantons, such as Zug or Appenzel, where labour was necessary to scrape a living from the land and where, as a result, people lived with nature and could never afford or imagine the luxuries of life. The Genevans and the French recognized how radical his vision of a transformed world was after the publication of the *Social Contract* and *Emile*. Soon after their appearance in 1762, both books were burnt for attacking religion and government.

Rousseau's *Social Contract* inspired legions of lovers of liberty to imagine an anti-commercial state ruled for the people. He was an enemy to democratic government, which he considered 'for Gods rather than for men'. He also opposed equality, believing that societies had to be divided into ranks, with the rich and able, naturally heads of families, contributing far more to politics. Women, he was certain, would be most happy in ruling the domestic realm and ought to focus on being mothers. Yet, for all of this, Rousseau's refusal to become the lackey of nobles and kings, his refusal to bow down to Protestant or Catholic authorities and his consistent condemnation of commerce, luxury, war and empire won him admirers everywhere. The precise nature of his politics was deemed uncertain, however, by many. This was because Rousseau, when called upon to judge contemporary conflicts, as he was in Geneva in the 1760s or Poland or Corsica, always avoided the revolutionary path. His deep sense that there was no point trying to reform what could never truly be changed was ever to the fore. This raised the question of whether he really was just a cynic. The fundamental problem was that the *Social Contract* remained unfinished. Rousseau promised in the book a second volume. The first part of what he called his 'Political Institutions' had described what a free state would look like. It was crucial, however, to explain how it might survive in a world of large and powerful states. Rousseau promised that he would deal with diplomacy and international relations in the second volume. His failure to publish it was a real problem for reformers. Rousseau had given them a vision of an altered world but had not explained how to get there. That is one of the reasons why Rousseau inspired revolutionary feeling while the practices that followed these sentiments were, in France, so far from anything Rousseau himself would have justified.

## Further Reading

Cranston, M., *The Noble Savage* (Chicago: University of Chicago Press, 1991).

Hont, I., *Politics and Commercial Society: Jean-Jacques Rousseau and Adam Smith* (Cambridge, MA: Harvard University Press, 2015).

Neuhouser, F., *Rousseau's Theodicy of Self-Love: Evil, Rationality, and the Drive for Recognition* (Oxford: Oxford University Press, 2008).

Sonenscher, M., *Before the Deluge: Public Debt, Inequality, and the Intellectual Origins of the French Revolution* (Princeton: Princeton University Press, 2007).

# 6

# Exclusion at the Founding: The Declaration of Independence

### Robert G. Parkinson

*We hold these truths to be self-evident, that all men are created equal, that they are endowed by their Creator with certain unalienable Rights, among these are the right to Life, Liberty, and the pursuit of Happiness …*

*He has excited domestic insurrections amongst us, and has endeavoured to bring on the inhabitants of our frontiers, the merciless Indian Savages, whose known rule of warfare, is an undistinguished destruction of all ages, sexes and conditions.*[1]

The Declaration of American Independence was always intended to speak to two separate audiences. The first, and perhaps primary, one was what Thomas Jefferson referred to in the document as a 'candid world', the Europeans he imagined who waited with anticipation to render their opinions about this massive colonial rebellion. In truth, the Declaration should have been written in French, for it was the court at Versailles that the Congress really meant to impress. The entire exercise was a work of legitimization, to put the American rebellion in a posture of righteous and justified resistance, supported by appeals to universal rights and Enlightenment principles. Though they were doing something innovative, American patriots wanted the 'candid world', especially the French, to consider their declaration of independence as nothing new, but rather a statement highly steeped in historical precedent and tradition. They sought to portray the American rebellion as a new Glorious Revolution, a repeat of perhaps the most hallowed event in the history of English liberty. The patriots laboured to present 1776 as 1688 redux.

That is the reason behind the opening two paragraphs, the Declaration's preamble. Ever since the tolling bells stopped announcing the news, scholars, politicians, historians, social activists and admirers throughout the world have tried to discern the true meaning of those paragraphs. Scores of students have wrestled over what or whom Jefferson intended by 'created equal', 'pursuit of happiness', 'self-evident', 'unalienable rights', 'all men'. Those analysts constitute another audience, the 'candid world' that pored over the Declaration and its meaning long after 1776. They were (and are) the candid posterity that drafted, adapted and shaped Jefferson's Declaration to fit their own circumstances. Abraham Lincoln was one of those students. Eight decades on, Lincoln continually invoked the preamble of Jefferson's Declaration as the unfulfilled promise of the American republican experiment. Many others in the nineteenth and twentieth centuries – in the candid posterity – invoked the Declaration's opening paragraphs to legitimize their own varying political and social agendas.

Yet, at the same time, this taking the Declaration out of its specific context thoroughly alters its intention and purpose. The 'candid world' outside North America at the time or the 'candid posterity' who fixated on the opening paragraphs ever since were not the only audiences Jefferson and the Continental Congress intended when they ordered the Declaration to be printed and read aloud in the summer of 1776.

In other words, since 1776 we have been mostly reading the Declaration of Independence wrong.[2] The Declaration of Independence was a political document meant to achieve specific domestic goals at a particular historical moment. It was a statement intended to cultivate popular opinion for the revolutionary movement at home, to solidify support among the minority of colonists who backed the 'common cause' and, more importantly, to convince the large number of inhabitants who considered themselves neutral or 'disaffected' that the patriots were right. To understand this, it is necessary to focus on the body of the Declaration, not the preamble. By broadening our attention away from the universalist opening lines to include an analysis of the twenty-seven grievances that comprise the Declaration's body – especially the last, climactic charge – we can grasp the purpose of the document.

Without a compelling, concrete list of grievances that resonated with all audiences, foreign and domestic, the preamble would have been impotent. The twenty-seven charges levelled at King George III were essential to the Declaration's immediate reception and were therefore quite carefully assembled. Instead of presenting the case chronologically, Jefferson grouped them for maximum effect. The first dozen reached back a decade or more into the imperial crisis, centring on abuses of executive authority. Many of these first charges were in and of themselves hardly inspiring enough to encourage farmers to rush to their muskets, but Jefferson was starting slowly. They were meant to incorporate as many local issues as people in the various thirteen colonies might have separately felt, meant to be a summary statement from all of the mainland provinces. So, therefore, while only New Yorkers really felt the particular repercussions of not paying for the supply of British troops, or even though Massachusetts was the only colony to suffer from the removal of their assembly and court records, Congress included them as a complaint from all rather than some, however minor they might appear.

The second dozen focused on a menu of tyrannical parliamentary acts and the king's willingness to enforce them, especially the Coercive and Quebec Acts. Here are the American complaints about taxes and perceived alterations in where the colonies stood in the constitutional apparatus of the British Empire. Whereas Jefferson listed each of the first-dozen grievances with a separate, personal accusation aimed at King George, beginning with 'he has', most of the grievances in this second set abandoned this patterned march of indictment by stringing together a list of eight infractions with colons, creating an effect of one collective, singular charge against the Crown.

As Jefferson pivoted into the past year of violence, the Declaration approached its apex. The verbs alone give it away. The accusations levelled at George earlier on were rather feeble: he had 'dissolved', 'obstructed' and 'refused'. In the final five presentments, the king's crimes were far more severe. In the concluding charges, Congress submitted powerful accusations that the king had 'plundered', 'ravaged' and 'destroyed'. These final charges carried a great deal of rhetorical and political weight; their acceptance by the 'opinions of mankind' could determine whether American independence was deemed legitimate and defensible or not.

The delegates to Congress grasped this importance. They tinkered with this last group of accusations more than all the other grievances during their editing sessions on 2–3 July. Other than a few touches to rearrange words or slice extraneous phrases, Jefferson's first twenty-two grievances entered the final Declaration largely intact. But as the stakes increased, so did Congress's attention. They edited the last five charges heavily, striking out one entirely from Jefferson's rough draft (on encouraging loyalists by offering them confiscated property), adding evocative phrases that deepened the king's crimes and, most of all, paring down to a few words Jefferson's long passage that blamed the king for the crime of 'waging cruel war against human nature itself' by continuing the African slave trade. When students lay Jefferson's rough draft against the final Declaration, it is no accident that most of the red ink is at this point, the document's climax.

There was more to Jefferson's pivot than just amplified resentment. When the Declaration moved from legislative acts to violent acts, the king suddenly had lots of helpers. To this point in the 'long train of abuses and usurpations', George had been the sole designer 'to reduce them under absolute Despotism'. Apparently, he had personally 'ravaged our coasts, burnt our Towns, and destroyed the Lives of our People'. In the final three grievances, the king had far more assistants outside the Commons or cabinet.

For the first time there were vague categories of numerous proxies acting on the king's account. Some of these aides could not be blamed; they were, after all, acting against their will: 'He has constrained our fellow Citizens taken Captive on the high Seas to bear Arms against their Country, to become the Executioners of their Friends and Brethren, or to fall themselves by their Hands.' Other proxies could not claim a similar absolution.

> He is, at this time, transporting large Armies of foreign Mercenaries to compleat the Works of Death, Desolation, and Tyranny, already begun with circumstances of Cruelty and Perfidy, scarcely paralleled in the most barbarous Ages, and totally unworthy of the Head of a Civilized Nation.
>
> He has excited domestic Insurrections amongst us, and has endeavoured to bring on the Inhabitants of our Frontier, the merciless Indian savages, whose known rule of Warfare, is an undistinguished Destruction of all Ages, Sexes and Conditions.

Here, at the climax, a panoply of enemies stands against the 'Free and Independent States'. The king was joined by willing assistants: rebellious slaves, hostile Indians and German mercenaries.

It was not surprising that Congress concluded its indictment with these particular charges. Since the news of Lexington and Concord had spread throughout North America late in April the year before, worries about what role African Americans and Indians might play in the now-war with Britain preoccupied patriots' minds. Starting in the summer of 1775, rumours of slave insurrections and Indian attacks swept through the American countryside, from the Canadian Frontier to the Carolinas. Accounts suggesting a myriad of British officials, from army officers and imperial agents to royal governors, were attempting to 'spirit up', 'tamper with' or 'instigate' Indians and African Americans to intercede in the fighting appeared almost without cessation throughout the year preceding independence.

Newspaper accounts – managed and promulgated by patriot leaders – then collected and substantiated those rumours. They were the first sustained group of war stories of the Revolutionary War. Patriot political and communications leaders played upon inherited fears of slave insurrections and Indian massacres as the terror of colonial American society, turning the British into the conductors of those nightmares. One of the victims of those stories, the British Superintendent for Indian Affairs in South Carolina, wrote from his forced exile to Florida, 'The newspapers were full of Publications calculated to excite the fears of the People. ... Massacres and Instigated Insurrections were Words in the mouth of every Child.'[3] In the autumn, rumours about the Crown begging for mercenary troops, first from Catherine the Great of Russia (unsuccessfully) and then from a group of German princes (successfully), also swept through the American colonies. For months before Jefferson sat down to draft the Declaration, stories about slaves, Indians and foreign mercenaries aiding in the violent suppression of the rebellion were narratives that were well known by many colonists across North America.[4] Patriot leaders continually invoked the use – or, to be precise, the potential use – of these groups as proxies of British tyranny. Those war stories were the essence of the king's attempt to destroy or enslave them, far more than just restricting their rights to jury trials or consent to taxation. Once the shooting started, patriot leaders described the plotting of British officials in America (from Indian agents and royal governors to naval captains and army officers) to encourage slaves, Indians and foreign mercenaries to murder them as the ultimate deal-breaker with the Crown. These ubiquitous stories were the centrepiece of the 'common cause' after April 1775. Indeed, in the case of the king's proxies – whether slaves, Indians or mercenaries – when Jefferson remembered five decades on that the Declaration neither aimed at 'originality of principle or sentiment' but was 'intended to be an expression of the American mind' his memory was well served.[5]

On 3 July 1776, John Adams wrote home to Abigail, 'The Second Day of July 1776 will be the most memorable Epocha in the History of America. I am apt to believe that it will be celebrated, by succeeding generations, as the great anniversary Festival.'[6] Adams, who would complain three decades later about Jefferson's wrest-of-glory as a '*coup de théâtre*', would not allow himself to grasp the importance of the Declaration as a necessary performance.[7] For him, it simply stated the obvious: when the king withdrew his protection, America was independent by default. The 'theatre', however, offered an opportunity to present heroes and villains not just to the 'candid world' but to colonists throughout North America. These final grievances sought to make the case that 'we' – the 'one people' who 'hold these truths to be self-evident' – were distinct from and superior to their 'British brethren'. It was a summary statement of the 'common cause'.

But it was nevertheless an exclusionary one. At the crucial founding moment, the definition of what it meant to be an American was a negative one: not-British. But the heated language of the Declaration's final grievances gave it other shapes, especially not-slave and not-savage. Those negative constructions reinforced the patriots' positive assessment of themselves as holding the moral, philosophical and political high ground in this conflict. Because those tropes plugged into deeply embedded colonial prejudices about Africans and Indians, however, they were more than just stock tropes about not behaving in manners that were slavish or savage. They had the effect of casting out real Indians and African Americans.

Outside Huntington, on the north shore of New York's Long Island, a crowd 'from all the distant quarters of the district' gathered on 22 July to show their approval for independence. After a public reading of the Declaration, the assembly celebrated by constructing a visual representation of the multiple enemies of the new United States of America. A newspaper report detailed the actions of that July afternoon:

> An effigy of [George III] being hastily fabricated out of base materials, with its face black like *Dunmore's* Virginia regiment, its head adorned with a wooden crown, and its head stuck full of feathers, like *Carleton* and *Johnson's* savages, and its body wrapped in the Union [Jack] instead of a robe of state, and lined with *gunpowder*, which the original seems fond of.

'The whole', the article concluded, 'was hung on a gallows, exploded, and burnt to ashes'.[8] In essence, the crowd of Long Islanders gave their own performance of the Declaration. They defended 'life, liberty, and the pursuit of happiness' by animating and then destroying both the king and his proxies simultaneously. The New Yorkers consigned all their enemies – the king, the 'merciless savages' and the 'domestic insurrectionists' – to the flames, leaving 'Americans' to stand outside and watch the blaze. The names of enemies listed in the article (Dunmore, Carleton and Johnson) were some of the notorious royal officials whom patriots had broadcast as being tied to slave insurrections and Indian hostility in colonial newspapers throughout 1775–6. For those Long Islanders, all their enemies – the king and his officers and their blackened and feathered proxies – were outside the social compact Jefferson sketched in the preamble and therefore enemies of the American people. Consigning them to the flames was the natural outcome of more than a year of hearing patriot leaders construct the conflict in that particular fashion. That expression of rage and exclusion defined those who were, for the first time, declaring something – that they were an independent people. It outlined the boundary between the people who were to be included in the 'we' and those who were not.

That this distinction and division occurred in the nation's founding document would be crucial in years to come. Jefferson and Congress made no exceptions in their announcement that all Indians were 'merciless savages', leaving no room for the thousands of Stockbridge, Oneida, Tuscarora, Catawba, Delaware or Shawnee Indians who supported the patriot cause. Nor did the Declaration leave any space for African Americans who served bravely in the Continental Army, the most racially integrated force the United States would embody until the Vietnam War. They too were all deemed enemies, all 'domestic insurrectionists' who sought to undermine the Revolution. The Declaration allowed for no nuance or gradations; it made bold assertions and lumped people into categories, cordoning off 'friend' from 'enemy', 'us' from 'them'. In addition to the central division cordoning off 'he' (the king) from 'we' (the American people), the final grievances also gave some evidence of who belonged to that latter group – and who did not.

As the Revolutionary War continued, patriot leaders continued to amplify stories in their newspapers of British agents 'instigating' with African Americans in the Deep South and 'tampering' with Indians throughout the backcountry. After Washington's forces routed the Hessians at Trenton, patriot leaders stopped amplifying stories of German mercenaries as fearsome destroyers and began portraying them as pitiful fellow victims of monarchical despotism. Their refusal to continue telling stories about Germans as King George's proxies opened up a space for their redemption. Not so with slaves and Indians. Though critical as the founding statement of the United States, the Declaration was but one of the ways patriot political leaders associated African Americans and Indians with British tyranny. Week after week in their local newspapers they read stories about *these* proxies (but not foreign mercenaries) undermining the cause of liberty and freedom throughout the remainder of the war. This too was foundational to the experience of the Revolution for many Americans.

Before they solidified in the nineteenth century, concepts of racial difference were under construction during the late 1700s. They were in part a reaction to the claims of natural rights and universalism posited by the Enlightenment and in subsequent revolutions in America, France, Haiti and Latin America. Here we, like Lincoln, can credit the Declaration's preamble for being a touchstone in that Enlightenment project. In this view, Jefferson's soaring words of 'all men' being 'created equal' fixed an agenda by which equality, democracy and human rights were imperatives that defined the modern condition. However, further down that very same page, Jefferson himself provided important evidence to challenge those universalist claims. The Declaration also forwarded an argument for exclusion and racial discrimination. By taking into consideration both sides of the Declaration – the preamble and the climactic grievances – we can see the central paradox of the American Revolution and the contradictions of race, citizenship, belonging and equality that Americans would face throughout the early history of the United States.

## Further Reading

Armitage, D., *The Declaration of Independence: A Global History* (Cambridge, MA: Harvard University Press, 2007).

Becker, C. L., *The Declaration of Independence: A Study in the History of Political Ideas* (New York: Knopf, 1940 [1922]).

Maier, P., *American Scripture: Making the Declaration of Independence* (New York: Knopf, 1997).

Wills, G., *Inventing America: Jefferson's Declaration of Independence* (Garden City, NY: Doubleday, 1978).

# 7

# Securing Liberty: The *Federalist Papers*

## T. G. Rodgers

*An enlightened zeal for the energy and efficiency of government will be stigmatized as the offspring of a temper fond of despotic power and hostile to the principles of liberty. An over-scrupulous jealousy of danger to the rights of the people, which is more commonly the fault of the head than of the heart, will be represented as mere pretense and artifice, the stale bait for popularity at the expense of public good. It will be forgotten, on the one hand, that jealousy is the usual concomitant of violent love, and that the noble enthusiasm of liberty is too apt to be infected with a spirit of narrow and illiberal distrust. On the other hand, it will be equally forgotten that the vigor of government is essential to the security of liberty; that, in the contemplation of a sound and well-informed judgment, their interests can never be separated; and that a dangerous ambition more often lurks behind the specious mask of zeal for the rights of the people than under the forbidding appearance of zeal for the firmness and efficiency of government. History will teach us that the former has been found a much more certain road to the introduction of despotism than the latter, and that of those men who have overturned the liberties of republics, the greatest number have begun their career by paying an obsequious court to the people, commencing demagogues and ending tyrants.*[1]

The *Federalist Papers*, written by James Madison, Alexander Hamilton and John Jay, are widely regarded as a classic, indeed the classic, work of American political thought. A justification for the Constitution of the United States, the *Federalist's* exegesis of republican government has been hallowed by the undiminished vitality of the Constitution as the heart of the American state. The Declaration of Independence and the Constitution may embody the deeds of the American Revolution, but it was the *Federalist Papers* that provided the most sustained prose vision of the revolutionary settlement. Yet such canonical status is problematic;

the *Federalist* was a polemical vision produced in a moment of great debate over the legacy of 1776 and the future of the nation.[2] The arguments posited by Hamilton, Madison and Jay were, in their own ways, revolutionary and yet appeared to turn the values of the Revolution upon their head. In its advocacy for the ratification of the Constitution the *Federalist* advanced the notion that liberty could only be preserved by endowing the new federal government with authority. The security of liberty was no longer to be guaranteed solely by the vigilance of the people but by the workings of a carefully constructed system of government.

Alexander Hamilton (1755–1804) was the instigator of the *Federalist* project and the most prolific contributor of letters, all written under the pseudonym 'Publius', which appeared serially in a number of New York newspapers between 1787 and 1788.[3] In *Federalist* No. 1 Hamilton introduced the underlying premise of the *Federalist*'s contribution to the ratification debate. The proposed Constitution, which had sprung secretly and unexpectedly from a forum charged with merely ameliorating the defects of the Articles of Confederation, sought to balance the cherished notion of liberty with the need for a more effective form of government. Fearing the seemingly inevitable tendency of power to enrich itself at the expense of liberty, the convention delegates who had convened in Philadelphia devised a plan that carefully balanced the different branches of government. This system of checks and balances introduced a fissiparous tension between the Legislature, Executive and Judiciary that would quash any attempt to engross power at the expense of the people. For the *Federalist*, and in particular for Hamilton, government was not merely something that had to be guarded against; rather, vigorous government was 'essential to the security of liberty'. This was a controversial statement given the ideological principles that had given birth to revolutionary fervour only a decade or so before.

For a complex event the Revolution's ideological origins were surprisingly coherent, or rather, the pattern of the many strands of political thought that comprised the fabric of revolutionary motivation boldly delineated an idea of republican virtue countering corruption and tyranny.[4] There was a dramatic interplay of ideas and events throughout the imperial crisis of 1765–75 as tit-for-tat acts by parliament provoked colonial patriot resistance, fuelled by an increasingly bellicose rhetoric on both sides of the Atlantic in pamphlets, newspapers and on the street. Arguably the most powerful denunciation of British measures and a strident call for independence was Thomas Paine's *Common Sense*, published in Philadelphia at the start of 1776. Paine's direct style conveyed a principle that chimed with the mood of the time; he began his treatise with the distinction between society and government, paraphrasing the notion of the social contract. Reminding his readers that the origins of government were prompted by 'wickedness' and the necessity of 'restraining our vices', Paine was adamant that 'government, even in its best state, is but a necessary evil'. Although the rest of *Common Sense* was concerned with revealing the rottenness of the English constitution and the advisability of making a clean break, Paine's distrust of government did not obviate its fundamental purpose, 'viz. freedom and security'.[5] Although the apparent division between Paine's distrust of government and Publius's advocacy of the same is, in this important respect, one of tone rather than substance, the tenor of *Common Sense* was to stir a profound hostility towards governmental power. The experience of the Revolution served to reinforce such feelings and hostility to anything that suggested arbitrary power, a wellspring of popular ideology that was to challenge the principles of the Constitution, especially by the Anti-Federalists.[6]

It was a fear of tyranny that had severely limited the scope of Congressional authority over the Thirteen States and the powers with which it could act. For the leading proponents of sweeping political reform, especially James Madison (1751–1836), the lack of authority possessed by Congress was a dismal embarrassment that only became more pronounced in the difficult post-war years of the mid-1780s. Even worse, events such as Shays's Rebellion in Massachusetts in 1786 raised the fear that law and order would be upset by the rule of the mob. Madison drafted a cogent summary of his principal concerns in April 1787; entitled 'Vices of the Political system of the U. States', the unfinished list of twelve points concentrated on the vexed relationship between the individual states and the Continental Congress. Point 7 identified the glaring omission in the existing settlement, a 'want of sanction to the laws, and of coercion in the Government of the Confederacy'.[7] A delegate to the Continental Congress, Madison shared with the cadre of senior Continental Army officers a profound frustration with the inability of the states to pull together on matters of profound mutual interest. As Madison elaborated under the heading of point 7, 'Even during the war, when external danger supplied in some degree the defect of legal & coercive sanctions, how imperfectly did the States fulfil their obligations to the Union? In time of peace, we see already what is to be expected.' Therefore, the remedy of the Constitution was to vest coercive authority over the states in the federal government; no longer could one state act against the good of the whole, nor stand by while others were in need.

The shift in the locus of sovereignty from the state government to the federal government, exemplified in the words 'We the People' that open the Constitution, was profound; and it was a transformation that alarmed the Anti-Federalists.[8] However, for the authors of the *Federalist*, it was the principal means by which domestic tranquillity could be assured harmoniously. As Hamilton explained,

> Government implies the power of making laws. It is essential to the idea of a law that it be attended with a sanction; or, in other words, a penalty or punishment for disobedience. If there be no penalty annexed to disobedience, the resolutions or commands which pretend to be laws will, in fact, amount to nothing more than advice or recommendation. This penalty, whatever it may be, can only be inflicted in two ways: by the agency of the courts and ministers of justice, or by military force; by the COERCION of the magistracy, or by the COERCION of arms. The first kind can evidently apply only to men; the last kind of necessity be employed against bodies politic, or communities, or States. (149)

The problem of the Confederation government was that it was not a collection of individual citizens but individual states; a situation that rendered force of arms inevitable.

> In an association where the general authority is confined to the collective bodies of the communities that compose it, every breach of the laws must involve a state of war; and military execution must become the only instrument of civil obedience. Such a state of things can certainly not deserve the name of government, nor would any prudent man choose to commit his happiness to it. (149)

Hamilton elaborated this point in the following number, No. 16, in which he explored the likely possibilities of individual states or groups of states resisting the demands of the national government. In such circumstances the attempt of the federal government to enforce its will would in all likelihood lead to war, doubtless resulting in the 'dissolution of the Union' (153). Given the brief experience of the ineffectual confederation government, the resort to arms to compel obedience was both unworkable and unlikely. If coercive sanctions against the states were unfeasible the obvious solution was to bind the national government to individual citizen; and vice versa. In so doing the federal government 'must itself be empowered to employ the arm of the ordinary magistrate to execute its own resolutions'. In short, the will of government was to be enforced, as in the states, through the wholly unexceptionable means of the courts, operating with neither more nor less efficacy than the existing means of compelling compliance to the laws of the polity. 'The government of the Union, like that of each State, must be able to address itself immediately to the hopes and fears of individuals; and to attract to its support those passions which have the strongest influence upon the human heart' (154). With a simple yet radical shift, the vigour of government would be mildly effected by its most proper arm, rather than by brutal and unwieldy force.

Hamilton and Madison, who were strongly agreed on this point of sovereignty, justified the federalist nature of coercive power with reference to the problems of the day and also to historical precedent. The Enlightenment values that informed the political principles of the *Federalist* also trumpeted the importance of historical precept.[9] The republicanism espoused by the patriots during the Revolution naturally led to great interest in classical examples and influences. Madison devoted three numbers (18, 19 and 20) to uncovering the flaws of the various republican confederacies of Ancient Greece and identifying the lessons for the present case. Of greatest alarm was the imbalance of power between the different states within the Amphictyonic league and the consequent lack of common will, a situation that led to 'the weakness, the disorders, and finally the destruction of the confederacy' (160). Classical precedents were particularly telling, given the democratic nature of the polities and the tragedy of their lapse into tyranny, but Madison also elaborated on contemporary examples from Europe. Whereas the Holy Roman Empire had been torn asunder by conflict between its members in the Thirty Years' War, the United Provinces (Netherlands) were only held together by external threats. All were cautionary tales of what ought to be avoided by the United States. Madison echoed Hamilton's prescription, arguing that historical example demonstrated that 'sovereignty over sovereigns ... as contradistinguished from individuals' was 'subversive of the order and ends of civil polity, by substituting *violence* in place of the mild and salutary *coercion* of the *magistracy*' (172).

If coercive authority was a necessary and an effective means of securing liberty it was nonetheless vulnerable to the abuse of tyranny. Vigorous government may have been the means of preserving liberty, but too vigorous an extension of power, anything that amounted to the suppression of liberty, would have been, in Madison's view, a remedy 'worse than the disease' (123). In No. 37 Madison expanded on the difficulties faced by the convention in achieving this delicate balance. The ingredients of effective government, energy and stability, could not be easily reconciled with the 'genius of republican liberty' (243). Whereas energy and stability required decisiveness and duration of office for those in power, republican liberty required deliberation and frequent recourse to the people. For Madison, the Constitution not only established an appropriate balance, but also was achieved by the delegates with 'unanimity almost as unprecedented as it must have been unexpected' (246); such confidence was born not merely from a belief in the fitness of the constitutional mechanism but also from the greatest safeguard against tyranny, the vigilance of the people themselves.

The precedent of resistance to intolerable coercion was clearly established by the events of the Revolution itself. Echoing Lockean notions of justifiable resistance, Hamilton wrote of the final recourse to the 'original right of self-defense' were the representatives ever to 'betray their constituents' (206).[10] Not only had this principle been established, the people's resolve and ability to safeguard their liberty had been tested and vindicated. In a defence of the construction of the House of Representatives (*U.S. Constitution*, Art I, § 2) in No. 55, Madison countered the notion that the initially small number of elected representatives would be inherently dangerous to liberty.

> I am unable to conceive that the people of America, in their present temper, or under any circumstances which can speedily happen, will choose, and every second year repeat the choice of, sixty-five or a hundred men who would be disposed to form and pursue a scheme of tyranny or treachery. (337)

Hamilton, in defending the proposed senate from the charge of aristocratic tendencies, similarly relied on the presumption that any attempt to counteract a republican spirit would be swiftly curtailed by the popular assembly, the House of Representatives, as had been demonstrated in Britain where the House of Commons had the ascendancy (374).

The sustained defence of the provisions of the Constitution was conducted in a rhetorical mode that dismissed fears of excessive governance as imagined, unreasoned or deliberately misconstrued. On the contrary, the unfolding of the Constitution's provisions detailed in the numbers of the *Federalist* emphasized time and again that the safeguards to liberty were secure. Whether it was in the separation of powers between the legislative, executive or judicial branches of the government; the terms of appointment to either branch; or the relationship between the Union and the States, historical precedent, current example and common sense were relentlessly marshalled to prove fears of tyranny groundless. So secure, in fact, was liberty that the genius of the republic was to be found in the distance that the Constitution opened between the passions of the people and the calm contemplations of government. It was a balance of which Hamilton could ask, 'What more can an enlightened and reasonable people desire?' (436).

Inevitably, not all citizens of the United States were as enlightened and reasonable in their support of the federal government as its architects could have desired. The language of states' rights became increasingly shrill as advocates for secession (and slavery) finally provoked the outbreak of the Civil War in 1861.

Yet it was the inner steel of authority within the Constitution, clearly identified in the *Federalist*, which undergirded the Union's coercive response against the secessionist rebels. More recently the concern with the 'original intent' of the founders has propelled the vision of Hamilton, Madison and Jay into the front rank of revolutionary texts; in particular, Madison's Nos 10 and 51 retain especial force. However, as the case of the Civil War demonstrates, it would be misguided to cherry-pick from the complex and nuanced writings of Publius merely the words and phrases that appeal to the purposes of the reader. The enthusiasm for liberty within the *Federalist* is carefully balanced by the vision of an energetic system of government, a government endowed with coercive authority and a government whose purpose was to be effective.

## Further Reading

Edling, M. M., *A Revolution in Favor of Government: Origins of the U.S. Constitution and the Making of the American State* (Oxford: Oxford University Press, 2003).

Madison, J., A. Hamilton, and J. Jay, *The Federalist Papers*, ed. Isaac Kramnick (London: Penguin Books, 1987).

Rakove, J., *Original Meanings: Politics and Ideas in the Making of the Constitution* (New York: Vintage, 1997).

Wills, G., *Explaining America: The Federalist* (New York: Penguin Books, 2001; original edn 1981).

# 8

# Revolution, Reform and the Political Thought of Emmanuel-Joseph Sieyès

Michael Sonenscher

*The plan of this work is quite simple. There are three questions that we have to ask of ourselves.*

*1° What is the Third Estate? –* **Everything***.*
*2° What, until now, has it been in the existing political order? –* **Nothing***.*
*3° What does it want to be? –* **Something***.*

These are the opening words of the single most famous pamphlet of the French Revolution: Emmanuel-Joseph Sieyès' *What Is the Third Estate?* or *Qu'est-ce qu'est le tiers état?* as the pamphlet was originally entitled when it appeared in Paris late in January 1789.[1] The three questions that Sieyès used to frame the pamphlet's argument were, substantively, questions about the subjects of reform and revolution, not only because of the relevance of these subjects to conditions in late eighteenth-century France, but also because they had already arisen in the context of a number of earlier political conflicts in Europe and the Americas during the two previous decades. The best known now is the American Revolution of 1776, with its outcome in the ratification of the Constitution of the United States of America, a process that took place at almost the same time as the French Revolution began. But the subjects of reform and revolution were also central to several other political conflicts that occurred in the decade before 1789, notably in the Swiss republic of Geneva, in the United Provinces of the Netherlands and in the Holy Roman Empire, as well as in the movement for electoral reform that arose in Britain during and after the American war. From this perspective, Sieyès' pamphlet was not only an intervention in French politics, but also an outcome of an older, European-wide discussion of established political regimes and how they could be changed. In this context, the political thought of Jean-Jacques Rousseau had a particular salience, both because of Rousseau's frequently repeated prediction that, as he put it in his novel *Emile* in 1762, 'we are approaching the state of crisis and the century of revolutions' and because of his unusually acute precision in identifying what, whether individually, morally or institutionally, was likely to be required to turn intense political conflict into peaceful political change.[2]

Sieyès' pamphlet registered both these aspects of Rousseau's thought. It was designed to be the means to establish what Sieyès was later to call a monarchical republic, meaning a political system in which sovereignty was democratic, or came from below, but where the government had the same pyramidal shape as the government of a monarchy, with a large electoral base and a single elected head. Sieyès was careful to distinguish this type of political system from what he called a republican monarchy, meaning a political system with a popular government and a single, royal sovereign. *What is the Third Estate?*, Sieyès later observed, was written to turn the inverted triangle of absolute government right side up. Its immediate purpose, however, was to address the two major problems thrown up by the political argument that began in France in the spring of 1786. These problems were a product of growing disagreement over the range of possible measures required to fund the French royal deficit. The first problem was about political legitimacy and political decision-making. Here, what mattered was the question of identifying who had the right to decide what to do about the deficit. The second was a problem about political implementation and political coordination. Here, what mattered was the question of identifying an agent and a sequence of steps able to deliver an outcome compatible with the answer to the first question. Sieyès' pamphlet was designed to answer both questions.

It is important, however, to see that the answers to the two questions pulled against one another very strongly. The answer to the first question, Sieyès emphasized, could not be France's king, Louis XVI, even though the French monarchy was, formally, absolute and, accordingly, could not be subject to a higher power. Although its unitary nature made it well equipped to deal with the second question, the same quality ruled it out as an answer to the first. But restoring the old French Estates-General, with its separate assemblies made up of representatives of the clergy, the nobility and the third estate (meaning the mass of people, from peasants and labourers to lawyers and bankers, who did not belong to the church or the nobility) was equally impossible. The number of separate agencies involved in this form of decision-making meant that reviving an assembly of the Estates-General to deal with the two questions was likely to produce many answers but no action. Instead, Sieyès argued, the right to decide what to do about the deficit had to belong to the whole French nation. In itself, the claim was not unusual. Many of the hundreds of pamphlets published before 1789 made something like the same claim, frequently insisting on the nation's right to call the royal ministry to account for its financial management and demanding that all three estates share equitably in the fiscal and financial sacrifices that were likely to be required to fund the deficit. Sieyès, however, made a further move, centred on the nature and power of the third estate. The third estate, he asserted at the very beginning of his pamphlet, was 'a complete nation'. This was the move that made his reputation. It explained why the answer to the question *What Is the Third Estate?* had to be 'everything' and why, by extension, the answer to the question of who had the right to decide what to do about the deficit turned out, daringly, to be simply the third estate. A nation, Sieyès explained, needed a range of private occupations and a number of public services to be a nation. The private occupations in question would encompass agriculture, industry, trade and the various professions, while the public services would include the army, the legal system, the church and the administration. Together, the combination of private occupations and public services amounted to what Sieyès called a representative system. All the activities required to make this system work were, he claimed, carried out by the members of the third estate, even if the members of the two privileged orders, the clergy and the nobility, were still nominally at the head of parts of the royal government. It followed that, since the members of the third estate were responsible for doing all the things that a nation needed to do in order to be itself, the third estate was a self-sufficient, independent nation and, like any 'complete nation', could not be subject to a higher power (94, 98). It was, in fact, just like a state.

It followed, Sieyès emphasized, that when, as the king had announced, an assembly of the three estates of the kingdom began to meet, the representatives of the third estate were entitled to take sole responsibility for deciding not only what to do about the deficit, but also to draft a constitution compatible with the sovereignty of the French nation. A constitution, Sieyès pointed out, consisted of an array of constituted powers, like a legislature, an executive and a judiciary, along with a body of rules and procedures to guide them. But these constituted powers also required a constituting power to give them life and legitimacy. This was the power that belonged solely to the nation and, since the third estate was a complete nation, the third estate alone was entitled to use its constituting power to establish a new system of government that would be designed to establish and maintain public and private liberty.

On these terms, the answer to the question of who had the right to decide what to do about the deficit was, therefore, the third estate. The members of the other two orders of the old French Estates-General, the clergy and the nobility, had no right or power to decide or act independently. They could, Sieyès emphasized, certainly abandon their separate status and distinctive privileges and join the nation formed by the members of the third estate. But there could not be two additional nations within the nation. France, Sieyès insisted, was a single nation and the third estate alone supplied all that it needed to be what it was. In this respect, too, the nation was just like a state.

The inclusive answer that Sieyès gave to the first question pulled, however, against the sequential practicalities raised by the second question. If the nation, or the third estate, or even the representatives of the third estate, had a sovereign right to decide what to do about the deficit, including a right to use the nation's constituting power to draft a constitution for a new system of government, it was still not clear how the nation, or the third estate, or even the representatives of the third estate, would go about making their decisions or how these decisions would then be implemented. Here, the difficulties involved in finding a way to deal with the collective-action problem were magnified by the problem of the deficit itself.[3] Funding the deficit meant raising taxes to pay interest and, by doing so, transferring resources from all or part of the nation to some or all of the nation's creditors. As it stood, the nation itself contained many different types of social, legal or regional privilege, many varieties of economic activity and many different forms of public and private property. In themselves, the range and variety of interests that the nation housed were a substantial obstacle to effective decision-making and coordinated collective action. Adding the further divisions of interest involved in raising taxes to fund the deficit amounted to magnifying the already considerable economic and social difficulties involved in using the nation's constituting power to give its government a stable constitution.

Sieyès was well aware of the dilemma. The more it could be argued that only the nation could deal with the problem of the deficit, the more difficult it was to see how the nation itself could actually act. He had, in fact, drafted a pamphlet designed to deal with the dilemma some six months before he published *What Is the Third Estate?* The pamphlet in question was written in July or August 1788 and was published to coincide with the meeting of the French Estates-General in May 1789 under the title of *Vues sur les moyens d'exécution dont les représentants de la France pourront disposer en 1789*. The near-contemporary English title of the work, *Views of the Executive Means, which are at the disposal of the*

*Representatives of France, in 1789*, captures its aim quite well.[4] It was designed to show how, given its right to deal with the problem of the deficit, the nation would be able to act. In it, Sieyès went to some lengths to explain why the action itself had to be limited in nature and sequential in character. Both qualities were required to reconcile political effectiveness with political legitimacy. The deficit, Sieyès argued, was either a threat or an opportunity. Under the existing system of government it would be a threat, not only because of the often unaccountable character of government expenditure, but also because of the unaccountable character of absolute government itself. At the limit, he warned, an absolute government could simply default on its debt or, worse, might even persuade an assembly of the French Estates-General to sanction a debt default if the measure was accompanied by a programme of patriotic fiscal reform designed to reduce the already heavy tax burden on the poor. If this were to happen, the deficit would certainly disappear, but so too would the opportunity to establish civil and political liberty in France. This, Sieyès argued, was why the way to avoid the threat was to grasp the opportunity and why treating the constitutional problem had to take precedence over treating the financial problem.

The way to manage the sequence was to establish a special assembly entrusted with the task of drafting a constitution. Unlike the old Estates-General, with its separate representatives of the clergy, nobility and the third estate, this assembly, Sieyès wrote, would be a single body with a single assignment, namely to draft a constitution for a new system of government. It would be a scaled-up version of an already partially established network of provincial assemblies, with no distinction between the three estates in how its members were to be elected or in how they would deliberate and decide. Importantly, it would also have no legislative power, but would simply present the results of its constitutional deliberations for ratification by the nation in a way that was similar to the concurrent process of constitutional ratification taking place in the United States of America. Once ratified, absolute government would give way to constitutional government and, once a constitutional government had been established, it would then be possible to deal with the deficit. This was the plan that Sieyès envisaged in the later summer of 1788. It followed the logic of the distinction between sovereignty and government made by Jean-Jacques Rousseau (and, earlier, by Montesquieu) and relied on a temporary, non-governmental agency to manage the process of political reform. The government itself would not be involved in the political transition, just as the sovereign nation would not be required to play a part in government. Although the plan asserted the sovereignty of the nation, it did not yet assert the sovereignty of the third estate.

By the winter of 1788 the situation had changed. Faced with objections by members of the clergy and the nobility to any modification to the established forms and procedures of the old Estates-General, the royal government backed down. It agreed to double the number of representatives of the third estate to the forthcoming assembly but allowed the clergy and nobility to continue to elect their own representatives and left open the question of whether these representatives were to deliberate and decide separately or as a single body when the Estates-General began to meet in May 1789. This was the context in which, late in January 1789, Sieyès published *What Is the Third Estate?* As he indicated in the rather rueful title of the fifth chapter of his pamphlet – 'What should have been done: first principles on this matter' – the putative process of constitutional reform had turned into a trial of strength (133). Here, the royal government appeared to have the trump card because it had the power (and, some argued, the right) to opt, *in extremis*, for a unilateral debt default. But Sieyès, in his *Views of the Executive Means*, had already shown that the nation had an equally deadly reply. It had the right and the power to seize control of the fiscal system and could start the process by issuing a unilateral proclamation announcing that all taxes would be paid provisionally until a properly constituted government had been established. *What Is the Third Estate?* simply showed that the threat could be readily transferred to the representatives of the third estate alone.

The spectre of mutually assured financial destruction raised by the residual power of the royal government on the one side and the fiscal leverage of the third estate on the other makes it easier to explain the anxiety, suspicion and fear that began to develop when the Estates-General assembled at Versailles in May 1789. On 17 June 1789, the representatives of the third estate adopted the title that Sieyès had suggested and unilaterally proclaimed themselves to be a national assembly. Three weeks later, the dismissal of the popular finance minister Jacques Necker brought the collision between the desperation of the royal government and the intransigence of the third estate to a head and ignited the insurrection that culminated in the fall of the Bastille on 14 July 1789. As Paris reacted to the news of Necker's dismissal, the assembly at Versailles issued a proclamation placing the deficit under the safeguard of the nation. The royal debt became the nation's debt.

Sieyès' relationship to the revolution that began in France when the Bastille fell was similar both to Rousseau's relationship to the intermittent political conflicts that had occurred in Geneva a generation earlier and to Immanuel Kant's relationship to the many expressions of support for events in France voiced all over the German-speaking parts of Europe after 1789. *What Is the*

*Third Estate?* was an assertion of political sovereignty. But like Rousseau earlier, and Kant later, Sieyès's prime concern was to secure and maintain a clear distinction between sovereignty and government. Governments would come and go, in keeping with the constitutional provisions supplied by the sovereign's constituting power. But adding sovereignty to government increased the risks of either a frozen political system or one whose divisions could become a real threat to political and social survival. Either possibility was part of the politics of reform because real reforms – whether electoral, financial, moral, legal, educational or religious – were usually likely to bring sovereignty into play. This was why the line separating reform from revolution was so hard to maintain and why, in the light of the danger of either political paralysis or political disintegration, Sieyès went to such lengths to keep sovereignty and government, or the constituting and constituted powers, as separate as possible. In this respect, his political thought also paralleled the thought of Immanuel Kant. Sovereignty, Kant wrote, could be autocratic, aristocratic or democratic, but government itself was simply republican or despotic. Paradoxically, however, the less inclusive forms of sovereignty lent themselves more readily to republican forms of government than their democratic counterpart, if only because in autocratic or aristocratic regimes the different numerical sizes of the sovereign and the government favoured a clear distinction between the legislature and the executive. The opposite was the case with democratic sovereignty. There, the sovereign was, numerically, also the government, making the legislature and the executive indistinguishable and requiring a high level of civic awareness and self-sacrifice to keep public and private interests aligned. This, Rousseau had pointed out, was why democracy was a political system that was suitable only for gods.

Sieyès' solution to the problem of finding a form of government able to coexist with a democratic form of sovereignty echoed Rousseau's. The constitution that he envisaged was similar in character to the one proposed by Rousseau in his posthumously published *Considerations on the Government of Poland*, with its emphasis on what contemporaries called a system of 'gradationed promotion', or a pyramid-shaped, multi-tiered, electoral process, with those elected from the level below forming a new electorate to elect the level above. The upper level of the pyramid would house a senate and a life-peerage made up of men (and, Sieyès speculated, women) who had been ennobled for distinguished public service and were, therefore, equipped with the moral authority to endorse or criticize plans for future reform. At its apex there would be an elected head of state, with all of the splendour, but none of the power, of an old style French monarch. Ordinary political power would be in the hands of a collectively responsible ministry, but there would still be room for a single decision-maker if there was a need for emergency power. The small size and collectively responsible character of the government would give it the power to implement reform, while its national electoral origins would give it the authority to do so. Sieyès, as has been said, described the whole system as a monarchical republic, as against the more recognizable idea of a republican monarchy. *What Is the Third Estate?* was designed both to bring this system about and to block its royal opposite. In this sense, establishing the right relationship between the adjective and the noun, in France, in 1789, was not just a textual moment.

## Further Reading

Forsyth, M., *Reason and Revolution: The Political Thought of the abbé Sieyès* (Leicester: Leicester University Press, 1987).

Furet, F., *Interpreting the French Revolution* (Cambridge: Cambridge University Press, 1981).

Sieyès, E. J., *Political Writings*, ed. Michael Sonenscher (Indianapolis: Hackett, 2003).

Sonenscher, M., *Before the Deluge: Public Debt, Inequality, and the Intellectual Origins of the French Revolution* (Princeton: Princeton University Press, 2007).

# The Declaration of the Rights of Man and of the Citizen, August 1789: A Revolutionary Document

Lynn Hunt

*The representatives of the French people, constituted as a National Assembly, and considering that ignorance, neglect or contempt of the rights of man are the sole causes of public misfortunes and governmental corruption, have resolved to set forth in a solemn declaration the natural, inalienable and sacred rights of man: so that by being constantly present to all the members of the social body this declaration may always remind them of their rights and duties; so that by being liable at every moment to comparison with the aim of any and all political institutions the acts of the legislative and executive powers maybe the more fully respected; and so that by being founded henceforward on simple and incontestable principles the demands of the citizens may always tend toward maintaining the constitution and the general welfare. In consequence, the National Assembly recognizes and declares, in the presence and under the auspices of the Supreme Being, the following rights of man and the citizen:*

1. *Men are born and remain free and equal in rights. Social distinctions may be based only on common utility.*
2. *The purpose of all political association is the preservation of the natural and imprescriptible rights of man. These rights are liberty, property, security and resistance to oppression.*
3. *The principle of all sovereignty rests essentially in the nation. No body and no individual may exercise authority which does not emanate expressly from the nation.*[1]

The Declaration of the Rights of Man and of the Citizen of 1789 set the modern human rights movement into motion. When the deputies of the National

Assembly asserted in the first article that 'men are born and remain free and equal in rights', they effectively endorsed the principle of equal rights expressed in the American Declaration of Independence of 1776. Yet unlike the American Declaration, which had no constitutional status, the French Declaration was drafted as the preamble to the first written constitution in French history. It set out the 'simple and incontestable principles' that should guide citizens in establishing any and all political associations. By insisting that the rights of man were universally applicable, rather than derived from a nation's history or customs, the 1789 Declaration ignited an enduring controversy that touched people around the world.

The immediate response of critics inside and outside of France clarified the stakes involved.[2] Detractors derided the Declaration as too abstractly philosophical and hostile to historic traditions. It would be dangerously destabilizing to societies long accustomed to aristocracy and monarchy, and most European societies were dominated by landed nobles and ruled by monarchs who inherited their thrones. If 'social distinctions may be based only on common utility', as the first article insisted, then status based on birth into a particular family, defining of both nobility and monarchy, would inevitably be called into question. In June 1790 the revolutionaries decreed an end to noble titles (noble tax exemptions had been eliminated even before the drafting of the Declaration), and in September 1792 newly elected deputies abolished the monarchy and established a republic. Although no one foresaw the end of nobility and monarchy in August 1789, traditionalists already sensed the threats posed by the principles of the Declaration.

French kings claimed authority based on continuation of the dynasty; maintenance of the Catholic religion; defence of traditional privileges, whether of aristocrats, the Catholic Church, particular status groups, regions or towns; and the dispensing of justice for all. In short, kings derived their legitimacy from the safeguarding of tradition, not from 'the preservation of the natural and imprescriptible rights of man' (art. 2), which by definition stood outside any given law codes or judicial institutions. Defenders of tradition considered past customs, institutions and laws the best foundation for government. For them sovereignty was inseparable from the dynastic ruler; it made no sense without a monarch. In its first four editions, the influential Dictionary of the French Academy defined 'sovereignty' as 'the quality and authority of the sovereign prince'. Only in its fifth edition of 1798 did the definition change to the more generic 'supreme authority'.[3] The Declaration thus effectively took sovereignty away from the king when it asserted that it emanated from the nation (art. 3).

It announced a fundamental upheaval on the basis of French government even while insisting that its principles applied to all governments everywhere. Other monarchs could not fail to take note.

As if to drive home its point that 'the principle of all sovereignty rests essentially in the nation', the Declaration made no mention of the French king, the Catholic Church or any other traditional French institutions. It offered general principles based on reason and did not refer to French history or Christian teachings. The rights of man derived from human nature itself. The deputies affirmed that they were making their Declaration 'in the presence and under the auspices of the Supreme Being', but they did not trace the rights of man back to the Christian God or to the Bible. The Supreme Being did not grant rights, in this view; it only oversaw the recognition and declaration of them.

Scholars have long argued about the sources of the universal claims made in the French Declaration.[4] Were the French deputies simply following the example of the American Declaration of Independence or making new kinds of claims based on the philosophy of the Enlightenment, in particular the ideas of the Genevan writer Jean-Jacques Rousseau? Although the American Declaration was immediately translated into French, by 1789 the French deputies were more concerned with the various state constitutions and especially the bill of rights attached to Virginia's new constitution.[5] The Americans had shown that natural rights could be used to justify revolutionary change, but they stopped short of basing their new government on the guarantee of rights; the United States Constitution drawn up in 1787 included virtually no mention of rights, and the United States did not ratify its own federal bill of rights until 1791.

In contrast, the French deputies took the notion of natural rights that had gained currency during the eighteenth century, called them the rights of man to signal their political potency and declared them the basis of any legitimate government. Where the American Declaration of Independence offered lists of specific grievances against the British King George III, the French Declaration focused exclusively on abstract claims about government in general. These universal claims had their source in Enlightenment philosophy. Rousseau's *Social Contract* (1762) provided a model of this kind of abstraction but not an explicit defence of rights or specific guidelines for the French constitution. The deputies combined natural rights, the American idea of declaring and Enlightenment philosophy's emphasis on universal values based on reason with their own distinctive understanding of the political meaning of the 'rights of man'.

Defenders of these universal claims of the Declaration responded to critics with tracts in many languages that brought the controversy to an ever-expanding audience.⁶ For supporters the universalism of the Declaration's assertions constituted their main appeal; the rights of man could be and were used to attack the privileges of aristocracy, the legitimacy of monarchy, the suppression of women, the enslavement of Africans and the colonization of peoples outside Europe. For this reason, the ideals of the 1789 Declaration resonated right into the twentieth century. In 1948, when the United Nations drew up its Universal Declaration of Human Rights, its first article deliberately echoed the French Declaration of 1789 by proclaiming, 'All human beings are born free and equal in dignity and rights.'⁷

The change of wording in the United Nations Declaration from man to human draws attention to one of many paradoxes to be found in the 1789 Declaration. 'Man' in 'rights of man' referred simultaneously to all humans and only to citizens – that is, to those who had the right to participate in politics. How could these universal and particular national claims be reconciled? Did the rights of man apply to women, to non-Catholics, to men who owned no property, all of whom had been traditionally excluded from participation in French governance? The self-evidence of the rights of man produced further paradoxes. If rights were so self-evident that only 'ignorance, neglect, or contempt' of them could produce 'public misfortunes', then why did the effort to draft a declaration cause so much disagreement? Finally, if the rights of man were indisputable, why were they not recognized as such before the end of the eighteenth century?

No ready answers to these questions will be found in the debates of the National Assembly about the Declaration. The deputies formed a constitutional committee on 6 July 1789, and it announced three days later that it would draft a declaration of rights as its first task. In the midst of rapidly unfolding events, the deputies argued about whether such a declaration was needed, whether it should be attached to a constitution and whether it should be accompanied by a declaration of duties (it was not). Over six days of heated debate in late August, the deputies managed to agree on 17 articles among 24 proposed by a subcommittee and then simply voted to table further discussion. Too many other urgent matters required their consideration.

The constitution to which the Declaration was attached was only ratified in 1791 and replaced two years later, yet the 1789 Declaration influenced opinion for generations. Even in English-language publications, 'rights of man' appeared much more frequently than 'human rights' until the 1940s.⁸ At an anti-slavery society meeting in Boston in 1836, for example, speakers denounced slavery as a sin and 'a violation of the rights of man'.⁹ When Ho Chi Minh declared the independence of the Democratic Republic of Vietnam in 1945, he cited the American Declaration of Independence and the French Declaration of the Rights of Man and of the Citizen in support of Vietnamese resistance to French colonial rule.[10] For him, and for many others, the idea that 'men are born and remain free and equal in rights' had lost none of its relevance.

The paradoxes of the 1789 Declaration actually contributed to its continuing influence. The rights of man may not have been self-evident to everyone in 1789, yet the act of declaring them, however muddled or inconclusive, gave them a kind of credibility they had not possessed previously. The term 'rights of man' became increasingly common in French from the 1760s onwards, but only among the educated elite, and even there it failed to arouse anything resembling unanimity, as the debates over the Declaration demonstrated. Yet once such rights were declared, the terms of discussion changed abruptly, even among those who thought the very idea of rights of man too 'metaphysical' because unrelated to actual laws. Now critics had to combat the extension of those rights rather than simply opposing the very idea of declaring them.

Because the Declaration referred both to 'man' and 'citizen', it created an inevitable but nonetheless productive tension between universal rights and their particular political expression. In principle the rights of man were universal (applicable to everyone in the world), natural (inherent in humans rather than in particular classes, races, religions or sexes) and equal (the same for everyone). In practice, however, the rights of citizens had to be defined by particular national and local laws determining the right to vote and hold office and regulating newly declared freedoms such as the right of expression or the practice of religion.

The potential conflict between universal claims and practical implementation became apparent almost as soon as the Declaration had been voted. Article 10 had guaranteed, 'No one should be disturbed for his opinions, even in religion, provided that their manifestation does not trouble the public order as established by law.' Conservatives hoped that this wording would permit the continued exclusion of non-Catholics from political participation. The practice of Calvinism had been illegal in France since 1685 and only in 1787 was a measure of religious toleration restored. When pressed by deputies explicitly citing the Declaration, however, the National Assembly granted equal political rights to Protestants in December 1789. Jews then petitioned for their political rights and after acrimonious debate they gained equal political rights in September 1791.

The granting of equal political rights to Jews, almost unimaginable before 1789, shows the immense moral force of the act of declaring rights. As the noble deputy Stanislas, Count of Clermont Tonnerre argued in December 1789, 'There is no middle way possible: either you admit a national religion … or you permit everyone to have his own religious opinion, and do not exclude from public office those who make use of this permission' (87). When opponents succeeded nonetheless in tabling the question of Jewish political rights, various Jewish communities submitted petitions invoking the Declaration in their favour. Rights were extended first to the Jews of southern France and then to all Jews in France. In contrast, many states in the new United States restricted the right to hold office and sometimes even voting to Protestants. Jews gained the right to sit in the British parliament only in 1858. Austria–Hungary granted political rights to Jews in 1867, Portugal followed in 1911 and Russia in 1917.

The dynamic did not stop with the question of religious minorities. In late October 1789 the deputies decided to limit the right to vote to men who were at least twenty-five years old; had lived for a year in their area; were not servants, accused of a crime or bankrupt; and who had paid taxes equal to three days of work. To hold office, a man had to pay taxes worth ten days work (a sum determined by local governments). In this way the deputies created a distinction between active and passive citizens. Only a few dissented, since the practice of limiting political participation to property owners was common everywhere in the eighteenth century. Yet some did protest and, after another upheaval in August 1792 toppled the monarchy, the new republican government removed the property requirement. Free blacks in the colonies demanded political rights, too, and so did advocates for women's rights. Free blacks eventually gained equal political rights, and slavery was officially abolished in 1794, but women did not obtain political rights until 1944.

The guarantee of freedom of opinion created a similar tension with the exigencies of the nation's survival, especially in a time of revolution, counter-revolution and war. Article 11 reads, 'The free communication of thoughts and opinions is one of the most precious of the rights of man. Every citizen may therefore speak, write, and print freely, if he accepts his own responsibility for any abuse of this liberty in the cases set by the law.' The universal principle of freedom of opinion therefore hinged on the particular limits set by the law. In 1792, after France went to war against Austria, pressures mounted for censorship of newspapers that were deemed counter-revolutionary and, after the proclamation of a republic, of publications considered pro-royalist. In times of war, virtually every state, however democratic in principle, reserves the right to censor publications that might undermine the nation's security.

As these developments show, the contentious debates provoked by the tension between universal claims and particular laws could only be temporarily resolved by legislative decisions. The particular laws would invariably be compared to the universal principles, as the Declaration insisted they should be, and since those particular laws reflected current customs and practices, they would often fall short of the universal principles and thus create demands for future changes in the laws. The question of who could vote and hold office, for example, drove political conflicts throughout the nineteenth and twentieth centuries. At the same time, individual rights and the needs of the nation might also come into conflict and could never be resolved once and for all.

While the steady drumbeat of demands for equal rights shows the power of universal claims, the inability of women to gain them demonstrates the tenacity of cultural habits and customs. The deputies came to see the logic of recognizing the equal rights of religious minorities, non-whites and men without property, but this logic did not extend to women, despite the efforts of a hardly few to explain why it must. Women were citizens in that they lived in a nation governed by laws that pertained to them, but in the view of the vast majority of people in the eighteenth century, women could only be passive citizens. Women supposedly lacked the moral autonomy necessary to participate fully in political life. When newly elected deputies drafted a republican constitution in spring 1793, a spokesman for the constitutional committee explained the common view: 'It is true that the physique of women, their goal in life [as wives and mothers], and their position [as dependent on their fathers or husbands] distance them from the exercise of a great number of political rights and duties.' But he also admitted the force of the arguments for women's rights: 'Perhaps our current customs and the vices of our education make this distancing still necessary at least for a few years' (133). The few years turned into 150 years, demonstrating the power of those 'current customs'.

The Declaration of the Rights of Man and of the Citizen is like a mirror we hold up to ourselves. It lays out universal principles that continue to inspire us and reflects ambiguities and contradictions that still haunt even the most democratic governments, those that supposedly hold to the conviction that all sovereignty lies in the nation and that all people possess equal rights. Just what those rights mean in practice remains as pressing a topic of discussion as it was in 1789.

# Further Reading

Hunt, L., *Inventing Human Rights: A History* (New York: W.W. Norton, 2007).

Hunt, L., *The French Revolution and Human Rights: A Brief Documentary History* (Boston: Bedford Books of St. Martin's Press, 1996).

Landes, J. B., *Women and the Public Sphere in the Age of the French Revolution* (Ithaca, NY: Cornell University Press, 1988).

Van Kley, D. (ed.), *The French Idea of Freedom: The Old Regime and the Declaration of Rights of 1789* (Stanford, CA: Stanford University Press, 1994).

# 10

# Paine's *Rights of Man* and the Religiosity of Rights Doctrines

Gregory Claeys

*Though I mean not to touch upon any sectarian principle of religion, yet it may be worth observing, that the genealogy of Christ is traced to Adam. Why then not trace the rights of man to the creation of man? ... The illuminating and divine principle of the equal rights of man, (for it has its origin from the Maker of man) relates, not only to the living individuals, but to generations of men succeeding each other. Every generation is equal in rights to the generations which preceded it, by the same rule that every individual is born equal in rights with his contemporary.*

*Every history of the creation, and every traditionary account, whether from the lettered or unlettered world, however they may vary in their opinion or belief of certain particulars, all agree in establishing one point, the unity of man; by which I mean, that men are all of one degree, and consequently that all men are born equal, and with equal natural right, in the same manner as if posterity had been continued by creation instead of generation, the latter being only the mode by which the former is carried forward; and consequently, every child born into the world must be considered as deriving its existence from God. The world is as new to him as it was to the first man that existed, and his natural right in it is of the same kind.*

*The Mosaic account of the creation, whether taken as divine authority, or merely historical, is full to this point, the unity or equality of man. The expressions admit of no controversy. 'And God said, Let us make man in our own image. In the image of God created he him; male and female created he them.' The distinction of sexes is pointed out, but no other distinction is even implied. If this be not divine authority, it is at least historical authority, and* shews that the equality of man, so far from being a modern doctrine, is the oldest upon record.

It is also to be observed, that all the religions known in the world are founded, so far as they relate to man, on the unity of man, as being all of one degree.[1]

How ought we to interpret this dramatic yet in some respects unexceptionable passage? Paine's extraordinarily influential claim has been termed 'one of the most important developments in the doctrine of rights in our own time'.[2] It occurred at a critical moment of both political and conceptual change in which modernity is often described as being declared in the description of all humanity, rather than only the privileged few, as rights-bearers. Yet both Paine's formulations and their reception reveal other levels of meaning. There is no doubt that this particular passage possessed a shocking, intoxicating quality. *Rights of Man* was a type of secular revelation. One reader termed Paine a 'second Jesus Christ'; in the words of the radical shoemaker Thomas Hardy, Paine's writings 'seemed to electrify the nation'. Universalistic rights claims were empowering in an extraordinarily dramatic manner. Well had the Unitarian radical Joseph Priestley reflected, capturing the spirit of the moment, that 'every man, when he comes to be sensible of his natural rights, and to feel his own importance, will consider himself as fully equal to any other person whatever'.[3] Yet this passage goes beyond empowerment to hint at redemption of a sort, at least of passionate hopes and expectations. It clearly involved a powerful emotion in which the apprehension of God's will plays a major part in the experience, if falling short of Priestley's vaunted millennium.[4] It indicates, too, that the religion of rights gained its moral force partly, perhaps even predominantly, by being entwined with a psychological process of individuation, which brought about a more intense desire for 'rights' as markers and assertions of identity.

This chapter will focus on several aspects of the religious context of Paine's *Rights of Man* (1791–2). Most historical accounts of human rights ideals in the later modern period deploy some variation on a secularization narrative. They see some type of shift from natural rights, grounded in natural jurisprudence and theology, and from discussions of historical rights, 'liberties' and 'privileges' of particular peoples, to secular arguments which impute rights to human beings as such. It is often contended that the phrase 'human rights' had not yet appeared in this period; in fact, while not yet widely deployed it was in use.[5] Thus it is widely accepted that the French Revolution 'marked the secularization of the concept by changing its name from "natural rights" to "human rights"'.[6]

Nonetheless the secularization hypothesis is liable to various challenges. It can for instance be suggested that many rights concepts rested on a pre-existing conception of human nature whose first premise, sometimes framed in terms of the 'natural dignity' of mankind[7] still defined 'human nature' in terms of divine natural law.[8] The reception of rights ideas in this period is thus interwoven with religiosity to a degree usually unexplored. We need hence to recall that the concept of revolution itself, defined in this period in a well-known account (the 1789 *Catechisme d'un peuple libre*) as a crisis in which peoples aged by suffering regained 'the vigor of youth, and escape the grip of death', was frequently associated in this period with the idea of regeneration. Rights ideas thus often remained more deeply infused with religious associations than we commonly acknowledge.

How does Paine fit into this story? Issued in two parts in February 1791 and February 1792, *Rights of Man* became the best-selling political tract ever published in the English language, selling at least 200,000 copies. It followed on from the Declaration of the Rights of Man and of the Citizen, drafted by Lafayette and ratified by the Constituent Assembly in August 1789. This had asserted that 'in respect of their rights men are born and remain free and equal'. It built, of course, on Lafayette's main model, the American colonies' Declaration of Independence, a document once attributed to Paine (who perhaps played a major role in drafting it). And it owes something also to Paine's *Common Sense*, which had done much to further the cause of independence in appealing to 'the equal rights of nature'.[9] *Rights of Man* also reacted directly to Edmund Burke's *Reflections on the Revolution in France* (1790), which denied that the chief function of civil society was to protect rights inherited from the state of nature and which described natural rights doctrines as 'metaphysical abstractions' which had spawned the 'monstrous fiction' of human equality.[10] Yet this monstrosity was also one of the foundation myths of both European and American culture and would become an essential dogma in modern republican civil religion as well as in socialism.

The two main meanings of rights claims before the French Revolution were rooted in the idea of rights as privileges and the wider idea of rights as rooted in nature and derived from God. Rights were deemed 'natural' insofar as they were possessed by all in the state of nature, defined by natural liberty. Thus Abraham Williams had written in 1762 that all men were 'naturally equal, as descended from a common parent', while John Dickinson wrote of rights that 'we claim them from a higher source – from the King of Kings, and Lord of all the earth'.[11] Though it had been used synonymously with 'liberty', 'claim', 'power' and so on in John Locke and others, 'right' here was not something granted and possibly withdrawn (except for criminals). It was rather an inheritance (often described as a 'birth-right') which, at least, all propertied white males received upon reaching maturity. Locke had also proposed both a secular and a religious conception of equality, the former based in a concept of personhood which stressed equal desires for happiness and capacity for rational reflection and the pursuit of rational ends. Every man had in Locke's view an equal right to natural freedom 'without being subject to the will or authority of any other men'. The 'rights of man' was certainly very rarely understood as such to imply the 'rights of women': the universal presumption is not yet present, if latent as a principle awaiting to be driven forwards by the embarrassment of the hypocrisy of restriction. The 'rights of man' were thus actually the 'rights of men' which were in turn chiefly 'the rights of Britons'. But some eighteenth-century writers did acknowledge that rights claimed as Christians and rights claimed as men could differ, despite the fact that their source was identical.

At the dawning of the Revolution there is evidence of a perceived tension between these two traditions. As Jonathan Israel has shown, one reason the French Declaration won out over a restatement of the English Bill of Rights of 1688 was that it did not have to have recourse to 'ancient rights and liberties'. Attempts to have 'God' inserted somewhere in the Declaration also failed, leaving the way open for a more universalistic interpretation of the document. Israel notes that the 'French Declaration clearly envisioned renewal of society on a completely new basis, not one inherent in the legal past of the nation (as is implied by the American declaration)'. This echoes Paine's own sense that a 'Regeneration of Man' was proposed by the Declaration.[12]

The case for seeing the emergence of these ideals in religious terms has often been stated. Alexis de Tocqueville described the French Revolution as 'a political revolution which proceeded in the manner of a religious revolution', emphasizing here precisely that doctrinal universalism which sought 'the regeneration of mankind ... to regulate the relations of man towards God, and the rights and duties of men towards each other, independently of the various forms of society', and exporting such ideals to all nations accordingly.[13] We might describe this process as the rebirth of the Christian ideal of equality as a theory of political equality based on rights, but still infused with a fervency characteristic of religion. Partially, at least, this was the dialectical, antithetical response to existing privilege, the citizen pitted against the aristocrat. Partly also it was a response to modernity as such, and the unsettling effects of urbanization, scarcity and the extension of market society.

Accounts of rights during the revolutionary period were, however, often suitably ambiguous with regard to religion. In describing 'the natural, inalienable and sacred rights of man' the 1789 Declaration had asserted that, respecting rights, 'men are born and remain free and equal'. This could mean that citizens possessed (an undefined) freedom and equality, defined in terms of rights, *at their own birth*. Or it could mean that mankind was collectively created or 'born' as a species in possession of such rights in a more metaphorical, Rousseauean sense of the word. Some assume that such claims did intend to refer to 'individuals by virtue of their humanity'.[14] But did this 'humanity' derive from being made in the image of God or from some other postulate? The former response was offered by Richard Price, a key target in Burke's *Reflections*. Price contrasted the 'rights of men' to 'prescriptive right' and wrote in his *Discourse on the Love of Our Country* of the 'general rights of mankind'. He argued that the American colonists' rights derived not from charters but 'from a higher source' and described the fundamental right of 'equality or independence' as emanating from 'their maker'. In the *Discourse* Price doubtless also wedded Christian enthusiasm to a radical approach to rights in proposing the superiority of universal benevolence over patriotism – that is, appealing to higher over lower rights.

Paine's chief concern was to refute Burke's insinuation that rights were merely conventional and emanated from 'musty records and mouldy parchments' (18). Thus he strengthened the tacit theological context of the 1789 Declaration, bringing it into line with accepted natural law usage rather than making it more overtly secular. This gave him a broader appeal than discussions of the rights of particular peoples. But it did not establish a psychological or 'humanist' rights claim as such, even if a person's rights were exercised, according to Paine, 'in right of his existence' (39). 'Existence' is still defined theologically rather than as a claim about personality, identity, psychology, physiology or 'humanity' as such. It is true that in 1777 Paine defined a natural right as 'an animal right; and the power to act it, is supposed, to be mechanically contained within ourselves as individuals'.[15] This gives us the hint of a psychological theory of rights separate from, if derivative of, the Creation. But it was not the strategy central to *Rights of Man*. Moreover, no declaration of rights could become truly universal unless it were freed from the framework of particular religions. Hence the irony of Paine's claim: deriving rights from 'Genesis' gave them a more universal basis than the particular rights of Britons, Frenchmen or Americans but still limited them to an account which, notwithstanding his comments about the 'unity of man', non-Christians might find difficult to accept. This strategy has been described as 'linking the humanistic basis of rights with a religious approach', and it is stressed that Paine saw the individual 'conceived as the rightful possessor of rights *qua* individual, and not because of ... his status as a member of an existing community'.[16] Yet Paine did not move towards the more secular strategy here, but rather if anything away from it. When he spoke of 'inherent' rights, as he did several times in *Rights of Man*, the reference was not psychological but to theologically rooted natural rights. Similarly, it is unwise to assume that 'the rights of man' were either intended to describe the most general attribution of rights to the species, or even prospectively desired to become universal, if one is to understand that claim to universality as having its basis in the essence of the human.[17]

It might be helpful at this point to describe briefly the religious context of Paine's ideas. The democratic language of equality of right and opportunity in the pre-Revolutionary American colonies had many religious sources. The quest for individual perfection, salvation and millennial happiness was often linked to collective endeavour and identity at a time of change, fear and challenge of various kinds. An intensified religiosity often termed 'enthusiasm' characterized the Great Awakening of the 1740s, which has often been described as 'the beginning of America's identity as a nation – the starting point of the Revolution'. Here a discourse focusing on rights, contractual self-government and antagonism to ecclesiastical hierarchy linked religion and politics. The New World represented a markedly utopian ideal in which respite from the sins of the old world loomed large psychologically. A sense of divine mission, millennial hope and escape from persecution united the more religious colonists and provided the basis for a growing conception of manifest destiny which would subsequently of course become central to America's national identity. A resurgence of evangelical zeal occurred after 1790. Such a coincidence was also present in the Second Advent movement of William Miller (Millerism), with the American development of Owenism and Fourierism, and with Shakerism and other forms of sectarianism. In Britain this 'enthusiastic' religiosity was often linked to Methodism and forms a significant undercurrent to the 'Rational Dissent' which we more commonly associate with eighteenth-century radicalism, but which was linked to millenarianism in the writings of Priestley and Price in particular. This would also fuel an unprecedented expansion of Protestant religiosity in the nineteenth century. Its presence helps us to understand the cathartic reaction by readers to Paine's *Rights of Man*, which clearly brought home or reinforced in startling fashion the message that religious doctrines could possess a strikingly direct political meaning. Paine's background as a sometime Methodist lay minister made it easy for him to deploy such arguments. There is also evidence that a number of Methodists were Paineites. But we can also conceive Paine as reimporting to Britain from the new United States a more enthusiastic fusion of religion and politics, focused on the idea of rights and infusing both the American and French revolutions with Providential and quasi-millenarian meanings.

Finally, it is worth reiterating that the publication of *The Age of Reason* (1794), with its withering assault on the 'Mosaic account' of creation and revelation more generally, potentially undermined a good part of the foundation of Paine's rights claims of 1791–2, as well as fatally wounding Paine's American reputation. Anxious to stake his claim as a deist, and to counter atheism, Paine nonetheless inadvertently moved rights arguments in a non-theological direction. If the account of human equality offered in 'Genesis' was some combination of 'fabulous' and 'traditionary', this concept too had to be rethought, for instance in utilitarian terms. The same rationale holds for his arguments respecting divine intentions concerning property rights in *Agrarian Justice*, where the earth is described as initially bequeathed by God as 'the *common property of the human race*', leaving 'every person born into the world' with the right to a means of subsistence.[18] The subversive nature of theological criticism in Paine's case ironically paved the way for seeing all rights as essentially conventional and aspirational, and rights-based movements as 'utopian' attempts to construct a social and political framework which *created* equality rather than assuming it was retrieving a long-lost divine intention. We should also recall in this context that the further welfare rights proposals offered in *Agrarian Justice* were *not* contingent on divine intent but included a 'principle of progress' and a theory of 'social debt' by which the rich as stewards of God's bequest always owed part of their wealth to society. Here, in particular, old-age pensions were justified on the basis of labour performed, not any humanitarian consideration as such, for Paine insisted that it was 'not of the nature of a charity, but of a right' (200). The religiosity of the moment of *Rights of Man* was passing and giving way to more secular accounts of rights, and now, not in 1791–2, Paine lent his assistance to the process.

It has been argued here that the theological context of Paine's claims on behalf of the 'rights of man' is central both to Paine's argument and to understanding the immense popularity of *Rights of Man*. In terms of the secularization of human rights arguments in the later modern period, Paine's strategy for going beyond revolution to 'the regeneration of man' (82) can thus be seen as a retrograde one. But this probably contributed substantially to the book's popularity in the 1790s.

It may also be that, like *The Age of Reason*, this was a move by Paine to stem some of the French revolutionaries' efforts to 'de-Christianise' society. The irony is that this is accomplished by a reinforcement of a theological context which many earlier Enlightenment thinkers had been concerned to erode and many later human rights theorists to dismiss. This context, in turn, was wedded to other meanings associated with the idea of regeneration, like the constitutional renewal urged by Paine (42).

## Further Reading

Claeys, G., *Thomas Paine: Social and Political Thought* (London: Unwin Hyman, 1989).

Claeys, G. (ed.), *Political Writings of the 1790s*, 8 vols (London: Pickering & Chatto, 1995).

Fruchtman, J., Jr., *Thomas Paine and the Religion of Nature* (Baltimore: Johns Hopkins University Press, 1994).

# 11

# Virtue and Terror: Maximilien Robespierre on the Principles of the French Revolution

Marisa Linton

*This great purity of the bases of the French Revolution, the very sublimity of its object is precisely what makes our strength and our weakness; our strength because it gives us the ascendancy of the truth over deception, and the rights of public interest over private interest; our weakness, because it rallies against us all the vicious men, all those who in their hearts plot to despoil the people, and all those who have despoiled them and want immunity, and those who have rejected liberty as a personal calamity, and those who have embraced the Revolution as a career and the Republic as their prey: hence the defection of so many ambitious or greedy men, who, since the beginning, have abandoned us along the way, because they had not begun the journey in order to reach the same goal. One could say that the two contrary geniuses that have been depicted here battling for control of the realm of nature, are fighting in this great epoch of human history, to shape irrevocably the destiny of the world, and that France is the theatre of this redoubtable contest. Outside our borders all the tyrants surround you; inside all the friends of tyranny conspire; they will conspire until the hopes of crime are exhausted. We must suffocate the interior and exterior enemies of the Republic, or perish with her; yet, in this situation, the first maxim of your policy must be to lead the people by reason, and the people's enemies by terror.*

*If the mainspring of popular government in peacetime is virtue, the mainspring of popular government during a revolution is both virtue and terror; virtue, without which terror is baneful; terror, without which virtue is powerless. Terror is nothing more than speedy, severe and inflexible justice; it is thus an emanation of virtue; it is less a principle in itself, than a consequence of the general principle of democracy, applied to the most pressing needs of the* patrie.[1]

Robespierre made this speech at the height of the French Revolution and his words need to be understood against the backdrop of that unprecedented time in human history. In August 1792 the monarchy had been overthrown. A new representative body, the National Convention, was installed on the basis of a democratic (male) franchise. Its first action was to declare France a Republic. While legislative power remained with the Convention, a proportion of the executive responsibilities of government devolved into the hands of the Committee of Public Safety, of which Robespierre was a member. The French armies were fighting a defensive war on several borders simultaneously against the foreign powers of Western Europe, including England, Austria, Prussia and Spain. Within France itself, the royalist and federalist uprisings of the previous year had, for the most part, been defeated by the revolutionary forces. Yet internal unrest continued, kept in check only by the recourse to terror, or the threat of terror, on the part of the revolutionary government. The nature of the revolutionary terror and the complex reasons why it developed are controversies that show no signs of abating.[2]

On the face of it, Robespierre seems an unlikely figure to be a revolutionary leader, and his own development into that role embodies the immense changes that the Revolution wrought. Before the Revolution he was a provincial lawyer, living an obscure and blameless life. Robespierre arrived at his place of pre-eminence in revolutionary politics through five years of dedicated political activity.[3] In the first years of the Revolution he was notable mostly for his humanitarian beliefs, his unwavering support for the principles of liberty and equality and his strong opposition to the death penalty, which he considered a barbaric form of punishment. He never changed his belief that such were the goals towards which the Revolution should be headed, yet, as this speech makes clear, he came to believe that in order to ensure the survival of the Republic, the revolutionaries must be prepared to adopt the ruthless tactics that their enemies would not hesitate to use against them were their positions reversed. The Revolution, he said, should be prepared to use the weapon of terror against its enemies.

There was no historical precedent to guide him. Robespierre was consciously feeling his way towards a theoretical understanding of the nature of the Revolution and what its defenders must do to meet the challenges that confronted them. In a report made the previous December, he had said: 'The theory of revolutionary government is as new as the revolution that has led to it. We should not search for it in the books of political theorists ... who did not foresee this revolution.'

He went on to contrast normal constitutional government with the exceptional circumstances of revolutionary government:

> The goal of constitutional government is to maintain the Republic; that of revolutionary government is to found it. The Revolution is the war of liberty against its enemies: the Constitution is the regime of victorious and peaceful liberty. ... Under a constitutional regime, it is sufficient to protect individuals against the abuses of public power: under a revolutionary regime, public power is obliged to defend itself against all the factions that attack it.[4]

Seven weeks later, in his speech 'On the principles of political morality', Robespierre set out the principles on which revolutionary government in time of war should be based. He included a passage that became some of the most quoted words of the French Revolution. These are the closing lines of the extract, where Robespierre brought together two very different concepts whose juxtaposition remains shocking – virtue and terror.[5] In the views of many subsequent commentators these words were notorious as marking the moment at which the modern concept of revolution was forged in the crucible of the French Revolution. This was the concept that there could be a moral justification for using violence in the cause of bringing about a better world.

Robespierre began his report by developing his vision of the kind of society that the Revolution was intended to bring about. It would be founded on: 'The peaceful enjoyment of liberty and equality; the reign of that eternal justice whose laws are written, not on marble or stone, but in the hearts of all men, even in that of the slave who forgets them and of the tyrant who denies them' (352). He then posed a series of rhetorical questions. What kind of government was best suited to bring about such a society? He answered: 'Only a democratic or republican government – the two words are synonymous' (352). He then asked: 'What is the fundamental principle of democratic or popular government, that is to say, the essential mainspring which supports it and makes it work?' He answered: 'It is virtue' (353).

Robespierre depicted the Revolution as a titanic struggle between the people who were endeavouring to found a Republic based on virtue and those who conspired against it. The combatants were 'battling for control of the realm of nature ... to shape irrevocably the destiny of the world'. In time of conflict, virtue in itself was not strong enough to ensure the survival of the Republic. At such a moment of crisis it was necessary to resort to 'terror, without which virtue is powerless'.

Virtue was a key term in eighteenth-century political thought. It meant to put 'public interest over private interest'. To be politically virtuous entailed abnegation of self, dedication to the public good and the rejection of both financial corruption and personal and familial ambition. This concept had two main derivations. First, there was the classical republican idea of virtue as the highest quality of a citizen; this notion was familiar to many in the eighteenth century (including Robespierre) through the formulations of Montesquieu, who said, 'I have called *political virtue* love of the *patrie* and of equality'.[6] Montesquieu saw the practice of this kind of virtue as an agonizing process, which entailed the denial of natural feelings: 'Political virtue is an abnegation of self, which is always a very painful thing.'[7] This classical republican conception of virtue can be contrasted with the second derivation, which was the belief in natural virtue, an idea that came into vogue from about the mid-eighteenth century. It was founded on the idea that people naturally sympathize with their fellow human beings and find the truest happiness through promoting the happiness of others.[8]

Robespierre voiced the aspirations of many revolutionaries when he spoke of the Republic of Virtue. The idea that the Republic should be founded on political virtue was one that many revolutionaries held – or professed to hold. Where Robespierre differed from some of them was in the strength with which he held to this belief and his conviction that a revolutionary politician's virtue should be authentic, rather than just a form of words.[9] Robespierre's report is haunted by fears of inauthenticity; of men who faked virtue as a means to their own self-advancement, who used the language of virtue to betray the Revolution from within while selling their services to royalists and foreign powers.

The concept of the Republic of Virtue was based on four distinct but interlinked elements. It was a political system, one that stressed equality through the participation of all citizens on the basis of their virtue. Secondly it was a moral system, founded on integrity, selflessness, political transparency and opposition to the institutionalized corruption of the Old Regime. Thirdly, it was an emotional community, a *patrie*, wherein citizens were linked by their love for their community and devotion to their fellows. Lastly, as Robespierre's words demonstrated, the Republic of Virtue was to be linked to terror and maintained, if necessary, by violence.

Robespierre distinguished between two aspects of republican virtue: these were virtue 'as it relates to the people and as it relates to the government' (355). Both were necessary for a republic. 'Happily virtue is natural to the people', so that, 'the people have no need for a great virtue; it suffices for them to love themselves' (355–6). However, the virtue of public functionaries, including political leaders, was much more problematic. They had the opportunity and the incentive to abuse their power for their own material benefit. Therefore:

> The government must weigh heavily upon its parts .... If there exists a representative body, a highest authority constituted by the people, it is up to it to inspect and ceaselessly control all the public functionaries. But who will curb the legislature itself, if not its own sense of virtue? (356)

For Robespierre, the Terror was not principally a weapon that the government used against the people; rather, the Terror's principal targets were public functionaries, not excepting members of the government itself. He envisaged terror as a means by which the government could police its own activities and those of its agents. In Paris, the central locus of the Revolution, much of the Terror was directed at public officials, including politicians. Ironically, they had more cause to fear the recourse to terror than most of the Parisian population.

In making this assertion Robespierre had some specific groups of revolutionaries in mind, though he did not refer to them by name in this speech. Rather than overt royalists or opponents of revolution, these were men who were part of his own group, the Jacobins. Over the winter of 1793/4 two new factions had emerged among the Jacobins. These were the Cordeliers (extremists who called on support from the *Sans-Culottes* to demand an intensification of the Terror) and the Indulgents (including Georges Danton and Camille Desmoulins), who were trying to moderate the Terror and return to regular government. Robespierre introduced his attack on them with the words: 'The internal enemies of the French people are divided into two factions .... They march under the banners of different colours, and by different routes: but they march towards the same goal: that goal is ... the triumph of tyranny' (359). From this point on, the second half of Robespierre's speech was devoted to a lengthy description of the activities and motivations of these groups. He claimed that, despite their surface differences, they were secretly in league with one another and working in concert with France's external enemies to undermine the Revolution from within. The speech thus became a prelude to the arrest and subsequent execution of the leaders of these groups. It was therefore a contribution to what I have characterized elsewhere as the 'politicians' terror' – an internalized and particularly ruthless form of terror, whose principal victims were revolutionary leaders.[10]

How was it that the man who had been so opposed to the death penalty had come to see terror as acceptable – indeed, as necessary? Robespierre's thinking must be set within the context of the war. In this speech he was turning from the war against foreign soldiers, in recognizable uniforms, to the idea of the enemy within, French people who were opposed to the Revolution but who disguised themselves by adopting the rhetoric of men of virtue. In the minds of the revolutionary leaders external and internal enemies were acting in concert: 'Are not the enemies within the allies of those without?' Fear of conspiracy was endemic to the French Revolution.[11] One should not underestimate the extent to which the rhetoric of conspiracy expressed a very genuine degree of anxiety, even though those fears were often directed against the wrong targets. Much of Jacobin politics needs to be understood in relation to fears of conspiracy – both real and imagined.

Fear of conspiracy had some basis in reality: the revolutionaries had suffered a series of betrayals. The foreign powers sheltered many French nationals, *émigrés* who had fled France and hoped to overthrow the Republic. Among their ranks were Louis XVI's two brothers. Moreover, two of the Revolution's leading generals, Lafayette and Dumouriez, had become *émigrés*. In Dumouriez's case this was only after his attempt to lead his soldiers to overthrow the Convention failed due to the soldiers' refusal to follow him. Other revolutionary leaders, including earlier leaders of the Jacobins, had subsequently been accused of having used their personas as leaders of the radical movement as a means to secure their own power, careers, wealth and personal ambition, rather than for the benefit of the people they purported to represent. Hence Robespierre's reference to 'so many ambitious or greedy men, who, since the beginning, have abandoned us along the way, because they had not begun the journey in order to reach the same goal'.

Robespierre's attitude to violence and terror shifted in response to a series of such events. A key moment came before the trial of the king in January 1793, when Robespierre had argued that the king – whom the revolutionaries regarded as a traitor to his people – must die to ensure the survival of the Revolution. Another turning point came in the weeks preceding the speech on virtue and terror. Robespierre had given some cautious support to Desmoulins' campaign to end the Terror and institute a committee of clemency, but this came to an abrupt end with the revelation that Fabre d'Églantine, one of the Indulgent group and a close friend of Danton and Desmoulins, had been manipulating Robespierre to distract attention from his own involvement in a major financial swindle involving the embezzling of funds from the East India Company.

## Virtue and Terror

The realization that he had been duped by Fabre seems to have traumatized Robespierre and changed his attitude towards the Indulgents, whom he now believed to have been acting from corrupt and self-interested motives rather than for the public good.[12]

What, then, did Robespierre understand by 'terror'? He claimed that terror wielded in the cause of virtue would be a form of justice, albeit harsh justice: 'Terror is nothing more than speedy, severe and inflexible justice.' For terror to be justice it was essential that the men entrusted with the power to wield it be motivated by virtue, 'virtue, without which terror is baneful'. If not, the risk was that the men in power would act for personal motives – to ensure the continuation of their own power and to use violence against their personal enemies.

The Jacobin version of terror was a legalized terror, an official state policy, enabled by laws passed by the Convention. It was brought about in part to avoid situations such as the massacres carried out by crowds who entered the Paris prisons in September 1792. As Danton said, 'let us be terrible in order to stop the people from being so'.[13] The resort to terror also emerged out of relative weakness and fear. The Jacobins had only a shaky legitimacy and innumerable opponents throughout France, ranging from intransigent royalists to more moderate revolutionaries who had seen power centralized and their politics superseded. Many people in France were already indifferent, if not openly hostile, to the Revolution. For many the Revolution now meant requisitioning of supplies, military conscription and the constant threat to their religion and traditional ways of life. Throughout the year of Jacobin rule, it was the *Sans-Culottes* who kept them in power. But the price of that support was the blood-letting.

Speeches about terror were not only about the recourse to actual violence, they were also, calculatedly, about the *threat* of violence. Annie Jourdan has stressed the ways in which the language of terror was used as a rhetorical device to intimidate enemies. Both Jean-Clément Martin and Jourdan have argued that much of what is commonly perceived as terror was more rhetoric than reality and that the revolutionary leaders envisaged the political violence which they established through legislation as being about enforcing justice.[14]

In the spring of 1794 the word 'virtue' was on the lips of all public officials, but it seemed increasingly meaningless in the face of the state violence and coercion that stood behind it. By the end of his life, even Robespierre began to doubt, not in the principle of virtue, but whether it was achievable. In his final speech, on 26 July 1794, he said: 'My reason, not my heart, is on the point of doubting this virtuous republic whose image I had traced for myself.'[15] The following day he was overthrown in a genuine conspiracy organized by other Jacobins. The day after that he was executed along with many of his friends and associates. The men who overthrew Robespierre were his fellow Jacobins, men who were as much – or in many cases more – tainted by the use of terror than Robespierre himself. Once he was dead, these surviving terrorists sought to bring about a collective amnesia regarding their own activities by laying all the blame retrospectively onto Robespierre. In the months that followed, the language of virtue began to go out of currency. Its emotional heights, along with the violent excesses committed in its name, would henceforth be associated with Robespierre and the Jacobin government. Never again was the idea of political virtue to enjoy the ascendancy accorded to it at the height of the French Revolution; other concepts, such as 'class struggle', would provide justification for future revolutionary terrors. In the popular imagination Robespierre rapidly became the embodiment of the French Revolutionary Terror. Yet he would never have been so influential had he not spoken for a wide swathe of society and government. When he spoke of conspiracies against the Revolution, of the threats to 'the *patrie* in danger' and the need for extreme measures, he voiced the fears of many at that time that France was about to be overwhelmed by foreign and internal enemies. The policies of the Jacobin Committees had, after all, been endorsed by the deputies of the Convention. Perhaps this is why he has been so vilified: in holding one individual culpable for the ills of the Terror, French society was able to avoid looking into its own dark heart at that traumatic moment.

## Further Reading

Campbell, P. R., T. E. Kaiser, and M. Linton (eds), *Conspiracy in the French Revolution* (Manchester: Manchester University Press, 2007).

Haydon, C. and W. Doyle (eds), *Robespierre* (Cambridge: Cambridge University Press, 1990).

Linton, M., *The Politics of Virtue in Enlightenment France* (Houndmills: Palgrave, 2001).

Linton, M., *Choosing Terror: Virtue, Friendship and Authenticity in the French Revolution* (Oxford: Oxford University Press, 2013).

# 12

# The Haitian Declaration of Independence: Recognition, Freedom and Anti-French Sentiment

Julia Gaffield

***The General in Chief***

***To the People of Hayti***

*Citizens*

*... [R]emember that you wish your remains to be interred near those of your fathers, when you have driven out tyranny; will you descend into their tombs without having avenged them? No, their bones would repulse yours.*

*And you precious men, intrepid Generals who, without concern for your own misfortunes, have rescued liberty by shedding your blood; know that you have done nothing, unless you give to the nations a terrible, but just, example of the vengeance that must be wrought by a proud nation after having recovered its liberty, and jealous of maintaining it; let us frighten all those who would dare to try to take it from us again: let us begin with the French .... Let them shudder when they approach our coasts, if not from the memory of the cruelties they perpetrated, then by the terrible resolution that we have entered into of putting to death, anyone who is born French, and who would soil with their sacrilegious foot the territory of liberty.*

*...*

*Let us walk in other footsteps, let us imitate those Nations who, carrying their solicitude to the future and not willing to leave an example of cowardice for posterity, prefer to be exterminated rather than lose their place on the list of free nations.*

*Let us ensure however that a missionary spirit does not convert us from our purpose; let our neighbors remain in peace, let them live quietly under the laws that they have made for themselves, and let us not go, as revolutionary firebrands, erecting ourselves legislators of the Antilles, constituting our glory by disturbing the tranquility of the neighboring islands; they have not, like the one that we inhabit, been drenched with the innocent blood of their inhabitants; they have no vengeance to claim from the authority that protects them.*

*Fortunate to have never known the scourge that destroyed us; they can only wish for our welfare.*

*Peace to our Neighbors, but annihilation of the French name, eternal hatred to France: that is our cry.*

…

*Done at the General Quarters at Gonaives.*
*the 1st January 1804*
*(Signed) J. J. Dessalines*

Just over a month after the French army evacuated the colony of Saint-Domingue, General-in-Chief Jean-Jacques Dessalines gathered his leading generals and proclaimed the Haitian Declaration of Independence on 1 January 1804 at Gonaïves. With this proclamation, Dessalines concluded the event that we have come to know as the Haitian Revolution.

The Haitian Declaration of Independence marked the end of the world's only successful slave revolution and therefore represents a spectacular triumph over unimaginable adversity. The proclamation, however, did not articulate ideals of individual rights or provide for the foundations of a modern democratic republic. Instead, it paved the way for militarized authoritarian regimes whose main focus was the maintenance of national independence and sovereignty rather than the rights of the nation's citizens. The Haitian Declaration of Independence assured the abolition of slavery in the country but, at the same time, it undermined individual freedom in the name of national independence.

The proclamation was also a call to arms and initiated a nationwide massacre of white French citizens. Haitians leaders, however, were careful to specify that they directed their rage and revenge exclusively towards the French. The other empires and nations of the Atlantic World, Dessalines and later leaders argued, had nothing to fear from Haiti's independence; they desperately needed foreign allies and could not afford to alienate other slave-holding nations in the Atlantic. The document, therefore, is very much a product of the immediate context that confronted Haitian leaders as they sought to join the community of nations of the Atlantic World. Dessalines was well aware that while the Declaration of Independence was a document that was officially addressed to the 'People of Hayti', it was also a public statement to the rest of the world. The Haitian government printed the document and distributed it to foreign officials, and newspapers around the Atlantic published excerpts of the text.

The Haitian Revolution had begun in August 1791 with a coordinated uprising by enslaved plantation labourers in the northern province of Saint-Domingue. The war quickly became an international affair and involved changing allegiances and battles between French, Spanish, British and rebel armies with enslaved soldiers, free people of colour and whites fighting for each. The rebellious armies succeeded in forcing the hand of the local French administrators and secured the abolition of slavery in the colony in 1793. The next year, the French National Convention ratified this decision and applied it to the entire French Empire. By the end of the eighteenth century, the Spanish and British forces had evacuated the island and the former slave (and slave-owner) Toussaint Louverture secured the top political position in the colony as the French-appointed governor general. Louverture issued a colonial constitution in 1801 that claimed near-autonomy for the colony but it maintained allegiance to the French Empire. In an effort to regain metropolitan control over the colony, Napoléon Bonaparte sent an expedition to Saint-Domingue to disarm the population and deport the leaders. It is also widely believed that Bonaparte instructed his brother-in-law General Victor Emmanuel Leclerc to reinstitute slavery in the colony; at the very least, rumours began to spread that this was the case.[1] It was at this point that the revolution became a war for independence.

The French generals leading Bonaparte's invasion in 1802 captured Louverture and sent him to prison in France. They then began to wage a war of extermination so that they could eliminate all of the 'brigands' in the colony and begin anew with more enslaved people purchased through the transatlantic slave trade. On account of this violence, Jeremy Popkin argues: 'If any group is to be held responsible for introducing the practice of racially motivated mass killing into Saint-Domingue, it is certainly the whites.'[2] The extreme war waged by the French encouraged the 'rebel' forces in the colony, now under the leadership of Dessalines, to respond in kind. The Haitian war for independence, therefore, was characterized by extreme violence on both sides. Eventually, Dessalines's army was able to capitalize on the disease that devastated the French army and by June of 1803 they had begun preparing for independence.

The Haitian Declaration of Independence of January 1804 announced to the people of Haiti and to the world that the island was no longer a French colony.

Unlike the United States' Declaration of Independence almost three decades earlier, the Haitian Declaration did not initiate a war of independence but rather brought one to an end. The document, however, like the American precedent, also sought to justify the colony's break from the metropole, but Dessalines emphasized the inherent differences between the French and the Haitians rather than their similarities. According to the Declaration, Haitians and Frenchmen were incompatible as citizens of the same country. At the core of this inherent difference was slavery: the French had 'drenched [the island] with the innocent blood of their Inhabitants'. Dessalines's proclamation inextricably linked national independence and the abolition of slavery; individual freedom was therefore subsumed within the authority of the state. Abolition of legal enslavement was the driving force behind the war for independence in Haiti, whereas in the United States 'freedom' referred to the metaphorical slavery of colonialism.[3]

When Dessalines and the leading generals declared independence, they were still reeling from recent events. 'Remember that you wish your remains to be interred near those of your fathers,' Dessalines cried, '… will you descend into their tombs without having avenged them? No, their bones would repulse yours.' Dessalines took the lead in initiating his version of the revenge that he claimed would satisfy their ancestors. Over the course of the first four months of 1804, Dessalines ordered his army to round up all of the white French citizens and kill them. A very small number of lives were spared. Foreign accounts of these killings suggested that they were the result of Dessalines's barbarism and a sign of the lasting dangers of slave rebellions and black power. To Haitians, however, the massacres symbolically signalled their newly secured freedom and independence by eliminating their former masters and colonial representatives. They also served practical purposes: the Haitian state would not have to fear continued challenges to their authority from within the island and the state could assume control of the land formerly owned by the white planters.[4] Finally, the massacres provided a warning to all who dared to challenge the abolition of slavery on the island. They had given the world 'a terrible, but just, example of the vengeance that must be wrought by a proud nation after having recovered its liberty, and jealous of maintaining it'.

While the Declaration of Independence initiated acts of revenge for the crimes committed by the French during the colonial period and revolution, Dessalines also made clear that this one act would not end the war. The war must be forever: 'eternal hatred to France: that is our cry'. The French had, after all, not admitted defeat when their troops evacuated the colony in 1803. Furthermore, in the years that followed, French civilians, military leaders and government officials engaged in a 'war of proclamations' in order to assert their sovereignty over their former colony.[5] Dessalines well understood that Haitian independence would come under attack and the threat of reinvasion led to a concentration of authority in Haiti under military rule and limited the expansion of individual rights and political participation. The defence of national independence proved to be more important than individual freedom. In the Declaration of Independence, Dessalines predicted the continued threat from the former metropole and sought to warn the French of their destiny if they dared reinvade the island.

Ironically, by closing the borders to foreign attacks and creating a society dominated by military and security needs, the Haitian government tried to protect the free and independent society that they hoped to create. This protection, however, limited the scope of the universal freedom that the state espoused. By safeguarding its coasts, the Haitian state created an inextricable link between freedom and independence and the geo-political territory that the state occupied. While colonial Saint-Domingue and current-day Haiti only occupy the western third of the island of Hispaniola, Haitian leaders after the revolution claimed that Haiti occupied the entire island. The Spanish had ceded the eastern side of the island to France in 1795 under the Treaty of Basel; when Dessalines and his generals declared the colony independent from France, therefore, the colony occupied the entire island. In practice, however, Haitian jurisdiction was confined to the western side of the island until 1822 when Haitian President Jean-Pierre Boyer invaded the eastern side.

Haitian leaders all presented their cause as a universal one, but their efforts in state formation and freedom took place in a constrained and circumscribed geopolitical space – one surrounded by empires committed to the maintenance of slavery.[6] The borders of the island, at least in rhetoric, represented the boundary between universal freedom and the pervasive slavery and colonialism in the rest of the Caribbean in the early nineteenth century. The rigid boundaries that Dessalines initiated between Haiti and the surrounding world, however, were open to non-white 'natives' of the island. Dessalines published newspaper advertisements in the United States and other French colonies encouraging nonwhite 'natives of Hayti' to return to the island.[7]

In order to assuage the fears of the governments and slave-owners in neighbouring islands and territories, the flow of non-white migration, the Declaration of Independence promised, would only be one way. 'Let our neighbours remain in peace, let them live quietly under the laws that they have made for themselves, and let us not go, as revolutionary firebrands, erecting ourselves legislators of the Antilles.' Dessalines and later leaders understood that if they exported the revolution, they might then face a coordinated attack from all of the European empires and the United States who had a vested interest in preserving their systems of slave labour. As Dessalines's efforts to increase the population suggest, Haiti's leaders were willing and keen to expand the scope of universal freedom by inviting non-whites to join the nation, but they were not willing to jeopardize their achievements by invading foreign lands.

Dessalines's counsel to Haitians not to disrupt the existing systems of neighbouring islands was also a direct promise to the governors of the surrounding islands and their superiors in Europe not to do so. By promising not to become 'legislators of the Antilles', Dessalines hoped to avoid wars with other countries that might usurp Haiti's independence and re-enslave the population. It was also a demonstration that the Haitian government was willing to participate in the established customary practices of the law of nations. Haitians would respect the jurisdictional boundaries of the Atlantic. In communicating with the nations and empires of the north Atlantic, therefore, Dessalines hoped to become, what Eliga Gould calls, a 'treaty-worthy nation', in order to join the community of European empires and the United States of America.[8]

In addition to articulating promises to foreign nations regarding the containment of the revolution, Dessalines also sought acceptance as a sovereign and independent country. In issuing a declaration of independence, Haitian leaders followed the precedent set by the United States. The rallying cry of the war for independence had been 'liberty or death', words written in bold letters across the top of the Declaration of Independence, and this motto, Dessalines argued, also applied to Haiti's participation in the community of nations of the (north) Atlantic. Let us 'prefer to be exterminated', Dessalines proclaimed, 'rather than lose [our] place on the list of free nations'. As was the case with the United States almost three decades earlier, Haitians had to participate according to the terms laid out by foreign governments. By issuing a declaration of independence, Haiti, like the United States, 'sought confirmation of their standing alongside other such states by justifying their secession and, in some cases, their recombination with other territories and peoples'.[9] Haiti needed foreign governments to accept and recognize its independence and sovereignty. The creation of a defined and limited state meant that Haitian leaders acknowledged the limits of their powers and declared their willingness to participate in the community of nations in the Atlantic World.

Dessalines remained in power in Haiti, first as governor general for life and then as Emperor Jacques I, for two and a half years. On 17 October 1806, rebels assassinated Dessalines. Following his death, a power struggle ensued between Henry Christophe and Alexandre Pétion. The country soon divided in civil war with Christophe ruling the northern department and Pétion the southern and western departments; both leaders, however, claimed to be the legitimate ruler of the entire country. This civil war lasted until 1820 when Pétion's successor Jean-Pierre Boyer reunited the country. Christophe and Pétion reiterated many of the central themes of nation-building and international diplomacy that Dessalines articulated in the Declaration of Independence.

All of the early Haitian leaders publicly assured foreign leaders and citizens that they would not export their revolution in order to secure universal freedom throughout the Caribbean. The continued emphasis on geography and the borders of the island highlights the symbolic and political importance of the physical space that Haitians had claimed as their own. These promises, however, did not mean that they did not try to increase the country's population as Dessalines had done. Twelve years after the Haitian Declaration of Independence, President Alexandre Pétion initiated the most extensive effort to recruit foreigners to join the Haitian nation. 'Haiti, argued Pétion, was a land where no one could be enslaved', Ada Ferrer highlights, 'and where arrival in and of itself conferred freedom and eventually citizenship'.[10] Pétion's 1816 constitutional revision included an article that would give all people of African and indigenous descent freedom and a path to citizenship if they made it onto Haitian soil. Pétion, however, like other Haitian leaders, promised that he would not export the revolution; but, by extending freedom and citizenship to non-whites in the Atlantic World, he was able to apply the universal freedom of the Haitian state to more people. In initiating these policies, Pétion, like Dessalines, hoped to increase Haiti's population, since it had been severely diminished by the thirteen-year Haitian Revolution.

While Haitian leaders attempted to participate in an international Atlantic community on the terms set by foreigners, the Haitian Declaration of Independence also created a unique Haitian state and nationality. 'Dessalines's Proclamation of Independence', Doris Garraway argues, 'indexes some positive criteria for Haitianness, notably in its frequent references to Haitians as "indigenes" and its figuration of liberation from slavery as a moment of collective rebirth within the "empire of freedom"'.[11] Dessalines addressed his Haitian audience as 'natives', despite the fact that over half of the enslaved population at the time of the revolution was African born. Furthermore, the Declaration named the country 'Hayti', meaning 'mountainous' in Taíno, the name previously used for the island before the arrival of Christopher Columbus in 1492. Haitians, Dessalines declared on 1 January 1804, were the rightful and legitimate inhabitants of the island. On the whole, however, Garraway concludes that in the Declaration of Independence Dessalines defined Haitian national identity via the exclusion of the French and the ongoing war against their former metropole.[12]

The Haitian Declaration of Independence had two central objectives: first, Dessalines proclaimed perpetual war against the French and initiated a nationwide massacre of the white French citizens who remained in the territory, and second, he tried to convince foreign governments that they should include Haiti in the community of recognized nations in the Atlantic World by promising not to interfere in their affairs. Both goals would contribute to the unification of the diverse population that had just become Haitian citizens and these citizens would never again see the yoke of slavery. Leaders in Haiti, however, struggled for decades to secure diplomatic recognition from foreign governments. France only recognized Haitian independence in 1825 in exchange for a large indemnity payment – to compensate the former plantation owners for their loss of property, including enslaved people – and favourable trade duties. During the period of diplomatic non-recognition, however, Haiti maintained its independence and sovereignty, and slavery never returned to its shores. January first is still celebrated as the day that Haiti won its independence from France.

## Further Reading

Dubois, L., *Avengers of the New World: The Story of the Haitian Revolution* (Cambridge, MA: Belknap Press of Harvard University Press, 2005).

Gaffield, J. (ed.), *The Haitian Declaration of Independence: Creation, Context and Legacy* (Charlottesville, VA: University of Virginia Press, 2015).

Garraway, D. (ed.), *Tree of Liberty: Cultural Legacies of the Haitian Revolution in the Atlantic World* (Charlottesville, VA: University of Virginia Press, 2008).

Geggus, D. P., *Haitian Revolutionary Studies* (Bloomington, IN: Indiana University Press, 2002).

Girard, P., *The Slaves who Defeated Napoléon: Toussaint Louverture and the Haitian War for Independence* (Tuscaloosa: University of Alabama Press, 2011).

# 13

# A Lesson in Revolution: Karl Marx and Friedrich Engels, *The Communist Manifesto*

Julian Wright

*We have seen above, that the first step in the revolution by the working class is to raise the proletariat to the position of ruling class to win the battle of democracy.*

*The proletariat will use its political supremacy to wrest, by degree, all capital from the bourgeoisie, to centralise all instruments of production in the hands of the State, i.e., of the proletariat organised as the ruling class; and to increase the total productive forces as rapidly as possible.*

*Of course, in the beginning, this cannot be effected except by means of despotic inroads on the rights of property, and on the conditions of bourgeois production; by means of measures, therefore, which appear economically insufficient and untenable, but which, in the course of the movement, outstrip themselves, necessitate further inroads upon the old social order, and are unavoidable as a means of entirely revolutionising the mode of production ...*

*When, in the course of development, class distinctions have disappeared, and all production has been concentrated in the hands of a vast association of the whole nation, the public power will lose its political character. Political power, properly so called, is merely the organised power of one class for oppressing another. If the proletariat during its contest with the bourgeoisie is compelled, by the force of circumstances, to organise itself as a class, if, by means of a revolution, it makes itself the ruling class, and, as such, sweeps away by force the old conditions of production, then it will, along with these conditions, have swept away the conditions for the existence of class antagonisms and of classes generally, and will thereby have abolished its own supremacy as a class.*

*In place of the old bourgeois society, with its classes and class antagonisms, we shall have an association, in which the free development of each is the condition for the free development of all.*[1]

Marx's idea of revolution as a fundamental change in social conditions, arising from the eternal struggle between the oppressed and the oppressor, is notoriously ambiguous. Did he mean to suggest that the change would always be effected through a forceful takeover of power? Or was that simply the necessity he foresaw in the mid-nineteenth century, given that the ultimate goal was for a more harmonious existence, the association that would promote the free development of each and thus the free development of all?

This ambiguity in *The Communist Manifesto* connects with the ambiguous context of socialism – and Marx's socialist activity – at the moment when the text was produced. The subtlety of Marx's commentary has lent itself to generations of reflection on the fundamental qualities of social struggle and social transformation as a driving force in history – since the late nineteenth century, that is. As Gareth Stedman Jones points out in his major essay on *The Communist Manifesto*, one of the key challenges for the reader of this enigmatic text is to see past the many layers of twentieth-century discussions of the text, to try and grasp its purpose and function in the 1840s. One of its most important developments was Marx's own decision to discard the format of a 'socialist catechism' and instead write a 'manifesto' that would allow a more discursive historical overview to develop through the text. This was itself a response to the historical mood of the 1840s, in which the significance of the French Revolution was developed more and more in historically informed political thought and through which the coming 1848 revolutions would in turn develop a rich historical meaning in their own time.[2]

Soon after its publication, rapidly moving political events would force the *Manifesto*'s authors to shift their positions more than once, during the crisis of the 1848 revolutions. As regimes tottered on the continent, Marx took up a position that would conflict with the grand historical overview he set out in Section I of *The Communist Manifesto*. Here, Marx and Engels argued that the overthrow of the bourgeoisie and the appropriation of their property by the organized, unified working class was paramount in socialist thought, action and militancy. Soon, however, they were campaigning for the uniting of the bourgeoisie and the proletariat. As revolution turned to defeat after the June Days in France, however, they returned to the original proposition, this time as pessimists rather than optimists. They had accepted that the overthrow of bourgeois capitalism was more necessary than ever, given the craven qualities of bourgeois leadership in 1848; but the contest with the bourgeoisie was seen as being darker and more bitter.

This double shift away from the positive, rallying cries of *The Communist Manifesto* gave the tone to the European socialist movement from the 1860s and 1870s, when German socialism in particular shaped socialist culture as a means of educating the working class. In the context of the later nineteenth century, social struggle between the middle classes and the working classes would be imprinted on the mind of socialist commentary and socialist activism as a fundamental feature of the modern European experience, notably through the bloody end to the Paris Commune in 1871.

The aftermath of those events provided the context for the first renewal of interest in *The Communist Manifesto*. The text was produced by a German court as evidence of the dangerous threat of the socialist movement at the trial of German Social-Democratic leaders in March 1872. The trial gave new publicity to a text which had almost disappeared from view, and Marx and Engels took the opportunity to present it with a new preface. They now questioned their original commitment in Section II of the *Manifesto* to an abrupt seizure of power on the part of the proletariat:

> In view ... of the practical experience gained, first in the February revolution, and then, still more, in the Paris Commune, where the proletariat for the first time held political power for two whole months, this program has in some details become antiquated. One thing especially was proved by the Commune, viz., that 'the working-class cannot simply lay hold of the ready-made State machinery, and wield it for its own purposes'.[3]

So, in 1847–8, Marx and Engels proposed that the working class would seize the levers of the state; but in 1872 they repudiated this? How can we grasp the importance of *The Communist Manifesto* if major historical and political statements such as this were to be turned upside down by their authors?

*The Manifesto* was above all a tool for rallying and educating a tight group of activists who moved between the Rhineland, Belgium, Paris and London. The trenchant, sharp-edged tone of the document, which comes across so strongly in the sardonic descriptions of other socialists in the third section of the text, should not simply be seen as a feature of Marx's personal style, angry and cutting as it was. This tone points to the central function of the text. *The Communist Manifesto* was an instrument that would carve out clear lines between the Communist League, a tight group of activists on whom Marx and Engels had attempted to impose their authority, and the confused and disparate socialist movement in Europe in the 1840s. As Engels would reiterate in 1888, that was a movement where a range of doctrines and political positions could be covered by the banner 'socialism', including elements of conservative thought that focused on social activism as a way of buttressing traditional systems of order. Marx engaged at length with German and French social thought in the 1830s and 1840s and his aim in *The Communist Manifesto* was to provide a framework through which communist activists could interpret that intellectual kaleidoscope – and mark themselves out from it.

Thus the purpose – to give identity and direction to the communist movement – helped to dictate the mode: a manifesto with trenchant political commentary and historical overview woven together. The trick of a phrase such as this is to give the impression that an eternal lesson in society and politics is being preached, one which future militants need to learn by heart:

> If the proletariat ... by means of a revolution makes itself the ruling class, and, as such, sweeps away by force the old conditions of production, then it will, along with these conditions, have swept away the conditions for the existence of class antagonisms and of classes generally.

The enduring fascination of the *Manifesto* throughout the early twentieth century stems to a considerable extent from the belief of future revolutionaries – in Russia, China and many other parts of the world – that phrases such as this contained the key to understanding the revolutionary programme of action.

As Marx would later explain, however, this sort of prognosis was not the main force of the text. The key purpose of the *Manifesto* was to create better understanding and better appreciation of the philosophical and historical context of modern socialist activity.

> What I did that was new was to prove (1) that the existence of classes is only bound up with particular, historic phases in the development of production; (2) that the class struggle necessarily leads to the dictatorship of the proletariat; (3) that this dictatorship itself only constitutes the transition to the abolition of all classes and to classless society.[4]

So, the *Manifesto* was not so much an instruction to action as an instruction to a better understanding of history. Marx's large theoretical conceptions throughout the 1840s were consistently framed within a debate, often with a specific author or small group of activists. *The Communist Manifesto* was no different.

The polemics that Marx had entertained with other socialist leaders such as Pierre-Joseph Proudhon and Wilhelm Weitling in the mid-1840s explain the force of *The Communist Manifesto*. The controversy with Weitling demonstrated that Marx and Engels wanted to emphasize the idea of class self-knowledge on the part of the proletariat. Where Weitling, after his return from prison in 1845, preached an increasingly vague philosophy of class reconciliation, they wanted to show the workers how capitalist economic evolution was driving the classes into an inevitable collision. In *The German Ideology*, Marx and Engels set out a long and devastating attack on the way German left-wing thought had been conceived. By 1846 they had established that the principal task for communist thinkers and activists was to create a consensus among communist and socialist organizations, using their scientific view of the class struggle as the basis for further expanding the proletariat's understanding of its position in the economy and in history.

Marx and Engels were insistent: propaganda needed to be controlled, if necessary stopped, because the poorly led workers' movement was in danger of having its hopes raised and then dashed by repression. Thus a purge of ill-constructed socialist formulae would lead to the expulsion from the movement of socialists who did not understand the real nature of revolutionary tactics. And fundamentally, the bourgeoisie would have to act first. Bourgeois democracy would be vital to the proletariat in the first instance. The Russian observer Amenkov described a telling scene. After Weitling had stumblingly attempted to answer the charge that his movement was led by idle hopes and vague platitudes, Marx's fist crashed to the table and his fundamental concern – that which underpinned his whole outlook – exploded from his mouth: 'Ignorance never did any one any good!'[5]

The French socialist Pierre-Joseph Proudhon would long suffer from the crushing blows of Marx's scientifically worked-through philosophical critique, which, Marx wanted to show, demonstrated the fundamental weakness of Proudhon's intellect. The two tussled closely in 1846–7. Proudhon foresaw (as later French commentators, including Jean Jaurès, would also agree) that Marx's understanding of revolution entailed the progressive misery of the working class, until such time as the capitalist system collapsed in on itself.[6] But the logical focus of his argument was dismantled by Marx's reply to his 'Philosophy of Misery'.[7] For Proudhon, the evil effects of competition needed to be replaced by a campaign to develop co-operation between the workers. Ultimately, Marx would argue, Proudhon was nothing more than an ameliorative socialist – someone who basically wanted to improve the system they found themselves in, rather than truly challenging it and working for its destruction. The brutality of the attack was striking, but the importance of rhetorical violence of this sort needs to be understood properly. In Marx's riposte, the workings out of his theory of historical materialism took another step forward.

In his sharply drawn account of Karl Marx, Isaiah Berlin suggested that Marx was a man who was not in tune with his age. Ideas of sympathy, sensitivity, heroism, personal experience and the whole issue of how an individual life was lived within social upheavals were of fundamental concern to the radicals, socialists, romantics and nationalists of the days leading up to the 1848 revolutions.[8] The capacity for Proudhon or Weitling to appeal to the mass movements of Western and Central Europe depended on their being in tune with these sentimental revolutionary qualities. But, as Berlin put it,

> Karl Marx ... lacked psychological insight ... this extreme blindness to the experience and character of persons outside his immediate range made his intercourse with the outside world seem singularly boorish ... he looked upon moral or emotional suffering, and spiritual crises, as so much bourgeois self-indulgence unpardonable in time of war.

Understanding the irascibility of Marx's dealings with the other socialist writers and activists of the 1840s is a fundamental part of appreciating the drive, rhythm and intensity of *The Communist Manifesto*. It points out that when he began to push for the organization of the Communist League, he did so as a man at cross purposes with so many of those he encountered. The point of this activity, as he saw it, was to put in place a framework that would provide an unalterable scientific structure to the way workers encountered the ideas of communism. This was the occasion for The Manifesto of the Communist Party, which members of the League were keen to see completed by early 1848. Begun by Engels, the work was rewritten, precisely to make it more forceful. This was not a manifesto for all times and places: it was a trenchant lesson for European socialists. This necessitated a strident and critical style, which could push out the cloudy, emotional rhetoric of the diverse utopian and other socialist ideals then current, replacing them with pointed and cogent understandings of how world history was evolving and of the place of the communist movement within that history. The drama of the opening sentences, and the twist towards the bourgeoisie, can only be understood properly as the slicing of a muddy debate with a sharp rhetorical flourish. That rich and chaotic debate between left-wing European intellectuals of the pre-1848 era is what frames this document. In order to hack through the verbiage of this debate, Marx emphasized his points in pungent statements that gave a dramatic account of world history. It was this rhetorical grandeur that made the text so apt, in later generations, to inspire a much wider, global attempt to construct a movement which would overthrow the capitalist economic system.

Was *The Communist Manifesto* a revolutionary text? Marx himself argued (just before the passage set out here) that his idea of communism was certainly a 'radical rupture with traditional property relations' – far more radical, indeed, than those ideas about property purveyed by his sparring partner Proudhon. Overall, the *Manifesto* was less a revolutionary tract, perhaps, than a text that sought to inform and shape understandings of a certain sort of revolution. The re-emergence of the *Manifesto* in the late nineteenth century as a later inspiration for a wide range of ideas of revolution should not, however, prevent us from seeing that Marx's fundamental aim was to prevent socialist revolutionaries embracing anything other than a properly scientific, historically informed view of revolution as the outworking of the forces of economic evolution and class struggle. And because so many of his closest colleagues in left-wing circles thought of revolution as something altogether more dynamic, more apt to be propelled and directed by emotional, fraternal and voluble groups of workers or others, our conclusion as to the revolutionary qualities of *The Communist Manifesto* must ultimately be that it was a very odd sort of revolutionary text in the 1840s. The distinctly awkward place it has in terms of Marx's own immediate political future in 1848 – where his ideas about the necessary course of action would change so quickly – is simply the natural corollary of understanding the *Manifesto*'s real purpose.

Where the *Manifesto* did touch on a genuine notion of revolution was in the rather rare passage we have examined here, which comes near the end of part two. Perhaps because the most important point of the *Manifesto* was to draw the gaze of fellow socialist activists away from deceptions and distractions, the moments when Marx focuses more carefully on the future are few and far between. Famously, there is very little in Marx's whole work to give socialists or communists, of his own day or subsequently, much idea of what a post-revolutionary future might look like. The 'free association of all' will in time replace the need for state and bureaucracy, creatures as they are of capitalism. It is only here that one of the key principles of Marx's theory of human experience in history makes its presence felt: the idea of individual human beings 'alienated' from their true nature was developed clearly in a number of Marx's writings during the 1840s. Here then there is a glimmer of the liberation of humans from their pitiful existence within capitalism. But so much of Marx's work – and the whole essence of *The Communist Manifesto* itself – was to try to bring the proletariat to a position of understanding, where it would avoid simply perpetuating and reinforcing the capitalist system that was every day creating alienation. Getting that idea into people's heads was ultimately far more important, in Marx's view, than distracting them with cloudy visions of the future; the 1820s, 1830s and 1840s had already been clogged up with such notions.

So these few sentences that give us a glimpse of Marx the visionary do not in the end define our response to the text a hundred and seventy years later. Understanding Marx's place in the cut and thrust of a movement which he worked so hard to master is a much more fruitful place to begin as we engage with this demanding, dramatic and didactic masterpiece of political literature. Its revolutionary qualities are complex, but above all it is a warning against revolution for the sake of upheaval. Upheaval, on a grand historical scale, must happen first – then and only then will the revolutionary process unfold. In the meantime, the working class needs to be imbued with understanding more than with fervour. Nonetheless, fervour, of a revolutionary kind, is there in every line of this text. It is there to drive the point home and cut through the hothouse atmosphere of the socialist and communist debates of the 1840s.

## Further Reading

The most important recent commentary on *The Communist Manifesto* is:

Stedman Jones, G., 'Introduction', to Karl Marx and Friedrich Engels, *The Communist Manifesto* (London: Penguin, 2002).

Three important biographies of Marx:

Berlin, I., *Karl Marx* (Oxford: Oxford University Press, 1939).
McLellan, D., *Karl Marx: His Life and Thought* (London: Macmillan, 1973).
Sperber, J., *Karl Marx: A Nineteenth-Century Life* (London: Norton, 2013).

# 14

# From National Backwardness to Revolutionary Leadership: Alexander Herzen's Book *On the Development of Revolutionary Ideas in Russia*

Derek Offord

*On the one hand, the Russian government is not Russian, but in general despotic and reactionary. It is more German than Russian, as the Slavophiles say, and that is what explains the sympathy and love with which other governments turn to it. St Petersburg is the new Rome, the Rome of universal slavery, the metropolis of absolutism; that is why the Emperor of Russia fraternizes with the Emperor of Austria and helps him to oppress Slavs. The principle of his power is not national, and absolutism is more cosmopolitan than revolution.*

*On the other hand, the hopes and aspirations of revolutionary Russia coincide with those of revolutionary Europe and portend their future alliance. The national element that Russia brings is the freshness of its youth and a natural leaning towards socialist institutions.*

*The impasse at which the states of Europe have arrived is plain to see. They need either to make a decisive leap forward or retreat further than they have. The antitheses are too inexorable, the questions too glaring and too far developed by sufferings and animosities for one to stop at half-measures or peace-making between authority and liberty. Yet if there is no safety for States in the form in which they presently exist, the manners in which they might die may be quite different. Death may come through palingenesis or putrefaction, revolution or reaction. The conservatism that has no aim but preservation of a worn-out status quo is just as destructive as revolution. It annihilates the old order, not by the raging fire of inflammation but by the slow fire of atrophy.*

> *If conservatism gains the upper hand in Europe, imperial power in Russia will not only crush civilization, it will destroy the whole class of civilized men, and then ...*[1]

Alexander Herzen's short book *On the Development of Revolutionary Ideas in Russia*, from which the above passage is taken, was first published in 1851. It is important to bear in mind that the book belongs to a cycle of works that appeared in Western Europe (in French, Italian, German or English, in the first instance) in the years immediately following the revolutionary uprisings of 1848–9 and the counter-revolutionary response to them, which included the dispatch of Russian troops in the summer of 1849 to crush the Hungarian Revolt. This cycle – which also contained articles or essays entitled 'Russia' (1849), 'The Letter of a Russian to Mazzini' (1850), 'The Russian People and Socialism' (1851) and 'Russia and the Old World' (1854)[2] – was directed primarily at a western public, which was largely ignorant of and hostile towards Russia, rather than at Russian readers. Herzen's aim in it was partly to win support in the west for the emergent Russian intelligentsia as it began during the age of Nicholas I (ruled 1825–55) to wage a struggle against the Russian autocratic regime. More broadly, Herzen wished to convince western readers that Russia, backward though it was, had admirable qualities. In particular, Herzen argued in his cycle, the socialistic instincts of the Russian common people and institutions that still survived in the Russian countryside, such as the peasant commune and the village assembly, provided foundations for the establishment of the new western doctrine of socialism. Thus Russia, Herzen wanted his readers to believe, was a new world, a fresh force which had the capacity to regenerate European civilization.

It is equally important, as we consider *On the Development of Revolutionary Ideas in Russia*, to be aware that Herzen's cycle of essays on 'Russian socialism', as he called the set of ideas I have outlined, is one panel of a diptych. The other panel offered a view of Western Europe, the 'old world'. This view unfolds in two further collections of essays, namely *Letters from France and Italy* and the work that Herzen regarded as his masterpiece, *From the Other Shore*.[3] Both of these collections incorporate Herzen's early first-hand impressions of the west, where he had arrived with his family, as a tourist, in 1847. (The nobleman's Grand Tour was to turn into permanent exile, because Herzen's sympathy for the European rebels of 1848 made it likely that if he returned to his native land then he would again – at best – suffer provincial exile, as he had in the 1830s and early 1840s.) In his *Letters from France and Italy* and *From the Other Shore* Herzen offered a crushing, contemptuous critique of modern European civilization, especially of the France of the July Monarchy of Louis-Philippe (1830–48), the Second Republic (1848–51) and the beginnings of Louis-Napoleon's Second Empire (1852–70). On the economic level, Herzen observed, Europe was characterized by heartless capitalism. On the social level, it was dominated by the mercenary bourgeoisie, which Louis-Philippe's minister François Guizot had famously advised to enrich itself. On the political level, 'liberals', who represented the interest of the bourgeoisie, were in the ascendant.

These two contemporaneous cycles of writings (one in which Herzen set out evidence that seemed to augur well for the establishment of socialist utopia in Russia and another in which he hoped to prove that the west was in its death throes) are complementary elements in a representation of Russia's national position and mission. I shall begin my discussion of the place of Herzen's book *On the Development of Revolutionary Ideas in Russia* within this corpus by summarizing its contents and the various models of revolution with which Herzen had to reckon. I shall then clarify Herzen's understanding of revolution at this period and consider his treatment of the emergent Russian intelligentsia. Finally, I shall point to the strong nationalistic complexion of Herzen's concept of revolution, which makes it easy to understand the aversion his views aroused in his more internationalist contemporaries Karl Marx and Friedrich Engels. It is no doubt this colouring, together with Herzen's rose-tinted characterization of the Russian peasantry in it, that accounts for the neglect of this work by Herzen's scholarly admirers, most notably Isaiah Berlin and his pupil Aileen Kelly, though it should also be said that the other authors of major scholarship on Herzen which I cite at the end of this chapter have not analysed it very closely either.[4]

Herzen begins his book with a chapter on 'Russia and Europe', affirming the paradigm that had become established in Russian thought in the 1830s and 1840s in the early stage of the debate between the so-called Westernizers (a group to which Herzen himself belonged) and Slavophiles.[5] According to this paradigm, 'Europe', or 'the West', despite its internal divisions, was a coherent entity against which 'Russia' was to be measured. Next, in a chapter on 'Russia before Peter I',[6] Herzen offered an idyllic account of the earliest stage of recorded Russian history, from the ninth century. The indigenous East Slav people, he argued, soon absorbed the Scandinavian Varangians, who, according to the foundation myth of the Russian state, had been invited to rule over them. They lived in harmony in rural communities, holding possessions in common and reaching unanimous decisions about community affairs under the guidance of patriarchal elders (25–6). In his third chapter, Herzen discussed Peter himself, his westernizing reforms and the formation of a European society in the age of Catherine II (1762–96). In Chapter 4, he considered the period between Napoleon's invasion of Russia in 1812 and the Decembrist Revolt of 1825, during which secret societies sprang up and a 'truly revolutionary opposition' to the tsarist regime first developed (66 ff.). The fifth chapter concerns the burgeoning literature (poetry, prose and journalism) in which independent public opinion began to find expression in the age of Nicholas. Herzen then considered, in Chapter 6, the recent dispute between Slavophiles and Westernizers (or, as Herzen defined the respective bodies of thought, 'Muscovite Pan-Slavism' and 'Russian Europeanism'). Lastly, he provided an epilogue in which he clarified the general thrust of his book, and it is from this part of the work that I have taken the passage that is the starting point for my reading of this text.[7]

In addressing the subject of revolution, Herzen had several foreign examples before him. There was of course the French Revolution of 1789 and the Jacobin turn that that revolution had taken in 1793. Herzen speaks with respect of the Jacobins in other writings of the period with which I am concerned, even when he is considering them at their most murderous. In a passage in the *Letters from France and Italy*, for example, he sympathetically compares the instigators of the revolutionary terror with those counter-revolutionary Frenchmen who brutally put down insurgents during the 'June Days' of 1848.[8] Then there was the revolution that ended the restored Bourbon monarchy in 1830. Most topically, there was the Parisian revolution of February 1848, which had overthrown Louis-Philippe and sparked insurgencies or unrest in Italian and German states and parts of the Austro-Hungarian Empire. Herzen refers explicitly to this revolution in the book examined here (119), although he naturally deals with it in greater detail in his writings about the west.

Russian history too was punctuated by events such as palace coups and the rise or fall of court favourites which sometimes amounted to 'revolutions' (47). Russia's most important revolutionary event to date, though, was the Decembrist Revolt of 1825, which had been inspirational for the young Herzen. This was a failed mutiny of military officers whose views ranged from constitutionalism and federalism on the American model, as commended by Nikita Murav'ev, to dictatorial republicanism on the Jacobin model, as advocated by Pavel Pestel. The tsarist state had also been periodically threatened in the seventeenth and eighteenth centuries by elemental peasant revolts, especially the Pugachev uprising (1773–4), which is mentioned several times by Herzen in his book (47, 51, 97) and the memory of which remained fresh among older generations when Herzen was growing up. More localized peasant disturbances still continued in the age of Nicholas (82). As for revolutionary ideas, socialism was gaining a following among the young men who regularly met in the St Petersburg home of a young nobleman, Mikhail Petrashevskii, in the late 1840s to discuss the ideas of Charles Fourier and other French utopian thinkers.[9]

However, we shall miss the larger meaning of 'revolution', as Herzen understands it, if we confine our attention to such overt examples of overthrow of political regimes, insurgency, popular unrest, peasant rebellion or socialist thought as I have mentioned, ignoring in the process the broad thrust of the corpus of work in which *On the Development of Revolutionary Ideas in Russia* is situated. We need, for instance, to note the arresting fact that even among the Russian tsars, Herzen believes, a revolutionary was to be found. Peter I was 'a Jacobin before the time of the Jacobins and a revolutionary terrorist', for revolution, on the broadest plane, is a complete transformation of an old way of looking at the world. Peter wrought such a transformation, or put into effect a 'great revolutionary idea', because he broke down the introspective, patriarchal world view of late medieval Muscovy (40, 42, 62).[10] Even Christianity was just as revolutionary in its early days as socialism in the modern age, Herzen argued at this time, because it helped to undermine the Roman Empire[11] (which is in Herzen's mind, it will be noted, as he speaks of Russian absolutism in the passage from his book that I have quoted).

Revolution, then, in Herzen's understanding of it, should not be construed as an exclusively political, economic or social transformation. It is notable that in the cycles of essays to which I have referred Herzen offers no very precise, concrete plans for change of these kinds. Nor, unlike his friend and close collaborator Nikolai Ogarev, did he reflect on the possible ways in which revolutionary forces might be organized for struggle. Rather he is concerned, as the title of his book suggests, with 'ideas'; he is an 'intellectual revolutionary'.[12] In fact, the sort of revolution with which he is chiefly preoccupied in his writings of the late 1840s and early 1850s, especially *From the Other Shore*, is personal: he stands for the emancipation of members of the intellectual, cultural and moral elite from the shackles of outmoded ideas and social conventions as well as from the chains placed on them by despotic political regimes.

To say all this is not to deny that social reform is an aspect of the revolution Herzen imagines (121). After all, as a political exile managing an uncensored press in London from the mid-1850s, Herzen would become a powerful voice in the movement to emancipate the serfs in Russia. We should also remember that in an autocratic state (of which the Russia of Nicholas I provided a classic example), as in more modern totalitarian polities, it is not so easy to separate the intellectual from the political sphere. Every thought and action that conflicts with a prevailing orthodoxy, such as 'Official Nationality' in mid-nineteenth-century Russia, is potentially subversive, or, as Herzen puts it, any challenge to authority is a revolutionary act (86). Nonetheless, it is hard to see Herzen as a revolutionary socialist in the normal sense if we take the term to imply firm support for a significant degree of economic and social levelling.

Herzen's elastic understanding of the concept of revolution helped him to challenge the prevailing contemporary perception of Nicholas's Russia as Europe's principal counter-revolutionary bulwark. It enabled him to argue that there were in fact 'revolutionary' forces at work beneath the surface visible to foreigners during the reign of the 'gendarme of Europe'. This 'revolutionary Russia', as Herzen calls it in the passage quoted, turns out to be a minority of the nobility who represent the 'individual principle' and therefore 'opposition to absolutism' (38–9). More precisely, it is a section of the Muscovite nobility to which Herzen himself belonged. Unlike the St Petersburg nobility, who served at court or in the government and were allegedly motivated by selfish ambition, these independently minded men refused to serve the state and occupied themselves instead with the management of their estates and with learning and letters (82–3). They were 'the intelligence of the country', the 'organs of the people' who helped the people to understand their true position (113).

And yet, Herzen's description of this emergent moral and literary force as 'revolutionary' seems highly problematic. The bulk of the diverse collection of writers and thinkers whom Herzen associated in his book with the rise of independent literature and thought in the age of Nicholas cannot be classified as 'revolutionary' in any normal sense of the term, even if we allow that 'revolution' for Herzen at this time may have consisted primarily in an intellectual transformation. It is reasonable to talk of the poems of the Decembrist Kondratii Ryleev as revolutionary but not the early poems of Aleksandr Pushkin (68, 76), the 'philosophical letter' of Petr Chaadaev, the historiography and criticism of Nikolai Polevoi, the poetry of Aleksei Kol'tsov, Nikolai Gogol's novel *Dead Souls*, Ivan Turgenev's *Sportsman's Sketches* or Dmitrii Grigorovich's story *Anton the Unfortunate*. Nor were the so-called Westernizers so unequivocally and uniformly revolutionary as Herzen hoped his readers would believe when in his sixth chapter he drew a clear distinction between these representatives of 'Russian Europeanism' and the Slavophiles, who yearned for the supposedly organic community of pre-Petrine Muscovy. The Westernizers had assumed the mantle of the 'revolutionary' Peter I, Herzen implied when he claimed Peter '*is in us*' (117). Admittedly, it could truly be said of the future anarchist Mikhail Bakunin, to whom Herzen's book is dedicated, that he was already 'revolutionary', and the literary critic Belinskii, 'furious Vissarion', privately expressed enthusiasm for socialism and the Jacobins during the 1840s. However, even within the Westernist camp such representatives of revolutionism were in a minority in mid-nineteenth-century Russia. Indeed, Herzen's intolerant critique of western economic, social and political life during the early years of his emigration helped to cause a rift within that camp, alienating erstwhile companions such as the historian Timofei Granovskii.

Herzen's characterization of a significant part of the Russian cultural elite as 'revolutionary' is bound up in the passage I have quoted with another problematic assertion, namely that 'Russia' had 'a natural tendency towards socialist institutions'. This supposed proclivity to socialism (which Herzen associated first and foremost with the peasantry), coupled with the 'freshness', the youthful vigour, that he attributed to the progressive nobility, constituted a distinctive 'national element' which Russia could bring to the mid-nineteenth-century European political ferment. The Russian government was not Russian, Herzen contended in the passage quoted, but the combined revolutionary forces of the socialistic peasantry and the progressive nobility definitely were. Thus revolution, for Herzen, was at bottom a nationalistic idea with roots in the Romantic age, in which European ethnic groups extolled their cultural distinctiveness. Pursuit of it was an enterprise in which a widely despised nation, taking advantage of the fact that her past was empty (112), might proudly lead the more advanced but now moribund civilization of Western Europe out of its present impasse. Lest any western reader should doubt that the key to Europe's salvation lay in Russia, Herzen introduced a threat about the consequences of rejection of his invitation to collaborate in the business of revolution. If Russia's autocratic regime remained unchecked, he opined, it would help the Habsburgs and the Hohenzollerns to crush revolution, destroying western civilization in the process (109, 113, 125). Herzen's ellipsis at the end of the last sentence in the passage quoted at the beginning of this chapter accentuates this air of menace.

It is debatable, then, to what extent and in what sense the libertarian Herzen of the late 1840s and early 1850s was revolutionary. Later, when confronted with the emergence of a more militant – and more plebeian – younger generation of socialists in Russia after the Crimean War, Herzen warned of the dangers of revolutionary destruction. Nonetheless, he did help to nurture in the Russian intelligentsia a deep and lasting antipathy towards capitalism, the bourgeoisie and liberal parliamentary democracy. He also laid a foundation for what would become known as 'Populism', according to which Russia might follow an independent path to socialism, bypassing the capitalist phase of economic development and exploiting the communitarian instincts attributed to the Russian peasant. The contribution of his book *On the Development of Revolutionary Ideas in Russia* to this foundation was essentially twofold. First, it yoked together in the imagination what Herzen saw as the two positive forces in Russian life, the progressive intelligentsia and the socialistic peasantry. Second, it exploited the paradigm of an opposition between Russia and Europe to persuade readers that seemingly backward Russia in fact had a vital role to play as revolution faltered in the 'old world'.

## Further Reading

Acton, E., *Alexander Herzen and the Role of the Intellectual Revolutionary* (Cambridge: Cambridge University Press, 1979).

Herzen, A., '*From the Other Shore*' and '*The Russian People and Socialism*', trans. Moura Budberg and Richard Wollheim (London: Weidenfeld and Nicolson, 1956).

Lampert, E., *Studies in Rebellion* (London: Routledge and Kegan Paul, 1957).

Malia, M., *Alexander Herzen and the Birth of Russian Socialism, 1812-1855* (Cambridge, MA: Harvard University Press, 1961).

Offord, D., *Journeys to a Graveyard: Perceptions of Europe in Classical Russian Travel Writing* (Dordrecht: Springer, 2005), Ch. 6.

# 15

# George Plekhanov and the Marxist Turn in Russia

## Christopher Read

*The desire to work among the people and for the people, the certitude that 'the emancipation of the working classes must be conquered by the working classes themselves' – this practical tendency of our Narodism is just as dear to me as it used to be. But its theoretical propositions seem to me, indeed, erroneous in many respects. Years of life abroad and attentive study of the social question have convinced me that the triumph of a spontaneous popular movement similar to Stepan Razin's revolt or the Peasant Wars in Germany cannot satisfy the social and political needs of modern Russia, that the old forms of our national life carried within them many germs of their disintegration and that they cannot 'develop into a higher communist form' except under the immediate influence of a strong and well-organised workers' socialist party. For that reason I think that besides fighting absolutism the Russian revolutionaries must strive at least to work out the elements for the establishment of such a party in the future. In this creative work they will necessarily have to pass on to the basis of modern socialism, for the ideals of Zemlya i Volya do not correspond to the condition of the industrial workers. And that will be very opportune now that the theory of Russian exceptionalism is becoming synonymous with stagnation and reaction and that the progressive elements of Russian society are grouping under the banner of judicious 'Occidentalism' …*

*Moreover, the so-called terrorist movement has opened a new epoch in the development of our revolutionary party – the epoch of conscious political struggle against the government. This change in the direction of our revolutionaries' work makes it necessary for them to reconsider all views that they inherited from the preceding period. Life demands that we attentively reconsider all our intellectual stock-in-trade when we step on to new ground.*[1]

George Plekhanov's pamphlet *Socialism and Political Struggle* (1883), together with its sister publication *Our Differences* (1885), stand at multiple intersections. They were written at a decisive moment, first in the evolution of Russia's political history, second in the development of Marxism in Russia and beyond and third at a critical point in Plekhanov's life (1856–1918). All three aspects interacted with each other. Plekhanov was well aware of the multiple turning points. In his own words, the 'change in the direction of our revolutionaries' work makes it necessary for them to reconsider all views that they inherited from the preceding period. Life demands that we attentively reconsider all our intellectual stock-in-trade when we step on to new ground.'[2] The remainder of the extract above summarized the new direction. What had brought about this moment of change and what was Plekhanov's response?

On 13 March 1881, Tsar Alexander II, initiator of the emancipation of the serfs in 1861 and an ensuing set of reforms of the judicial system, army service and local administration, was mortally wounded by the second of two bombs thrown at his carriage. The assassination was hardly surprising. It followed several near-misses in the preceding three years. Members of the leading terrorist group, Narodnaya volya (The People's Will), had blown up a reception room in the Winter Palace, derailed a royal train and tunnelled under the main thoroughfare in St Petersburg, Nevsky Prospekt, filled it with explosives and waited for the tsar to pass over the spot. But it was, as the terrorists intended, a shock. However, it was not the shock they had planned for. Their motives were complex but a key notion was that, by cutting down figures of authority, with the tsar as the ultimate target, the terrorists would encourage the downtrodden peasantry, deceived by the false promises of emancipation since it brought them not the desired land so much as debt, to take action against their local tyrants. Instead, the peasantry were confused, and to no little extent horrified, by the ghastly death of the omnipotent, but not invulnerable, autocrat. If anything they were sympathetic to the dead tsar and his family.

Alexander's son and heir, Alexander III, and his entourage believed the root cause of the assassination was an excess of reform and they set about undoing what they saw as the damage which had been done. Limited concessions to noble and elite representation were reversed. Under the lugubrious and reactionary gaze of the Procurator of the Holy Synod, Konstantin Pobedonostsev, a policy of 'russifying' the empire was undertaken to quash the recalcitrant minorities. Pogroms were set up against Jews. From the revolutionary perspective, two decades of expansion had come to a halt and for more than ten years the movement was moribund.[3]

In his 25,000-word pamphlet of 1883, Plekhanov became one of the first to take stock of the situation and laid out directions which influenced the Russian revolutionary movement for a generation. Plekhanov himself had followed the trajectory of that movement. To simplify, it had come of age in the 1860s, fuelled by disappointment at the limited scope of reform. In particular, nothing was done to even hint at a constitution and modification of the outworn and increasingly anachronistic autocratic system. Incredibly, even into the twentieth century, Russia had wide-ranging censorship, complete bans on all political parties, no legal form of politics and no national assembly even for the elite. Activist intellectuals in the 1860s were outraged at the absence of any progress in this direction. Many turned to revolution as the only solution. However, it was soon realized that a small group of angry intellectuals would carry no political weight. The solution appeared to be to take up the cause of the peasantry, Russia's vast majority. In the words of the first teacher of the movement, Peter Lavrov (1823–1900), they would become the 'mind, honour and conscience' of the Russian people.[4] The new tendency became known as populists (*narodniki* in Russian). At first, under the guidance of Peter Lavrov, they thought it would be sufficient to propagandize the peasants by explaining their revolutionary strategies to them. For a variety of reasons this had failed to excite peasant discontent by the mid-1870s. Some populists believed it was necessary to simply carry on over a much longer period. Land and Liberty, a small breakaway group, including Plekhanov, thought otherwise. A bolder, more dramatic effort was, they argued, to include, in limited circumstances, terror. It was in the wake of the failure of this second strategy by 1881 that Plekhanov came to his re-evaluation and move to new principles.

The extract above, by which Plekhanov introduced his contribution to what he called the reconsideration of all inherited views, encapsulates his response. The key propositions are: (i) to retain the concept that the working masses will achieve their own emancipation; (ii) a spontaneous peasant uprising[5] such as that the narodniks had worked for would not take place; (iii) it was necessary to form a party, though details of what this meant were sparse; (iv) industrial workers would be at the heart of the new strategy; (v) ideas of a 'separate path' for Russia, what he calls 'exceptionalism', should be abandoned; (vi) Russia's future lay in following the 'western' model, what he calls 'Occidentalism' (also translated as 'westernization'). Plekhanov's final point is perhaps the most difficult to grasp today but was of the utmost significance to Russia, and arguably to the subsequent history of Marxism in general. It is (vii) to realize there was a new epoch ushered in by the terrorists, that of '*conscious political struggle*'[6] which, especially to us, begs the question 'what did they think they had been doing prior to that?' Incidentally, though it is not explicit at this point, Plekhanov broke with terrorism as a counter-productive tactic. This scepticism is only hinted at here in his dismissive phrase 'so-called terrorism'.[7] Instead, Russian revolutionaries needed 'to pass on to the basis of modern socialism', a concept we will need to explore further.

The proposition that the working masses, a formula that included industrial and agrarian workers and, in Russian conditions, a significant part of the peasantry, should achieve its own emancipation was a standard Marxist proposition.[8] Marx had argued that revolutionary class consciousness would evolve organically among the proletariat as they contemplated their situation in the capitalist structure. They would realize their struggle was not against individual employers but against the system itself. Proposition (iii), on the need for a party, risks contradicting this view. Marx himself had spent little time thinking about such a requirement. Forming a party was not necessarily a contradiction, in that such a party could be composed of the working masses, but the implication and practice which Plekhanov had in mind was that intellectuals like himself would have a significant role in organizing and, albeit reluctantly in theory, leading such a party. In practice, this contradiction dogged the harmonious development of such parties in Russia and beyond. It also had implications for the crucial notion of 'political struggle' to which we will shortly return.

Propositions (ii) and (iv) are also linked. In a straightforward and highly understated way, Plekhanov, in these two statements, consigned the whole preceding history of the Russian revolutionary movement to the dustbin of history. The assumption of the narodniks and narodism,[9] as Plekhanov calls it, had been to instigate a 'spontaneous' peasant uprising. There is of course an unacknowledged contradiction here, too, in that the incendiary actions of the leading narodnik propagandists and/or terrorists mitigated the idea of 'spontaneity'. However, the idea was that, while narodnik action might set such a revolution in motion, it would, they surmised, be too vast for them to control. In that sense it would be 'spontaneous'. Be that as it may, Plekhanov was announcing a revolution in the revolution. Peasants would no longer be the major focus. Instead, the urban, industrial working class would be the main target of revolutionary action and the locomotive dragging history forward. This was a remarkable proposition in that, in the 1880s, Russia had a miniscule industrial working class, which was barely 2–3 per cent of the population against the overwhelming mass of peasants who constituted some 85–90 per cent. The notion, therefore, seemed far-fetched and was one of the key reasons why

Plekhanov had only the tiniest handful of supporters in the decade following the publication of *Socialism and Political Struggle*.

Propositions (v) and (vi) are two aspects of one concept. As an extension of his turn away from the peasantry Plekhanov also breaks with what was considered another major foundation of narodism: that Russia would follow its own path of development which would be different from the west. In particular, most narodniks believed Russia could avoid capitalism and move directly from its current quasi-feudal set-up to socialism. There were many reasons for this, one of which was that the survival of communal and redistributive land holding among the peasantry constituted a major step towards a socialist society. Ironically, almost at this very moment, Marx appeared to be siding with the narodniks.[10] Nonetheless, Plekhanov threw his entire weight behind ideas of westernism (*zapadnichestvo* in Russian, translated as 'Occidentalism' above), that is, that Russia had no special path to follow but would, by and large, follow the other leading powers through capitalism and industry to socialism.

And so, on to the final proposition, that there was a 'new epoch of conscious political struggle' which would enable the revolutionary movement and Russia 'to pass on to the basis of modern socialism'. Since this was the proposition which inspired Plekhanov's title for the pamphlet it obviously had considerable meaning for him. What was it? For Plekhanov, this proposition encapsulated and underpinned all the rest. In Marx's lifetime (he died, coincidentally, at almost the same moment as Plekhanov published this pamphlet)[11] workers' struggles had tended to take place outside the state. This was not least because Marx had argued bitterly with Mikhail Bakunin in the First International over the latter's prioritizing of the struggle against the state over 'economic' struggle in the form of class struggle conducted through trade unions and the like. For Plekhanov, a key legacy of his own narodnik past was that the future lay in the realm of political struggle, that is, in Russia's case, the need for a constitution as a basis for everything else. Hence the need for a political party. And when Plekhanov talks about 'modern socialism' he means worker-based Marxism. This also implies a break with all forms of Russian exceptionalism because they have become 'synonymous with stagnation and reaction'. It also embodied his firm rejection of terrorism as a counter-productive form of revolutionary activity which merely provided the state with an excuse to repress with a high degree of public approval.

Anyone familiar with Russian Marxism, particularly in its Leninist form, will immediately recognize all of the above propositions. They were firmly embodied in Bolshevik and Menshevik ideologies by 1917. Not for nothing is Plekhanov often described as 'the father of Russian Marxism'.[12] However, the path to acceptance of his ideas was steep and stony. For almost a decade Plekhanov was almost isolated. At one point he is said to have joked, while he and some companions were enjoying rowing a boat on Lake Geneva, that, if the boat sank, it would be the end of Russian Marxism. Nonetheless, In September 1883 Plekhanov joined with his old friend Pavel Axelrod, Lev Deutsch, Vasili Ignatov and Vera Zasulich in establishing the first Russian-language Marxist political organization, the Emancipation of Labour Group (*Gruppa Osvobozhdenie Truda*) but it remained tiny and uninfluential throughout most of the reign of Alexander III (1881–94).

As Alexander's reign came to an end, hope was renewed in wide sectors of elite Russian society, from liberal landowners to revolutionary intellectuals. The new tsar, Nicholas II, was quick to quash such expectations. In a key speech in January 1895 he claimed that expectations of reform were 'senseless dreams' and that it was his firm intention 'to uphold the principles of autocracy as firmly' as his late father.[13] Even so, society was stirring. In the early 1890s a distinct Social Democratic trend, along the lines defined by Plekhanov in 1883, began to separate itself definitively from narodism. Plekhanov himself had engaged in bitter polemics over the new direction in 1885 in his well-known work *Our Differences*, but it was only eight to ten years later that he began to have a substantial following. As Plekhanov had done in the 1880s, followers of the new tendency were at pains to define their distinctiveness compared to the narodniks/populists. Between 1890 and 1903, Social Democracy, though it remained small and isolated, emerged as an established political/intellectual tendency and as an embryonic political party. In particular, a young polemicist from the deep provinces, Vladimir Ulyanov, better known as Lenin, took up the theme. The first substantial surviving items from Lenin's ever-sharp pen were polemics against the narodniks, notably his articles 'What the "Friends of the People" Are' and 'The Heritage We Renounce' (1898).[14]

It also defined itself, in a polemic that is often misunderstood today, against the 'economist' tendency which prioritized economic struggle over political struggle – the very distinction which Plekhanov had initially rebelled against. The debate against the economists around 1900–5 contains many of the propositions supposedly directed by Bolsheviks against Mensheviks. In particular, Lenin's seminal early work *What Is to Be Done?* was initially read as a classic Social Democratic demolition of the economist tendency before it was reread as an attack on the 'Menshevik' conception of a political party.[15] Even though considerable argument swirled around them, the new movement embraced the guidelines laid down by Plekhanov. It looked exclusively to Marx and the Marxist tradition for inspiration. It prioritized the working class as the foremost power advancing the revolution. It developed into a political party which sought to establish a constitution as a step towards socialist revolution. It rejected the populist idea that Russia could evade the capitalist stage of social development. It scorned any notion that Russia was an exception to the economic laws of historical advance. It completely rejected terror as an effective revolutionary tactic.

These remained the principles of the Bolshevik Party when it came to power. It was still inspired by the 'conscious' and 'modern' form of socialism focused on political struggle as outlined by Plekhanov. It went further and established them as definitive principles of international communism and, as such, they had a great influence on the history of the twentieth century and may still have life in the future. Ironically, Plekhanov himself broke with Lenin long before his death in 1918, alienated by the heavy-handed, ruthless, authoritarian and undemocratic streak he perceived in his former protégée.

## Further Reading

Baron, Samuel H., *Plekhanov in Russian History and Soviet Historiography* (Pittsburgh: University of Pittsburgh Press, 1995).

Baron, Samuel H., *Plekhanov: The Father of Russian Marxism* (London and Stanford: Stanford University Press, 1963).

Haimson, Leopold, *The Russian Marxists and the Origins of Bolshevism* (Boston, MA: Beacon Press, 1966).

Read, Christopher, *Lenin: A Revolutionary Life* (London and New York: Routledge, 2005), Chs 1–5.

Walicki, Andrzej, *The Controversy over Capitalism: Studies in the Social Philosophy of Russian Populism* (Oxford: The Claredon Press, 1966).

# 16

# Ordinary Miracles: Lenin's Call for Revolutionary Ambition

Lars T. Lih

*[1] But a circle of inspiring leaders [korifei] such as Alekseev and Myshkin, Khalturin and Zheliabov are capable of political tasks in the most genuine and practical sense of the word – precisely because their impassioned preaching meets with an answering call from the masses awakening in an elemental fashion, and the leaders' seething energy is taken up and supported by the energy of the revolutionary class. [2] Plekhanov was a thousand times right when he not only identified the revolutionary class, not only proved the inevitability and unavoidability of its elemental awakening, but also presented to the 'worker circles' a great and noble political task. [3] But you refer to the mass movement that arose afterwards in order to lower this task – in order to narrow the energy and sweep of the activity of the 'worker circles'. [4] What is this, except an artisan's infatuation with his own artisanal limitations? [5] You brag about your practicality and you don't see (a fact known to any Russian praktik) what miracles for the revolutionary cause can be brought about not only by a circle but by a lone individual. [6] Or do you think that our movement can't produce real leaders [korifei] like those of the seventies? Why? Because we're unprepared? [7] But we are preparing ourselves, we will go on preparing ourselves – and we will not stop until we are prepared!*
*[8] True, over the stagnant waters of 'an economic struggle against the owners and the government', a layer of slime has unfortunately formed – people appear among us who get down on their knees and pray to elementality, gazing with beatitude (as Plekhanov put it) on the 'posterior' of the Russian proletariat. [9] But we will be able to free ourselves from this slime. [10] And it is precisely at the present time that the Russian revolutionary, guided by a genuinely revolutionary theory and relying on the class that is genuinely revolutionary*

> and that is undergoing an elemental awakening, can at last – at last! – draw himself up to his full stature and reveal all his heroic [bogatyrskii] strength.

The process by which certain passages from a famous book become emblems of the book as a whole is not a straightforward one. In the western academic tradition, Lenin's *What Is to Be Done?* has come to be represented by two or three passages where Lenin seems to be expressing his worries about lack of revolutionary fervour among the workers.[1] The rest of the book might as well not exist. In Russia, the passages regarded as central in the west are the ones that do not exist. In 2005, a book of Russian political quotations was published in which Lenin has the most extensive entry – 216 items – but his famous (in the west) remarks about the limitations of the 'spontaneous worker movement' do not appear.[2]

The quotations that constitute the Russian memory of *What Is to Be Done?* create a dramatically different sense of Lenin's outlook – not worry about workers but exhilaration about their elemental awakening, combined with a call for revolutionaries to think big.[3] One of these quotations begins with the words 'in a tight little band, hands firmly joined, we are treading a steep and narrow way'. This passage was set to music by Sergei Prokofiev in his *Cantata for the 20th Anniversary of the October Revolution*; the propulsive energy of Prokofiev's setting is an excellent commentary on the spirit of *What Is to Be Done?*[4]

If I had to choose one passage from *What Is to Be Done?* to be ceaselessly recycled in textbooks and histories of Russia, I would pick the textual moment analysed here. It helps us understand why the young underground activists who were the book's first readers were so thrilled by it. One such activist, N. Valentinov, broke with Lenin soon thereafter. Yet he later reminisced that, in his youth, he and his fellow activists were attracted by 'struggle, risk and danger'; for this reason, '*What Is to Be Done?* struck just the right chord with us and we were only too eager to put its message into practice'.[5] Any interpretation of Lenin's book must account for this enthusiastic reaction.

Our passage also shows Lenin's idiosyncratic blending of aggressive polemic with what another early reader (Aleksandr Potresov, who also later became a determined foe of Lenin) called political poetry. In order to understand the impact of *What Is to Be Done?* on its target audience, we must have a sense of this poetry. In order to have a sense of the poetry, we must first wade into the polemical context.

*What Is to Be Done?* was written in late 1901 and early 1902 in order to propagate Lenin's plan for achieving a widely held goal: creating a nationwide party structure out of the existing scattered and isolated underground organizations of Russian Social Democracy. Lenin was a prominent member of the *Iskra* group, named for an underground newspaper printed in Western Europe and smuggled into tsarist Russia. The *Iskra* editorial board represented a coalition between the founders of Russian Social Democracy (Georgii Plekhanov, Vera Zasulich, Pavel Axelrod) and younger activists who had practical experience in underground work (Lenin, Iulii Martov, Aleksandr Potresov).

*Iskra*'s highly ambitious political programme was to create a national party structure, secure it a strong base in the burgeoning mass worker movement and thus give Russian Social Democracy an important role – perhaps even a leading role – in the imminent overthrow of the tsarist system. In support of these optimistic perspectives, Lenin and his comrades could point to an upsurge of politicized worker protest that had taken place in the early months of 1901.

By the time Lenin sat down to draft his book, *Iskra*'s programme had been subjected to withering criticism by a rival group of Social Democratic émigrés associated with the journal *Rabochee delo*. This group argued that *Iskra*'s political aims were too ambitious, since 'political tasks in the actual and practical sense of the word – that is, in the sense of a rational and practical struggle for political demands – are not in general accessible to worker circles' (see sentence 1 for Lenin's paraphrase). In a way extremely typical for Lenin, he seeks to refute *Rabochee delo*'s 'no we can't' with his own 'yes we can'.

In the passage we are analysing, Lenin rhetorically addresses these critics with an argument that can be paraphrased as follows:

You say that small underground circles cannot rally the Russian workers around the banner of an all-out fight against tsarism? This is true, perhaps, of an underground organization made up of people like yourself: people who whine about the difficulties facing them and use the workers as an excuse for their own lack of ambition and refusal to think big. But what if the underground organization was made up of genuinely inspiring leaders such as those who created Narodnaia volia (People's Will) in the 1870s? Those were true heroes with ambitious aims, although the situation they faced back then prevented them from achieving their full potential. But today we have exactly what they lacked: a mass movement that is seeking *us* out – the revolutionaries of today – with the same energy that we revolutionaries have always sought them out.

Yes, there are practical difficulties that confront a persecuted, illegal underground organization that is trying to reach out to the masses. But instead of treating these difficulties as a challenge, you let them overwhelm you. You use the presence of the mass movement as an excuse to *lower* your ambitions.

Precisely at the present time, even a lone activist who thinks big and who is able to convey to his audience the grandeur of his revolutionary dreams can achieve miracles!

The above paraphrase gives the logical outline of Lenin's argument. He wants to show that his opponents have set their sights too low, and he points to the heroic revolutionaries of the 1870s who accomplished great things (Lenin assumes that his audience agrees with this assessment). He then argues: think how much more they could have accomplished with the advantage we enjoy, namely, support from a growing mass movement full of energy and enthusiasm.

To back up his argument and inspire his readers, Lenin deploys an extensive battery of rhetorical devices, all of which rely on the contrast between high and low – between great and noble tasks versus stagnant lack of ambition. A review of these devices will help put our passage in its full context.

One of Lenin's favourite techniques throughout his writings is to take a formulation of his opponents' and turn it against them. One of the *Rabochee delo* group, Aleksandr Martynov, had advanced as a tactical slogan the idea of 'an economic struggle against the owners and the government' – that is, using economic grievances to stoke anti-tsarist sentiment among the workers. The *Iskra* group objected that workers were already capable of responding to directly political appeals. Lenin loves to take a slogan like Martynov's and repeat it so often that it begins to lose meaning and appear ridiculous. The appearance of Martynov's slogan in our passage (sentence 8) is due to this rhetorical technique. The words 'worker circles' and 'practicality' are also taken directly from *Rabochee delo* (sentences 3, 5). Lenin wants to expose his critics as people who talk about 'practicality' as a way of condescending to the *praktik* – that is, the activist out on the frontlines of local underground organizations. In contrast, Lenin evokes the paradoxical image of the *praktik* as miracle-worker (sentence 5).

A more subtle and fundamental example of this ideological jiu-jitsu is Lenin's use of 'elemental' (*stikhiinyi*). Anyone picking up *What Is to Be Done?* will get the impression that Lenin was obsessed with the concept of *stikhiinost*. Indeed, scholarly consensus regards such an obsession as established fact.[6] Nevertheless, this impression is an illusion, due entirely to Lenin's habit of sarcastic repetition of his opponent's phrases. The only reason *stikhiinost* is prominent in *What Is to Be Done?* is because the term was used in September 1901 by Boris Krichevsky, a leading member of *Rabochee delo*. Lenin showed very little interest in the topic of *stikhiinost* either before or after this particular polemical joust.

The best English translation of *stikhiinyi* is 'elemental'. The etymological origin of the Russian word is the Greek *stoikheion* or 'element'; both the

Greek and its Latin equivalent became associated with 'force of nature', a connotation that *stikhiinyi*, its Russian descendant, still retains. Nevertheless, in English translations of *What Is to Be Done?*, *stikhiinyi* is most often (but never consistently) translated as 'spontaneous'. There were practical reasons for this rendering. The polemics of *What Is to Be Done?* gave rise to constant use of the noun form *stikhiinost* (otherwise a rather rare word in Russian when compared to the adjective). Unfortunately, 'elemental' has no familiar noun form ('elementality' is the best I could come up with), whereas 'spontaneous' does. Furthermore, the phrase '*stikhiinyi* element' is a common one in *What Is to Be Done?* And so, out of a purely practical translation problem arose a great subject of theoretical debate: Lenin's attitude towards 'spontaneity'.[7]

As mentioned, the word 'elemental' is centrally connected to the idea of a force of nature – a metaphor that can go in many directions. A force of nature can be seen as unfocused, unorganized, violent and destructive. When this set of connotations is in the forefront, Lenin is 'against' elementality – as was Russian Social Democracy as a whole, which saw its task precisely as organizing and channelling originally chaotic worker protests. In fact, the Menshevik wing of Russian Social Democracy was considerably more focused on the need to overcome elementality than was the Bolshevik wing.[8]

The metaphor of a force of nature can also be mobilized to evoke the idea of a mighty and irresistible power that is working, not against you, but for you. To understand our passage, we have to see that Lenin uses 'elementality' in both negative and positive senses. The negative sense is associated with his polemical opponents, who (according to Lenin) pray to elementality – that is, they not only passively accept the given situation, the current limitations, but they do so almost as a matter of principle. Lenin relays Plekhanov's joke about idealizing the proletariat from behind, with no sense that the proletariat itself is moving on (sentence 8).

The positive connotations of 'force of nature' – as inevitable, unstoppable, transformative power – are mobilized in the image of the 'elemental awakening' of the workers, an image used three times in our passage (sentences 1, 2, 10). This particular force of nature is working *for* us, so we should have the confidence to think big – this is the heart of Lenin's message, not only in *What Is to Be Done?* but also throughout his writings.

Lenin repeated *ad nauseam* not only his opponents' formulations but also his own newly minted polemical coinages. One example that resounds throughout *What Is to Be Done?* is 'kowtowing to elementality', a variant of which is found in our passage (sentence 8). Another example is *kustarnichestvo*, which I have translated as 'artisanal limitations' (other renderings include 'amateurism', 'primitivism'). A *kustar* is a traditional Russian craftsman, working for a local market with little or no division of labour. When applied to party organization, the *kustar* metaphor referred to local party committees that were isolated and separated from each other, due to the absence of nationwide organizational structures. With this meaning, the term became part of the standard lexicon of Russian Social Democracy. In our passage, *kustarnichestvo* plays an additional role as yet another evocation of thinking small and unambitiously (sentence 4).

Opposed to the *kustar* in Lenin's system of images is the *korifei*, an exalted word for 'leader' (sentences 1, 6). Its etymological origin is the coryphaeus, the leader of the chorus in Greek tragedy.[9] As examples of *korifei*, Lenin lists 'Alekseev and Myshkin, Khalturin and Zheliabov'. These populist revolutionaries from the 1870s have specific connotations that are mobilized by Lenin in his argument. First and foremost, they were 'inspiring' due to selfless dedication and their 'impassioned preaching' of ambitious revolutionary goals (sentence 1). The four leaders evoked by Lenin symbolize the union of workers and intelligentsia that was a key aspect of the new mass movement Lenin saw arising. These leaders also represent a shift in populist thinking from aiming at purely economic revolution to working for a political one, even if this new commitment was expressed first of all in the dead-end tactic of individual terrorism (the assassination of Alexander II in 1881). Finally, all of these *korifei* ended badly, personally and politically: death in Siberia or on the scaffold, combined with a stalled and demoralized revolutionary movement.

There is an autobiographical aspect to Lenin's evocation of populist *korifei* that might have resonated with some of his readers. Lenin's older brother Aleksandr Ulyanov was himself an inspiring and dedicated revolutionary leader who got embroiled in a futile attempt to assassinate the tsar in 1884 and died on the scaffold. Where Aleksandr failed, Vladimir was determined to succeed – because in the following two decades a genuine mass movement had sprung up, and Russian revolutionaries had also discovered Marxism, a 'genuinely revolutionary theory' (sentence 10). This evolution in the Russian revolutionary tradition is vividly incarnated in Plekhanov, whom Lenin cites not only as an authority but also as a living link between the *korifei* of the 1870s and the *praktiki* of the new century (see Christopher Read's discussion in this volume of Plekhanov's adoption of 'modern socialism').

Lenin's rhetorical opposition between high ambition and low routine even finds expression in sound effects. Alliteration of *v* and *k* adds to the solemnity of 'great and noble' tasks (*vysokii i velikii*) (sentence 2). In contrast, the hissing *z*'s and *i*'s of 'to lower' (*prinizit*) and 'to narrow' (*suzit*) strengthen the imagery of reptilian sloth (sentence 3). An even lower life form is evoked by the image of slimy pond scum (sentence 8). In contrast to all this creeping, crawling stagnation is the heroic *bogatyr* who strides forth to do battle in the final sentence. The *bogatyri* were the giant marvellous heroes of the Russian folk epics. Lenin could have chosen no better word to evoke his romantic conception of the Social Democratic *praktik* as people's hero.

The scholarly consensus concerning Lenin's worry about workers arises from focusing attention on a few of Lenin's formulations about *stikhiinost/* elementality/'spontaneity', while completely ignoring the overall system of images that governs Lenin's rhetoric throughout *What Is to Be Done?* – a rhetoric that continually contrasts high ambition to low routine, to the decided advantage of the former. If our passage had been chosen as the exemplary textbook quote from *What Is to Be Done?*, we would have a very different and much more accurate idea of Lenin's outlook.

'It is precisely at the present time that the Russian revolutionary ... can at last – at last! – draw himself up to his full stature' (sentence 10). The repeated 'at last' reveals the emotional investment that Lenin put into his argument and that so impressed the first readers of *What Is to Be Done?* The same emotional investment is manifest throughout Lenin's career. We will conclude our consideration of his 1902 book with a passage from early 1919, when Lenin still thought the Russian Revolution would quickly spread to Western Europe (he was soon to be disillusioned):

> Comrades, behind us there is a long line of revolutionaries who sacrificed their lives for the emancipation of Russia. The lot of the majority of these revolutionaries was a hard one. They endured the persecution of the tsarist government, but it was not their good fortune to see the triumph of the revolution. The happiness that has fallen to our lot is all the greater. Not only have we seen the triumph of our revolution, not only have we seen it become consolidated amidst unprecedented difficulties, creating a new kind of government and winning the sympathy of the whole world, but we are also seeing the seed sown by the Russian revolution spring up in Europe.[10]

Lenin's hopeful words in 1919 provide a gloss on our passage from *What Is to Be Done?*, a gloss that brings out the essential political poetry without the dross of momentary polemics. In both passages, the ongoing force of history has made meaningful the sacrifices of earlier generations of Russian revolutionaries (including Lenin's brother Aleksandr Ulyanov). In 1919, Lenin asserts that the isolated *praktiki* of 1902 did in fact accomplish miracles: the Russian proletariat, led by the party, has carried out a revolution that is now inspiring the whole world. No wonder so many of the first readers of *What Is to Be Done?* were themselves inspired by Lenin's injunction to think big.

## Further Reading

Lih, Lars T., 'How a Founding Document was Found, or One Hundred Years of Lenin's *What Is to be Done?*', *Kritika* 4, no. 1 (Winter 2003): 1–45.
Lih, Lars T., *Lenin Rediscovered* (Chicago: Haymarket Books, 2009).
Miliukov, Paul, *Russia and its Crisis* (Forgotten Books: 2012). Written in 1903 in English for American audiences by a prominent Russian historian and liberal opposition leader, this book is the best introduction to the immediate historical background of *What Is To be Done?*
Tucker, Robert C., 'Introduction: Lenin and Revolution', in *The Lenin Anthology*, ed. Robert Tucker (New York: Norton, 1975). Robert Tucker was one of the few historians to grasp the power of Lenin's romantic self-image.

# 17

# Revolution and Evolution: Kropotkin's Anarchism

George Crowder

*Anarchism is a world-concept based upon a mechanical explanation of all phenomena, embracing the whole of nature – that is, including in it the life of human societies and their economic, political, and moral problems. Its method of investigation is that of the exact natural sciences …. When philistine naturalists, seemingly basing their arguments on 'Darwinism', began to teach, 'Crush whoever is weaker than yourself, such is the law of nature', it was easy for us to prove first, that this was not Darwin's conclusion, and by the same scientific method to show that these scientists were on the wrong path; that no such law exists: that the life of animals teaches us something entirely different, and that their conclusions were absolutely unscientific. They were just as unscientific as for instance the assertion that the inequality of wealth is a law of nature, or that capitalism is the most advantageous form of social life calculated to promote progress. … The anarchists conceive a society in which all the mutual relations of its members are regulated, not by laws, not by authorities, whether self-imposed or elected, but by mutual agreements between the members of that society and by a sum of social customs and habits – not petrified by law, routine, or superstition, but continually developing and continually readjusted in accordance with the ever-growing requirements of a free life stimulated by the progress of science, invention, and the steady growth of higher ideals. … We understand the social revolution, not at all as a Jacobinist dictatorship [but] as a widespread popular movement, during which in every town and village within the region of the revolt, the masses will have to take upon themselves the task of rebuilding society … without awaiting any orders and directions from above.*[1]

Anarchism aims at a society without the state, but that is not the same thing as a society without rules.[2] Contrary to the popular misidentification of anarchism with 'anarchy', or chaos, an anarchist society would be ordered, but ordered by rules freely accepted by people rather than by laws coercively imposed upon them by government. For the classical anarchists, who reached their peak of influence around 1880–1914, human oppression is principally due to three institutions: capitalism, religion and (most importantly) the state. Since each of these oppressive institutions supports the others, all have to be abolished in order for the good society to emerge. The desirable society will be characterized by individual liberty from coercion and ignorance and by economic equality instead of class domination.

Opposition to capitalism locates the anarchists within the mainstream of the socialist tradition alongside the Marxists. Like the Marxists, the anarchists are revolutionaries rather than reformers, believing that the social changes that are needed are too radical to be accepted by the dominant classes without a struggle. Where the anarchists differ crucially from the Marxists, however, is in their rejection of state authority even as a transitional means to the necessary social revolution.

The revolutionary stream in anarchism is balanced by another aspect, namely its intellectual debt to the eighteenth-century Enlightenment. The Scientific Revolution of the seventeenth century had shown the power of human reason to explain the natural world. Galileo, for example, had demonstrated how modern scientific method, combining empirical observation with mathematical calculation, could overturn the old Aristotelian (or 'Scholastic') understanding of cosmology. The Enlightenment and its nineteenth-century heirs sought to apply the same methods to the study of human society, both to explain society more satisfactorily and ultimately to improve or even to perfect it.

The classical anarchists saw themselves as standing in this line of succession. In part this explains their characteristic hostility towards religion, which they, like the Marxists, usually associated with outmoded and harmful superstition. It also goes some way towards explaining the anarchists' optimism about the prospects for the future free society. If science can lay bare the basis of human morality then we should be able to identify moral laws of nature on which we can all agree just as we can agree on the descriptive laws of nature uncovered by the Scientific Revolution. Laws that command agreement need not be enforced.

The thought of Peter Kropotkin exemplifies all these general anarchist tendencies but he is especially interesting in his attempt to integrate the revolutionary and scientific elements of anarchism. Born in 1842 into the aristocracy of tsarist Russia, the young Kropotkin received a military education that one might have expected to lead anywhere but to anarchism. However, by the mid-1870s he had emerged as a leading anarchist revolutionary, active in Russia, Switzerland and France. As a result of his membership of the first International Workingmen's Association, which was proscribed in France, he was imprisoned at Clairvaux from 1883 to 1886. After his release he emigrated to England, where he settled in London and devoted himself to writing. His advocacy of anarchism and his fascination with the natural world, especially through the lens of Darwinism, come together in several works, of which *Modern Science and Anarchism* is a good example.

Much of *Modern Science and Anarchism* is devoted to attacking existing social, political and economic institutions and to sketching the anarchist alternatives. On the critical side Kropotkin focuses on what he sees as the nexus between capitalism and the state. The basic anarchist objection to capitalism is the standard socialist claim that economic inequality leads to class domination. In this connection Kropotkin neatly observes that the 'laissez-faire' principle celebrated by orthodox political economists in the tradition of Adam Smith in reality applies much more to the capitalists than to the working class, whose liberty is typically curtailed by taxes, monopolies and restrictions on the right to strike (182–3).

What is distinctive of anarchism, however, is its opposition to the state. For Kropotkin as for other anarchists, capitalism survives only because it is kept in place by the coercive force of government; if capitalism is to be abolished, the state must be abolished (181). The evil of the state extends beyond the maintenance of capitalism. Its essence is compulsion or coercion: while any society needs rules, the distinguishing mark of the state is that it turns 'customs', or freely accepted rules, into 'laws', which Kropotkin understands as rules coercively enforced by centralized, specialist authorities (175). Laws usually serve the interests only of those dominant groups who make them. But even when laws are directed towards desirable ends they undermine our capacity for genuinely moral action because we obey them out of 'fear of punishment' rather than from a sense of their rightness (157). In short, 'the State represents the negation of liberty and spoils even what it undertakes to do for the sake of general well-being' (165). These problems persist regardless of the form taken by the state. 'Representative' government suffers from them as much as dictatorship, and even an ostensibly 'socialist' government would have the same defects.

But Kropotkin sees that anarchism needs more than a critique of the state; it also needs a positive account of the alternative stateless society. As he expresses it in the selected passage, this will be organized 'by mutual agreements between the members of that society and by a sum of social customs and habits' (157). Kropotkin envisages the good society as a series of 'communes', or small communities in which property is held in common, each internally structured by rules freely accepted by its members and all externally related by a system of free federation.

Kropotkin does acknowledge a division within anarchist thought between two main versions of the ideal social structure, corresponding to two rival accounts of economic distribution. On the one hand there is the 'mutualism' favoured by Pierre-Joseph Proudhon and his followers, which rewards people in accordance with how long they spend at work (160). This scheme Kropotkin regards as unrealistic, in part because of the difficulty of equating the value of work with the amount of time spent working. He prefers the 'communist' alternative, in which goods and services are produced in common and distributed according to need (171–4). In this he agrees with the Marxists.

As noted earlier, however, Kropotkin and other anarchists depart from the Marxists over the question of how the transition is to be made from the existing capitalist state to the stateless communist future. Kropotkin accepts that the transition must be by way of revolution rather than parliamentary reform, but he implicitly condemns the Marxist account of revolution as authoritarian, and he replaces it with a characteristically anarchist theory emphasizing popular spontaneity. He also seeks to integrate this with an evolutionary explanation based on a distinctive interpretation of Darwin.

To focus on the evolutionary aspect first, this has to be set, as already mentioned, against the background of a general anarchist commitment to Enlightenment values of reason and scientific method. Thus, Kropotkin describes anarchism as 'a world-concept based upon a mechanical explanation of all phenomena, embracing the whole of nature' and claims that 'its method of investigation is that of the exact natural sciences' (150). He contrasts this scientific approach with 'the metaphysical fictions of old', which include, of course, religious views but extend also to 'the dialectical method' – a slap at the philosophical–historical speculations of Hegel and Marx (152). Rather than such predetermined patterns in history, it is 'the method of induction and deduction', so successful at explaining the natural world, that will also explain the social world. After all, 'the life of societies' is part of 'the phenomena of nature' (150).

The particular form in which science is most helpful to anarchist inquiry, Kropotkin believes, is that of Darwinism. Kropotkin was writing at a time when Charles Darwin's master-idea of the evolution of species by natural selection was widely accepted as a model for theories in a range of fields – ethical, economic and political. But in these connections the dominant interpretation of Darwin, 'social Darwinism', was rejected by Kropotkin as a grotesque misunderstanding. For the social Darwinists, such as Herbert Spencer, the central message of Darwin is that nature is an arena of competitive struggle among individuals and groups which leads inexorably to 'the survival of the fittest' (Spencer's phrase).[3] This was thought to justify competitive institutions and practices such as laissez-faire economics and imperialist international relations. Kropotkin summarizes this message as 'Crush whoever is weaker than yourself, such is the law of nature', and he dismisses it as the conclusion of 'philistine naturalists' who have got Darwin all wrong (153).

The true lesson from Darwin, Kropotkin argues, is 'that the life of animals teaches us something entirely different' (153). Although he does not go into detail in *Modern Science and Anarchism*, Kropotkin explains elsewhere that the central message is one of 'mutual aid', the title of one of his most influential books.[4] In this view it remains true that the realm of nature is one of a struggle for existence, but this is primarily not a struggle among individuals or groups within a species but rather the struggle of a species as a whole to survive in an often-hostile environment. 'Besides the law of Mutual Struggle, there is in Nature the law of Mutual Aid, which, for the success of the struggle for life, and especially for the progressive evolution of the species, is far more important than the law of mutual contest.'[5]

For Kropotkin, then, Darwin really teaches the importance, and the naturalness, of co-operation rather than competition. The political implications of Darwinism point not in the direction of economic laissez-faire and imperialism but rather towards libertarian communism – that is, towards anarchism as Kropotkin understands it. Powerful tendencies towards voluntary co-operation lie deep within human nature. These have been submerged or distorted by artificial institutions like the state, which is a 'superstructure' invented to serve the selfish interests of the few (192). But mutual aid survives in human experience like an underground stream.

Indeed, Kropotkin believes that mutual aid is gradually but increasingly winning through in contemporary society. Here he refers to the emergence of 'thousands upon thousands of free organisations for all sorts of needs: economic (agreements between the railway companies, the labour syndicates, trusts of employers, agricultural co-operation, co-operation for export, etc.), political, intellectual, artistic, educational, and so on' (168–9). None of these arrangements depends on the state; all draw upon the natural instinct to co-operate.

However, Kropotkin's anarchism does not rely on evolution alone; we must also 'promote evolution' in the desirable direction through revolutionary action (154). In so doing we should learn from the mistakes of past revolutions. The great French Revolution of 1789, the Europe-wide revolutions of 1848, the Paris Commune of 1871 – the ultimate failure of all of these is due, Kropotkin argues, to their reliance on the methods of government in attempting to plan, inspire and direct the course of the revolution. As William Godwin recognized as early as the 1790s, the use of 'governmental authority' has always 'acted as a retarding force upon the revolutionary movement' (154). The Jacobin Committee of Public Safety and even the Council of the 1871 Commune served only to perpetuate the ways of the state, becoming incipient states in their turn.

The true social revolution must itself take a form that anticipates the kind of society it is intended to inaugurate – that is, the revolution must be 'a widespread popular movement' that ignites spontaneously among the people of 'every town and village within the region of the revolt' (188). Rather than led or directed by any kind of distinct authority, it must be the pure expression of 'the collective spirit of the masses' (189).

Kropotkin does allow, however, that such a revolution has to be preceded by a period of 'incubation' in which the trail is blazed by the isolated protests of individuals and small groups: 'Not one, or two, or tens, but *hundreds* of similar revolts have preceded *and must precede* every revolution' (190). Again, though, these 'partial revolts' must be spontaneous rather than deliberately organized by anything like a central authority, since 'the character of every revolution is determined by the character and aim of the uprisings by which it is preceded' (191).

Although Kropotkin does not say so explicitly, he may have in mind here a partial defence of 'propaganda by the deed', the anarchist practice of inspiring revolution by actions as well as words. Notoriously, propaganda by deed came to be associated with the assassinations and bombings that terrorized Europe in the name of anarchism around the turn of the twentieth century. Kropotkin did not approve of these actions but he was inclined to explain them as understandable acts of desperation.[6]

Does Kropotkin's kind of anarchism represent a fundamental redefinition of revolution? Here two issues are striking: whether the state is a necessary tool of revolution or an obstacle to its achievement and whether anarchists like Kropotkin are neorevolutionaries or not revolutionaries at all.

There is no doubt that the anarchists depart from the statist pattern laid down by the French Revolution and later taken up by the Bolshevik

Revolution – indeed, they do so self-consciously and deliberately, for the reasons given. But that scarcely disqualifies them as revolutionaries, since they clearly demand radical social change that requires an emphatic break with the past. Nor are they opposed to violent means where those are judged to be necessary, although it must be open to question whether violence is essential to revolution. The case of Kropotkin becomes more complex at the point where he tries to combine revolution and evolution, 'internal war' with mutual aid, immediate with gradual change. It is this nexus that raises the thorniest critical questions for Kropotkin's view.

Kropotkin's reinterpretation of Darwin is interesting and one might say a more humane reading than that of the social Darwinists, but it suffers from similar problems. A standard objection to thinkers like Spencer is that they try to extract their ethical and political conclusions from a thesis that is essentially descriptive or factual rather than normative, thereby violating 'Hume's law' against deriving 'ought' statements from 'is' statements. Even if competition and violence are prominent features of the natural world it does not follow that we ought to promote these; perhaps we ought to restrain or manage them.

Similarly, even supposing that mutual aid is a significant factor in nature as Kropotkin claims, it is a further step to argue that it ought to be emphasized more than other factors and values. There may be good reasons to promote mutual aid, but those reasons are not given simply by pointing to mutual aid as a fact. Kropotkin cooks the books when he refers to mutual aid as a factor not merely in evolution but in 'progressive' evolution – presumably that evolution of which we approve. His thesis mixes up claims of fact and claims of value.

Further, if mutual aid really is as potent an evolutionary force as Kropotkin says it is, why should we, and how can we, 'promote' it? This seems to be the role of revolution as Kropotkin conceives it: to supplement or expedite the mutual-aid developments that are already present in the underlying pattern of social evolution. But supplementing or expediting an evolutionary process would be like supplementing or expediting the law of gravity.

On the other hand, Kropotkin's social revolution is itself a kind of evolutionary process, since it cannot be led, planned or inspired by anything like a central authority; rather, it must arise spontaneously from 'the people'. Such a view looks prescient as a critique of Marxism–Leninism, under which the vanguard party did indeed reconstitute itself as a new oppressive state. But the price for the anarchists' revolutionary purism was the frustration of waiting for the proper social revolution to occur under its own volition. Evidence of that frustration can perhaps be seen in the excesses of propaganda by deed.

The deepest level of difficulty for Kropotkin's view, and for anarchism in general, concerns the possibility of agreement. For Kropotkin and the anarchists, state coercion is unnecessary because people are capable of agreeing on the rules that will govern them without the use of force. Behind this is an assumption of something like the ancient doctrine of natural law, the idea that there is an objective law of morality inherent in human nature. In Kropotkin's version this will be revealed by modern scientific method, in particular using the evolutionary model of Darwin.

But what if, as so many people have believed in recent times, there is no such natural law? Conceptions of natural law depend on ideas of human nature, which are widely disputed. Or what if there is such a law but it is highly generic, leaving room for reasonable divergence of opinion over more detailed principles and applications? Perhaps there are natural principles of morals and politics but these are sometimes conflicting rather than harmonious, calling for hard choices that once again invite disagreement and conflict.[7]

Again, whatever ethical principles there may be, it is questionable whether they can be identified by the natural sciences. While the sciences observe the world objectively, from the outside as it were, moral and political life is lived from the inside, bounded and informed by particular languages and cultures.[8] These vary and the variations divide people. All human beings can agree that 2 + 2 = 4 and that water boils at 100 degrees Celsius. But the desirability of social institutions depends to some extent on local and historical conditions, and even on personal experiences, that cannot be captured in an abstract and objective scientific law. This is not to say that there are no objective and universal goods or that agreement is never possible in these and other cases. It is to say that the methods of the natural sciences are unlikely to substitute for the kind of local, historical and personal judgements that are unavoidable in morals and politics and that always tend to divide people.

Even where there is substantial agreement on the rules to be followed, experience suggests that we cannot rely on everyone to follow those rules consistently. As John Locke points out, people are apt to favour their own interests when they interpret and apply the rules.[9] Disputes break out, and these are best settled by an independent authority – government.

The currently dominant view in political theory is that there are too many points at which disagreement and conflict can arise for modern societies to dispense with coercive laws. It is hard to avoid the conclusion that Kropotkin's optimism runs aground on this hard truth.

## Further reading

Crowder, G., *Classical Anarchism: The Political Thought of Godwin, Proudhon, Bakunin, and Kropotkin* (Oxford: Oxford University Press, 1991).
Kropotkin, P., *The Conquest of Bread and Other Writings*, ed. Marshall Shatz [1892] (Cambridge: Cambridge University Press, 1995).
Kropotkin, P., *Memoirs of a Revolutionist* (Boston: Houghton Mifflin, 1899).
Miller, D., *Anarchism* (London: Dent, 1984).

# 18

# Revolutionary Cultivation: Liu Shaoqi's *How to Be a Good Communist* (1939) and the Rejection of Confucian Tradition

Jonathan J. Howlett

*Confucius said:*
'At fifteen, I had my mind bent on learning. At thirty, I stood firm. At forty I had no doubts. At fifty, I knew the decree of Heaven. At sixty, my ear was an obedient organ for the reception of truth. At seventy, I could follow my heart's desire, without transgressing what was right.'

Here Confucius was relating the process of his steeling and self-cultivation. He did not regard himself as a born 'sage'.

*Mencius said:*
'When Heaven is about to confer a great office on any man, it first exercises his mind with suffering, and his sinews and bones with toil. It exposes his body to hunger, and subjects him to extreme poverty. It confounds his undertakings. By all these methods it stimulates his mind, hardens his nature, and remedies his incompetencies.'

What Mencius said also refers to the process of steeling and self-cultivation that a great man must undergo. As Communist Party members have to shoulder the unprecedentedly 'great office' of changing the world, it is all the more necessary for them to go through such steeling and self-cultivation. …

Steeling and cultivation are important for every Party member, whether he be a new member of non-proletarian origin or even a veteran member of proletarian origin. This is because our Communist Party did not drop from the heavens but was born out of Chinese society and because every member of our Party came from this squalid old society of China and are still living in this society today. …

That is the reason why Communist Party members must undertake self-cultivation.[1]

Liu Shaoqi's *How to Be a Good Communist* was first delivered to the Institute of Marxism–Leninism in the Chinese Communist Party's (CCP's) remote wartime base at Yan'an in Shaanxi province on 8 July 1939. In this speech, Liu emphasized the importance of individual party members undergoing a sustained period of 'self-cultivation' and 'steeling' in order to forge them into true communists. This was a Leninist text that borrowed heavily from the Soviet model, urging discipline and sacrifice in the pursuit of victory. In the ideological context of the time, Liu's calls for the reordering of society – focusing in particular on changing the relationships between individuals and political organizations – were firmly revolutionary. Liu was among the founding members of the CCP and he excelled in the role of theoretician and organizer, first as an underground activist in trade unions and in enemy-controlled 'White areas', and later as a member of the party secretariat, before finally assuming a position as the second highest government official under Mao Zedong after the establishment of the People's Republic of China in 1949. He fell from power during the Cultural Revolution.

Interpretation and reinterpretation of *How to Be a Good Communist* played a key role within the cycle of exaltation and defamation that defined Liu Shaoqi's career. Few texts have been as influential in the history of communist China. The promotion of the speech began when a revised version was included in the collection *Rectification Documents*, first published in 1943 during the Zhengfeng (rectification) Campaign in Yan'an. It had a physical life as a widely disseminated object: copies of it found their way into millions of hands as the party recruited new cadres and attempted to remould its existing cadres throughout the war with Japan (1937–45), the Chinese Civil War (1946–9) and the first decades of communist rule. In communist 'New China' the speech was circulated widely and featured prominently in the domestic media: it was published as a book and in 1951 was translated in to English for distribution overseas. Following the Great Leap Forward (1958), a disastrous leftist adventure, Liu ascended to the position of head of state. The speech was revised and republished in 1962 and was serialized in the leading newspaper *People's Daily* and the journal *Red Flag*. Usually this kind of circulation was reserved only for texts by Mao.[2]

Liu went from being Mao's most useful ally and heir apparent to dying an ignominious death under house arrest in 1969 as the highest ranking casualty of the Cultural Revolution. In the spring of 1967 criticism of Liu focused on *How to Be a Good Communist* as evidence of his having put Soviet-style bureaucratic careerism and party supremacy above the needs of the people. The attacks culminated in an editorial titled 'Treason to the Dictatorship of the Proletariat is the Essence of the Book on "Self-Cultivation of Communists"'. The cycle came full circle when, following Liu's posthumous rehabilitation by Deng Xiaoping's 'reform faction' in February 1980, three of his works, including *How to Be a Good Communist*, were declared 'Marxist works of great significance'.³ The speech was again circulated widely to reinforce the importance of political discipline in the face of economic liberalization and as a tacit criticism of the Cultural Revolution.

Liu's references to Confucius and Mencius were particularly sensitive and these are the parts of the speech that were criticized most strongly during the Cultural Revolution. They are often referred to by scholars who analyse the tension between 'radical' Mao and 'conservative' Liu and by those who seek to find continuities between Chinese Communist ideology and Confucian statecraft. In revisiting *How to Be a Good Communist* it is important to explore two main lines of enquiry: the first of these is to consider the speech as a product of the revolutionary moment of its delivery – that is, to contextualize it historically, divorcing it from the meaning applied to it as it was variously promoted and denounced. Second, it is necessary to place Liu's references to Confucius within the context of the speech as a whole. Cultural Revolution-era critics used these quotes to damn Liu, and western scholars have deployed them in support of explanations of communist behaviour as being based on an inherited Confucian world view, but those who make reference to the quotes often ignore the fact that they are deployed within the context of an argument that is iconoclastic and anti-Confucian in its call for a revolutionary reordering of society.

Liu spent 1938–9 at Yan'an and among his duties was serving as director of the Cadre Training Department. It was in this capacity that he presented *How to Be a Good Communist*. In the early 1940s, he went on to play an important role in the Zhengfeng Campaign that cemented Mao's position as paramount leader.⁴ The Zhengfeng Campaign was an intense period of party reform designed to instil ideological uniformity among new and established cadres and it marked the introduction of the extensive use of small-group 'study' and criticism meetings in China. 'Study' often led to the expulsion or punishment of dissenters. It was focused largely on the *Rectification Documents* collection, which contained sections from *How to Be a Good Communist* focusing on the unconditional subordination of individual interests to those of the party and on correcting 'mistaken ideologies'. Liu's was one of eighteen texts, the rest included seven by Mao, six Central Committee resolutions (usually credited to Mao), two Soviet documents (one by Stalin) and two by other party leaders. This collection, which was to become required reading for hundreds of thousands (later millions) of cadres and new recruits, emphasized the importance of tying theory to practice and of applying Marxist–Leninist doctrine to Chinese realities.⁵ As such, it criticized the 'dogmatism' of the Moscow-trained 'returned Bolsheviks' faction. Liu's contribution was rather dry: the first American translator to tackle it described it as 'tortuously written'.[6]

After 1949, the Communist Party-state put a great deal of effort into constructing the narrative of its revolution and western observers sought to explain the success of the revolution in a similarly teleological manner. For both, the great texts of the movement served as markers on the road to victory in 1949, and as such, analysts sought to explain wider phenomena (state- and party-building, military successes etc.) through texts, rather than seeing the texts as reflections of historical events. It is important then that we consider Liu's *How to Be a Good Communist* as a historically contingent text, written in a period of uncertainty and borrowing heavily from Soviet models. We may perhaps then be able to escape reading the text backwards from Liu's fall (the 'Good Communist' deposed).

When the speech was delivered in July 1939, China had been at war with Japan for two years and the communists had been fighting for survival against the nationalist regime since 1927. Their 'Long March' (1934–5) had delivered them to their remote base area in the caves of Yan'an but had left them vulnerable. Between 1937 and 1945 a fragile peace, the 'Second United Front', held between the CCP and the Nationalists as the country experienced total war. Thus when Liu quoted Mencius' saying that when Heaven is about to confer a 'great office' it 'first exercises [the recipient's] mind with suffering, and his sinews and bones with toil' he was reassuring his audience of war-weary cadres that victory would one day be realized despite their present trials.[7]

Between 1937 and 1940 the party membership had increased at a rapid rate and this had exacerbated one of the party's most pressing concerns: instilling a sense of common purpose in cadres from diverse backgrounds. In response to this problem, the Mao faction launched the Zhengfeng Campaign to instil a new orthodoxy and discipline and to consolidate their leadership position. The new orthodoxy was essentially the affirmation of Marxist–Leninist principles as a guide for action (opposing peasant radicalism or intellectual liberalism) and the Sinification of the theory, relating it to Chinese practice. This was an attempt to forge an ideology and organization suitable for guerrilla warfare across scattered 'base areas' forging 'good communists' who could act independently but with iron discipline.[8]

While some scholars have interpreted the Zhengfeng era 'Sinification of Marxism' as a rejection of the Soviet model, with Mao's party seeking a new direction by grafting communism to Chinese belief systems, others have maintained that this was really a response to Comintern leader Georgi Dimitrov's 1935 call for national parties to adapt to their own surroundings.⁹ In this context, we can see that Liu's speech was arguing towards an immediate goal: strengthening party control over its cadres during a desperate struggle for survival. Liu's references to Confucianism in the speech should be read in this light: as directed by the Comintern, he was simply deploying Chinese cultural references to introduce unfamiliar concepts.

The mixture of Leninist principles and references to the Confucian classics in Liu's speech meant that for Cold War 'China watchers' this was a key text in explaining how an 'alien' ideology had managed to successfully take root in China despite that nation's strong indigenous traditions. Today, the text is still often referred to by those who seek to demonstrate Confucius' continuing influence.¹⁰ Teemu Ruskola, for example, argues that the CCP shared the Confucian preference for ruling society by internalized morality rather than by the rule of law and that *How to Be a Good Communist* simply served to replace the Confucian *Analects*. This view is seemingly evidenced by Liu's quotations from the classics.¹¹ Chen Weigang suggests in *Confucian Marxism* that Liu believed 'that "proletarian consciousness" was identical to the ethical qualities as prescribed in the Confucian ethical tradition' and that there was a 'rigorous effort to mesh "a new Communist ethic" with Confucian thought'.¹² There has long been a tendency to see Confucianism as the key to unlocking the secrets of Chinese society, but as with most historical labels, use of the term 'Confucianism' has the power to obscure complex historical realities and to suggest shared values frozen in time.¹³

A common observation is that while the title of the 1951 English translation is *How to Be a Good Communist*, a direct translation of the Chinese version would be '*On the Self-Cultivation of the Communist Party Member*'. Boorman suggests, however, that the English title was chosen so as to avoid the ambiguity of the original. In deploying these overt references to Confucian models was Liu really calling for the emulation of Confucian practices?

In section five, Liu foresees the dawning of a new era, one in which the realization of communism brings into being 'the best, the most beautiful, and the most advanced society in the history of mankind' (40). He goes on to say that the new society can be actualized only when communism triumphs over the exploiting classes 'along with all of their influences, traditions and customs' (41). This kind of utopian talk was unusual from Liu, a consummate pragmatist. It is clear that while he was making use of Confucian references to express new ideas about discipline in the Chinese context, he certainly was not calling for a perpetuation of tradition. Against the charge that Liu may have been inadvertently reproducing the lessons learnt during his Confucian schooling, we should note that throughout the text Liu consistently advocates a complete rejection of all ideology except Marxism–Leninism. He argued that man was a product of his environment and as such good communists should strive to reject all inherited influences of which they were aware (12–13). The 'exploiting classes' had ruled for thousands of years, he said, perpetuating 'backwardness, ignorance, selfishness, mutual deception, mutual antagonism, mutual slaughter etc.'. This was hardly an endorsement of the ideology of the Confucian order (43).

While the references to Confucius and Mencius in section one of the speech grabbed the headlines, Liu's call in section five for the establishment of a completely new value system is seldom mentioned by scholars. Elsewhere, Liu draws a clear distinction between 'revolutionary cultivation' and self-cultivation on the Confucian model (9). In section three, he quotes Zeng Zi, a follower of Confucius, as saying 'I reflect on myself three times a day' in support of the point that China had a long history of introspective self-awareness and he noted that a key feature of this reflection was the writing of mottoes to encourage contemplation (23). He criticizes such techniques, saying:

> These scholars and religious believers exaggerate the function of subjective initiative, thinking that so long as they keep their general 'good intentions' and are devoted to silent prayer they will be able to change the existing state of affairs, change society and change themselves under conditions separated from social and revolutionary practice. This is, of course, absurd. We cannot cultivate ourselves in this way. We are materialists and our cultivation cannot be separated from practice. (23–4)

For Liu the separation of theory from practice was 'one of the biggest evils bequeathed to us by the education and learning of the old society'. We should be conscious, therefore, that while Liu praises the 'excellent and useful teachings' of the sages, he also says that people preached righteousness and 'acted like out-and-out robbers and harlots in everything they did' (26–7). While the teachings of the sages may have been 'excellent', Confucianism was for the old society and Marxism–Leninism would define the future (13–22). 'Revolutionary cultivation' was necessary to bring about a new form of morality.

There are certainly many parallels between Liu's 'revolutionary cultivation' and Confucian self-cultivation, but we should not mistake the medium for the message. Despite presenting a more sophisticated analysis than most,

Nivison suggested that Liu's 'conscious didactic use of Chinese tradition is something that is itself entailed and called for by an acceptance of that tradition'. For Nivison, Liu was 'merely urging that Marxist "sages" be imitated in the Confucian manner'.[14] In fact, *How to Be a Good Communist* denounces Confucianism and posits true 'revolutionary cultivation' in opposition to it. The idea that a form of 'Confucian communist' ideology determined the success of the Chinese communist revolution seems to have a greater explanatory appeal to some scholars than historical accounts emphasizing the contingent nature of the events that led to victory in 1949. Defeat was a likely prospect on several occasions, but the communists' eventual success conferred legitimacy on their revolutionary 'model'. Documents from the preceding decades were then seen in the West as important texts to be analysed in the search for the ideological and organizational origins of victory. Liu's speech was a product of its time and it addressed two main concerns of the Yan'an era: the training of individuals to build a strong organization and the adaption of Marxist–Leninist theory, matured in the Soviet Union, to Chinese realities. The text could be read as an attempt to transplant a Leninist revolutionary model and graft it to a Chinese host – indeed, references to Confucius, Marx, Lenin, Stalin and Mao are often juxtaposed, but we should note that in all cases the correctness of Marxist and Maoist theory is emphasized while Confucianism is simply engaged with as a useful rhetorical device.

Liu wrote that 'every member of our Party came from this squalid old society of China' (12–13) and so in making their revolution manifest they could not avoid becoming exposed to social evils. 'Revolutionary cultivation' was Liu's suggested means of warding off these corrupting influences; his method was later denounced as 'counter-revolutionary'. The way in which he had presented his arguments, including the language he used and the examples he chose, aided his critics. In embedding his ideological argument in the local context, Liu left himself exposed to accusations that he had been contaminated by the very traditionalism he was trying to eradicate. We should perhaps follow Boorman in observing that even revolutionaries are 'creatures of time and place, prisoners of folkways, culture and language'. We should not mistake a common language and pool of cultural references for an innate Confucianism.[15] The CCP were, above all else, engaged in a fundamental reordering of relationships between individuals and groups in society. The significance conferred on the references to the Confucian classics came later when they were seized upon by Liu's Cultural Revolution critics and by Western scholars who sought to explain Chinese history through the lens of Confucianism.

## Further Reading

Boorman, Howard L., 'How to be a Good Communist: The Political Ethics of Liu Shao-Ch'I', *Asian Survey* 3, no. 8 (1963): 372–83.

Communist Party of China, *Mao's China: Party Reform Documents, 1942-46*, trans. and intro. Boyd Compton (Seattle: University of Washington Press, 1952).

Dittmer, Lowell, *Liu Shaoqi and the Chinese Cultural Revolution* (Armonk, NY and London: ME Sharpe, 1998).

19

# Between Socialist Futures: Mao Zedong on the 'Ten Major Relationships'

Daniel Leese

*Both inside and outside the Party a clear distinction must be made between right and wrong. How to deal with people who commit errors is an important question. The correct attitude should be one of allowing people to make revolution. When people commit errors, we must adopt the policy of learning from past mistakes in order to avoid future ones and curing the illness in order to save the patient so as to help them to correct their mistakes. Ah Q zheng zhuan (The True Story of Ah Q) is a fine piece of writing. I would urge comrades who have read this story before to reread it and those who haven't read it to read it carefully. In this story Lu Xun writes mainly about a peasant who was backward and unawakened and whose biggest fear was the criticism of others ... consequently putting him in a very passive position. ... It is no good if we bar people in society from making revolution. Nor is it good to prohibit those who have joined the Party and who have made errors from correcting their errors. We should allow people to make revolution. ... For the revolution, it is always better to have more people. Except for an extremely small number who cling to their mistakes, repeat them frequently, and refuse to mend their ways, the majority of those who have erred can correct their mistakes. Just as people can become immune to typhoid once they have had it, those who have erred may make fewer errors. ... On the contrary, it is those who have not erred who are in danger and need to be more vigilant; because they do not have such immunity, they are prone to become cocky.*[1]

Mao Zedong's speech 'On the Ten Major Relationships' was delivered to an enlarged meeting of the Chinese Communist Party's (CCP's) leading body, the Politburo, on 25 April 1956 amid a turbulent international situation. Two months earlier, Nikita Khrushchev had embarked on his de-Stalinization course, sharply criticizing the former Soviet leader and icon of world communism for his brutal dictatorship and extravagant personality cult. The secret speech triggered uncertainty about the future course of the Soviet Union and world communism, which was to result in calls for national variants of socialist construction as well as upheavals in several East European countries such as Poland and Hungary. The CCP leadership had not anticipated this change of direction and was at pains to develop an independent stance towards the Stalinist legacy and the future course of communism. The revolutionary past had been dealt with in a high-profile article written under Mao's personal guidance, published as 'On the Historical Experiences of the Dictatorship of the Proletariat' in the *People's Daily* on 5 April 1956, which acknowledged Stalin's mistakes but found them of secondary importance compared with his contributions to socialist construction. Outlining the future path of the revolution in China remained a more delicate task. By 1955, the CCP leadership had firmly consolidated its domestic grip on power and commenced with the transition to socialism by accelerating the collectivization of agriculture as well as transforming private property to collective and state ownership. Despite various clashes regarding specific policy measures, the CCP began self-confidently to depart from the Soviet model of development and to search for an alternative way of securing the victory of the socialist revolution in China.

The speech also occurred at a unique point in the development of Mao Zedong's political thought: it was delivered immediately after the consolidation of the communist dictatorship and the implementation of the first five-year plan, which had strongly relied on the Soviet model, and prior to the late Maoist mass campaigns of the Great Leap Forward and Cultural Revolution. Based on several weeks of discussions with representatives from different sectors of the party-state, it represents the most comprehensive blueprint Mao was to develop for revolutionary China's future after the founding of the People's Republic in 1949. The speech was not made publicly available contemporaneously. In December 1965, State President Liu Shaoqi approached Mao Zedong to suggest that the speech be made available to cadres above county level. Mao explained that he was 'not completely satisfied'[2] with the speech but allowed Liu to circulate speaking notes as an internal study document. The proximity of these speaking notes to the actual speech cannot be ascertained because the original notes are held in the hermetically closed Central Party Archives. The textual history is further complicated by the fact that Mao delivered a second speech on the same topic just a week later on 2 May 1956 at the Supreme State Conference. According to the official edition of Mao's post-1949 manuscripts, upon Liu's request the speaking notes of this second speech were reprinted for study purposes in 1965.[3] The reprint of the first speech leaked out to marauding students during the early Cultural Revolution and it was unofficially reprinted by different Red Guard organizations in 1967. These texts present the earliest available edition of the speech. In July 1975, the recently rehabilitated Deng Xiaoping approached Mao with the request of publishing the speech, which by now had been redacted by one of the party's foremost propagandists, Hu Qiaomu, in order to have it included in the upcoming fifth volume of Mao's *Selected Works*. For a second time, Mao opted to delay publication. Therefore, the speech was only officially published after Mao's death. The redacted version appeared on the front page of the *People's Daily* in commemoration of Mao Zedong's birthday on 26 December 1976 and was republished as part of the fifth volume of Mao's *Selected Works* the following year. Despite later rumours, interim party leader Hua Guofeng does not seem to have tampered with the content.[4] However, he made strong political use of the speech's tone of moderation and of 'bringing into play all positive factors and mobilizing all forces that can be utilized to achieve greater, faster, better, and more economical results in building socialism' (45) in order to consolidate his rule in the wake of the purge of the 'Gang of Four'.[5] While the original speaking notes still have not been published, the two available editions are fairly congruous in terms of general argument, although the latter version is much more explicit in its criticism of the Soviet Union. Our reading relies on the earliest extant edition of the text, the Red Guard reprint, since the unpolished character of the speaking notes bears a closer resemblance to Mao's contemporary rhetoric than the later redacted version.[6] The specific passage under review here, however, differs only marginally between the two editions.

The main objective of the speech was to outline a set of ten major 'relationships' (*guanxi*) understood as dialectical 'contradictions' (*maodun*), a crucial pillar of Mao's political thought, characterizing the current state of the Chinese revolution. These relationships included economic aspects, such as the relative percentage of investments in light and heavy industries or the unequal development of coastal versus inland regions, the relationship between agriculture and industry as well as between economic and defence construction, but also social and political contradictions, including the relationship between centre and localities, between revolution and counter-revolution, the relationship between Han Chinese and minority nationalities and the ties between China and foreign countries. Our excerpt pertains to section nine, an outline of the relationship between right and wrong, a task deemed crucial for both revolutionary practice and as an epistemological means of obtaining truth. According to the perception of the CCP leadership, Khrushchev's harsh criticism of Stalin had violated the most basic standards of truth. The previously proclaimed infallibility of the Soviet leader had hampered initiatives at lower levels, while the secret speech had simply aimed at erasing Stalin's legacy with one blow.

China was to follow a different path. According to Mao, the success of the Communist Party dictatorship depended on closely following the 'mass line' (*qunzhong luxian*) by way of distinguishing right from wrong in each policy field through an endless process of dialectical reasoning. Hence, wrong judgements were bound to occur once in a while. Mistakes were not to be perceived as bad, but rather as an opportunity to correct former standpoints through sustained and 'well-intentioned' criticism (59). Always fond of biological metaphors, Mao compared this process to active immunization against typhoid fever. It is important to note that Communist Party members were by no means exempt from making mistakes. Yet while previously, for example, during the so-called 'rectification campaign' of the early 1940s, the method of 'curing the patient in order to save the patient' (58) had applied to internal criticism only, by 1956 Mao was willing to widen the circle. Representatives of democratic parties were to be allowed to voice opinions 'as long as what they say make[s] sense' (55). A few days later, he would for the first time use the phrase of 'letting one hundred flowers bloom' in arts and literature, and of 'let[ting] a hundred schools of thought contend' (70) in academic circles, in order to allow for unorthodox appraisals of the present situation.

The main gist of the passage is directed at paving the way for local initiative and mobilization. Mao explicitly refers to a character from Lu Xun's famous novella *The True Story of Ah Q*, which is set in a small township of Eastern China during the 1911 Xinhai Revolution. The nameless anti-hero, Ah Q, is portrayed as inherently passive. He is held in contempt by his fellow citizens and continuously bullied and maltreated. Mao specifically points out his fear of being criticized by others, for example, for the 'ringworm scars on his scalp' (58), which he did not want others to talk about, yet his behaviour resulted in the very opposite. Mao here is mainly interested in showing how passivity engenders negative personal consequences, and also how certain local authorities decide on who is allowed to join the revolution as a sort of elitist privilege. He does not dwell on the question of whether the 'Ah Q spirit', the inability to face one's shortcomings and to turn defeats into unfounded expressions of moral superiority, should be read as a symptom of the Chinese national character. For Mao the immediate point of comparison is domestic politics. The Red Guard edition offers former

CCP leader Wang Ming and the 'dogmatists' as examples of those who barred people who were considered to have committed political errors from making revolution. Since Mao himself had been among those criticized in the early 1930s, there is clearly an element of personal vendetta involved. Yet besides these clearly subjective motives, the speech displays elements of cherishing popular revolution and a contempt for bureaucratic routines that foreshadow Mao's later policy choices. He calls for giving greater leeway to lower-level units and even voices the idea of reducing party and government institutions by two-thirds (54).

What makes this speech so special in the development of Mao's political thought is that it explores the role of contradictions within Chinese state and society without yet framing everything under the overarching concept of class struggle.[7] It does not neglect the basic idea of contradiction as the primary force propelling history forward, and yet change is not solely equated with violent struggle against perceived enemies. Mao proceeds in dialectical fashion to challenge the current status quo by probing alternatives. He opts for strengthening heavy industry by first spurring the level of consumer goods production in order to raise the people's living standards (47). He calls for budget cuts in the military sector in order to free capacity for economic construction, thereby creating positive side-effects for the military such as an indigenous automobile industry: 'How good it would be if one of these days we could ride to meetings in cars of our own make' (49).

The correctness of the dictatorship of the proletariat or the importance of eliminating its enemies is by no means negated: 'In a great revolution embracing six hundred million people, the people would not have approved if we had not killed off a bunch of [local despots]' (57). However, preference should be given to reforming this 'rubbish … into something useful' (57), since chopped-off heads could not be replaced. Finally, within international relations, China should stop slavishly following the Soviet model and rather try to adapt the strong points of each nation, irrespective of whether it belonged to the socialist or capitalist camp. In his earthy rhetoric, Mao in a follow-up speech yet again chose a biological metaphor: 'A fart can be fragrant or stink. We can't say that all the Soviet Union's farts are fragrant. At this time, when other people say that something stinks, we have been following them, and also say that it stinks. We should learn whatever is applicable, good things [even if they are] in capitalist [countries], should be studied' (71). Currently, the Chinese remained 'poor' and 'blank' (60), owing to the legacy of imperialist oppression and a belated revolution. Yet again, these weak points should be utilized as means of mobilizing all positive forces in achieving new victories of the Chinese revolution without becoming arrogant or cocky: 'We still need to learn from others. Even ten thousand years from now we [will] still need to learn! What's wrong with that?' (61).

This dialectical process of reasoning is vintage Mao: challenging the current status quo by creating alternative spaces of discourse, watching things unfold and thus continuing to hold a strategic advantage within inner party decision-making processes. No factor could be decided upon by itself but always in dialectical relation with other factors, mutually impacting on each other and incessantly shifting the balances in an endless process of moderating and accelerating policy decisions. Therefore, the revolution according to Mao was by no means over with the establishment of the People's Republic in 1949. His concept of revolution rather referred to a continuous process of social transformation which China had just started to embark upon and was literally to continue for ten thousand years. Shortly after, Mao would use Trotsky's idea of the 'permanent revolution' (*bu duan geming*) to convey this understanding of continuous change, which in a sense mirrored classical connotations of the Chinese term for revolution, *geming*, indicating both stellar movements and changes in dynastic leadership.[8] By 1956, Mao felt sufficiently confident to call for greater local independence and for constructive criticism of party rule in order to unite the largest part of the Chinese populace along the path towards a Chinese future characterized by integrating the 'universal truths of Marxism–Leninism with the concrete practice of revolution in China' (60). This optimistic view of continuing social transformation without class struggle was shattered by the failure of the Great Leap Forward. It was replaced by increasing scepticism regarding the true intentions of his fellow party leaders, whom he suspected of harbouring 'revisionist' sentiments, which ultimately might lead to a return to capitalist relations of production. This observation was not without factual basis as post-1978 developments reveal.

Why then would Mao stop his former top lieutenants Liu Shaoqi and Deng Xiaoping from making the speech publicly available? The main reason probably rests with the ambiguity enshrined in the ten major relationships. On the one hand, the speech could be read as a statement of moderation, of striking a national balance in economic construction, and it was indeed this aspect that fellow leaders like Zhou Enlai emphasized when propagating the content of Mao's speech in 1956–7.[9] The interests of Deng Xiaoping in 1975 were likewise directed at countering the overarching rhetoric of class struggle, which had come to dominate Chinese political discourse from the early 1960s. Mao resented being overtly pushed in this direction of moderation at the expense of highlighting the second element argued for in the speech: incessant popular revolution and social transformation.

While official party evaluation has come to the conclusion that this speech 'initially summed up our experiences in socialist construction and set forth the task of exploring a way of building socialism suited to the specific conditions of our country'[10] and dropped the concept of 'revolution' in favour of 'reform' (*gaige*), the speech could just as well be read as a statement for doing away with the privileges of the party bureaucracy, of 'narrowing the "scissors differential"' (52) between agricultural and industrial production and, finally, for thinking about ways of doing away with the Communist Party dictatorship altogether. As part of the sixth relationship, that between party and non-party, Mao without naming his source harks back to Lenin's writings on *State and Revolution* from 1917 and argues that parties, as products of history, will eventually 'wither away' (54). While by 1956 Mao was still convinced that the dictatorship of the proletariat was needed to suppress foreign and domestic enemies, ten years later at the outset of the Cultural Revolution and against the background of recent developments in the Soviet Union, which he interpreted as a revisionist return to capitalist policies, Mao had come to the conclusion that conditions were ripe to experiment with new forms of governance. He called upon 'all positive forces' within society, mainly the country's youth, to smash first old culture and then party institutions. No other communist leader went so far as to call for the destruction of the party-state he himself had been instrumental in bringing about. Inklings of this thought may already be found in the 'Ten Major Relationships', although crucial elements such as class struggle and revisionism are still missing.

'On the Ten Major Relationships' has received scant attention in western scholarship in recent decades. Current readings of the speech in Chinese-language scholarship clearly favour an economic reading. Elements of popular revolution and social transformation are downplayed. Instead, new political challenges are singled out as sets of 'major relationships' or 'contradictions', which are to be solved by the omniscient party. Even party leaders such as Jiang Zemin continue to build on the legacy of the speech by defining their own sets of major relationships.[11] The passage quoted above gave the post-Mao leadership a pretext for claiming the possibility of correcting mistakes committed under Communist Party rule and of returning to the path of raising the people's living standards through economic construction. On the other hand, more than any other section of the speech, the passage reveals the danger of elevating the party above the masses, of becoming self-content and neglecting political participation and popular criticism. It is here that our reading departs most obviously from standard interpretations of the speech by party historians.

The quote ends with a cautioning against claims of infallibility and the danger of becoming 'cocky' as a consequence. The possibility of committing and learning from mistakes for the late Mao Zedong was clearly a privilege applying to anyone but himself. In splendid isolation, the ageing dictator unleashed forces he proved unable to direct towards positive ends, resulting in a period of cruel persecutions and suffering, shaded by the rhetoric of popular revolution and 'great democracy'. The return to an economic reading of the speech after 1976 has by no means ended the existence of the dialectical contradictions sketched out in the 'Ten Major Relationships', and as abuses of party privileges become increasingly rampant, revolutionary readings have regained attractiveness for those left behind by the post-Mao reforms.

## Further Reading

Badiou, A., *The Communist Hypothesis*, trans. D. Macey and S. Corcoran (London: Verso, 2010), pp. 101–67.

Leung, J. K. and Michael Y. M. Kau (eds), *The Writings of Mao Zedong, 1949-1976. Volume II, January 1956 – December 1957* (Armonk: M.E. Sharpe, 1992), pp. 43–66.

Wei, Q., "'Lun shi da guanxi' de xingcheng he chuanbo" [Formation and Distribution of *On the Ten Major Relationships*], 6 March 2013, *Gongshi wang*, online available at: http://www.21ccom.net/articles/lsjd/lsjj/article_2013030678420.html (last access 15 May 2014).

Žižek, S. (ed.), *Mao Zedong on Practice and Contradiction* (London: Verso, 2007).

# Frantz Fanon's *The Wretched of the Earth*: Embodying Anti-Colonial Action

Xavier Guégan

*We believe that the conscious and organized undertaking by a colonized people to re-establish the sovereignty of that nation constitutes the most complete and obvious cultural manifestation that exists. It is not alone the success of the struggle which afterward gives validity and vigor to culture; culture is not put into cold storage during the conflict. The struggle itself in its development and in its internal progression sends culture along different paths and traces out entirely new ones for it. The struggle for freedom does not give back to the national culture its former value and shapes; this struggle which aims at a fundamentally different set of relations between men cannot leave intact either the form or the content of the people's culture. After the conflict there is not only the disappearance of colonialism but also the disappearance of the colonized man.*

*This new humanity cannot do otherwise than define a new humanism both for itself and for others. It is prefigured in the objectives and methods of the conflict. A struggle which mobilizes all classes of the people and which expresses their aims and their impatience, which is not afraid to count almost exclusively on the people's support, will of necessity triumph. The value of this type of conflict is that it supplies the maximum of conditions necessary for the development and aims of culture. After national freedom has been obtained in these conditions, there is no such painful cultural indecision which is found in certain countries which are newly independent, because the nation by its manner of coming into being and in the terms of its existence exerts a fundamental influence over culture. A nation which is born of the people's concerted action and which embodies the real aspirations of the people while changing the state cannot exist save in the expression of exceptionally rich forms of culture.*

> *The natives who are anxious for the culture of their country and who wish to give to it a universal dimension ought not therefore to place their confidence in the single principle of inevitable, undifferentiated independence written into the consciousness of the people in order to achieve their task. The liberation of the nation is one thing; the methods and popular content of the fight are another. It seems to us that the future of national culture and its riches are equally also part and parcel of the values which have ordained the struggle for freedom.*[1]

*The Wretched of the Earth* (1961) is the last book of the Martinique-born psychiatrist and Algerian National Liberation Front (FLN) activist Frantz Fanon before he died from leukaemia complications in 1961. Alongside his *Black Skin, White Masks* (1952) and *A Dying Colonialism* (1959), *The Wretched of the Earth* is considered as one of the key texts that analysed, reflected and embodied the anti-colonial action of the post-war period. Originally written in French, Fanon's body of work was translated into many languages in the 1950s and 1960s, and is now recognized as having influenced anti-colonial and national liberation movements around the world. Indeed for many, *The Wretched of the Earth* has been considered as 'the bible of the decolonization movement' (Stuart Hall) or even 'the bible of liberation movements across the world' (Michael Burawoy).[2] In 1963 Sartre said of Fanon that everything was still to be said. Much has been written on his life and his work since then, but there is still more to do. There have been several phases in the rehabilitation of Fanon as a key thinker and activist of the movement for anti-colonial revolution and as a key figure in the canon of postcolonial thinking.[3] Alongside Jean-Paul Sartre, Aimé Césaire, Albert Memmi and many others, Frantz Fanon became known during the 1950s for his psychological analysis of the suffering of colonized peoples, for his actions with the FLN and as a public intellectual on the international scene. He became posthumously famous in the 1960s and early 1970s for his analysis of the struggles and conflicts in French Algeria and more broadly in colonized Africa and post-independence Third-World countries, and as such he was an inspiration for independence movements around the globe – including the Black Power Movement in the United States. Although Fanon's writings served as an inspiration during that period, in the late 1970s and 1980s his name nearly disappeared from the academic world as well as from the general portraiture of the *decolonization* period. Then, his endorsement of violence, mainly through *The Wretched of the Earth*, was considered problematic and his penetrating analysis of the social psychology of colonialism obliterated; 'Conservative writers have reacted against his views on violence and leftist intellectuals have dismissed his revolutionary statements as outdated and naïve.'[4] It was in the 1990s that Anglophone postcolonial studies began to rehabilitate Fanon as an intellectual and thinker. Postcolonial academics and writers saw in Fanon a postcolonial voice that is as important and relevant today as it was during the 1950s and 1960s. His attack on colonial inhumanity is seen as still being relevant owing to the inhumanity that has been experienced in a neocolonial and postcolonial global world.[5] Then in the 2000s – after years of neglect – the figure of Fanon returned to Francophone academic fields to be celebrated as 'the man of action', the revolutionary, albeit to the detriment of his position as a theorist or 'man of thought'.[6]

The 1961 original edition of *The Wretched of the Earth* begins with a preface by the French philosopher and political activist Jean-Paul Sartre and is then divided into five parts, which are themselves divided into subsections, and a conclusion. The above extract is from the last section of 'On National Culture: Reciprocal Bases of National Culture and the Fight for Freedom'. The text was written a year after 'The Year of Africa' and during the time of independent national movements and what has been called the period of decolonization of the late 1940s and 1950s. Despite Algerian independence still being a year away, Fanon foresaw the imminent end of the Algerian War and French colonial rule. In the book he also considers the other countries that were still under colonialism, such as Angola, and the victims of an 'inner' racist colonialism, such as those living under apartheid in South Africa. *The Wretched of the Earth* is thus a work that explains three phases: the consequences of colonialism and the logic and organization of anti-colonial fights (movements, communities and individuals); the fights still to be won; and the challenges and transitory phases in independence and post-independence victories and regimes. For Fanon, as for others,[7] the fight against colonial regimes and the inner fight in newly independent countries were equally important.

Although, since the early 1990s, *The Wretched of the Earth* has been consistently used as a core text in postcolonial studies and theories, its style does not share the complicated and sometimes cryptic jargon that has so often been highlighted as a characteristic of postcolonial schools. The language is straightforward and yet playful (though never redundant); the words are powerful and the images are clear. Here is a vivid analysis of the psyches of both colonizer and colonized, a lucid portrait of the period and a reading that invites reaction and action – a manifesto. Fanon's writing may well be very significant in the postcolonial canon, but *The Wretched of the Earth* was first and foremost an anti-colonial revolutionary text.

Fanon writes from the perspective of a society that struggles. In this extract – and throughout *The Wretched of the Earth* – he establishes that the colonized not only have to fight against the colonizer to reclaim their land, identity and social unity, but they also have to make a choice: what kind of nation will they create? This new national struggle is defined by the very principles of the Revolution and Liberation movement. Fanon's theoretical action highlights western humanist principles, those developed before the time of nineteenth-century colonization, in connection with modern ideologies of the creation of the nation without the subterfuge of the '*mission civilisatrice*'. He emphasized a decolonized 'National Culture' that needed to re-affirm precolonial cultural and religious traditions as well as the culture of the fight and of anti-colonialism during the colonial time, while avoiding the resurgence of tribalism and elitist classes.

What became obvious to Fanon was that the colonized men and women were dehumanized by both the process of colonialism itself (which was founded on violent conquest and the annexation of lands and bodies) and a dogmatic hypocritical Euro-centricity that justified the negation of the Other, thus alienating the mind and spirit of the indigenous societies. The mechanisms of colonial domination, as Fanon explains, are based on an oversimplification of the conquered people through a 'cultural obliteration … made possible by the negation of national reality' (236). The colonial world is thus a Manichean world where the West uses its own set of values to define the Other in negative terms and to declare indigenous populations insensible to ethics (41). Therefore the colonized see their customs becoming illegal, see themselves being expropriated from their lands, and soon they are alienated from their tradition, their past and ultimately their own humanity. As a result in this colonial world they constantly question themselves: 'in reality, who am I?' (250). In parallel to this dogmatic and totalitarian system, by introducing the capitalist structure established in the West, the colonizer introduced another unequal system with an industrial bourgeoisie and an educated and political elite, which repressed the proletariat and masses. Consequently the colonized became psychologically and physically dehumanized and socially and economically under the control of a globalized capitalist system.

Consciousness and identity are thus both crucial themes in Fanon's understanding of the fundamental principles required for colonized people to be able to become free and to create – or recreate – a nation. Yet throughout the book, and particularly in this chapter, he wanted to alert the activist to the fact that national consciousness was not the same as nationalism (247) and that the two should not become identical. He was indeed worried about 'the monologic tyranny of nationalism'[8] and hoped to prevent detractors from confusing anti-colonial violence with dictatorships of the kind that appeared, for example, in the fascist regimes of inter-war Europe. He was keen to ensure that after liberation post-independence movements did not develop into autocratic regimes. 'Nationalism is not a political doctrine, nor a program. If you really wish your country to avoid regression, or at best halts and uncertainties, a rapid step must be taken from national consciousness to political and social consciousness' (203).

Fanon asks us to remember what Humanism means but also where it came from originally within our consciousness and understanding of what a modern nation is. The Enlightenment and the French Revolution, the working class and the struggles within capitalism, feminism, the fight against racism, but also against tribalism, are themes that recur in Fanonian thought and which are seen as crucial for the rise of a true people nation: a nation shaped by the decolonization process, not just in Africa but also from a common experience shared with South America and Asia.

Tribalism, the bourgeoisie and elitism are for Fanon the inner enemies of a true independent nation. Tribalism had been encouraged by colonial powers in order to use chiefs and clans against each other to justify their rule: 'By its very structure, colonialism is separatist and regionalist' (94). Colonizers used their domination to dispossess the local peasantry of their land. The need for a peasant revolution to reclaim that land – in connection with some of the ideals of previous revolutions – is thus a crucial phase instead of the national bourgeois road, which he considers dangerous because of the possible progressive degradation of the political order, ending in dictatorship and repression: 'The psychology of the national bourgeoisie is that of the businessman, not that of a captain of industry; and it is only too true that the greed of the settlers and the system of embargoes set up by colonialism have hardly left them any other choice' (150). We also see that Fanon explores the frustration newly independent populations might experience when they realize that nothing has changed; and the only way to avoid this feeling is by creating a truly national culture while fighting colonialism, and afterwards neocolonialism. There is a Marxist vision in Fanon's anti-colonial revolution, which highlights the ills of capitalism – a capitalism that has the United States as its champion – but throughout the text it is also clear that Fanon does not support the socialist models emanating from Moscow (contrary to what Sartre advocates in his preface). Most of the colonized countries can only recover political as well as economic freedom by focusing on the peasant rather than the worker. The difference with the 'bourgeois revolution' of 1789 is that the

French peasants benefited substantially from the upheaval (75), whereas a big majority within the undeveloped countries did not see such changes. The reasons are that both middle classes and working classes are generated by westernized industrialization (111); therefore, the truly independent nation can only emerge from the peasants if it is to avoid becoming a 'semi-colonial' state during the period of independence (172). The elites remain a difficult group for Fanon to assess, despite the fact that he was himself a 'creation' of the French colonial elitist machinery. As for Albert Memmi, the new elites have to be sincere and 'outlaw' the profiteers (177) instead of leading the newly formed nation into an autocracy. Consequently Fanon believes that only through a revolution of the masses can the colonial order be overthrown.

In this context violence becomes necessary to the process. Because colonialism is a system of domination held together by violence, anti-colonial violence is thus the only effective liberating means to dispose not just of colonial rule but also of the old colonial systems and principles. 'The colonized man finds his freedom in and through violence' (86); Grant Farred has stressed that 'Fanon's claim is unambiguous: without violence, no decolonization; without violence, no subjectivation of the decolonized'.[9] However, violence is redundant after the decolonization process as long as the masses remain in charge and are involved in the organization of an egalitarian society.[10] The anti-colonial revolution and violence transform consciousness and help to build a national solidarity, and for Fanon this is a decisive process.

Yet, Fanon also emphasizes that after independence the newly independent nations often continue to suffer. This is the result of their being 'underdeveloped' countries. When colonized, people had to fight against the colonizer to become independent, but as newly freed people, they have now to fight the world superpowers and their global economies. A common and often popular mode of thinking from the old metropoles at the time of decolonization was again a brutal feeling of superiority: 'If you want independence, then take it and go back to the Middle-Ages' (94). Fanon also reminds us that at the time of the emergence of European nation states in the nineteenth century, these countries were all at more or less the same level of industrialization and the respective national bourgeoisies were in possession of most of the wealth as well as of the financial, commercial and scientific institutions. The bourgeoisie represented the most dynamic social class, and its rise to power enabled the emergence and democratization of industry, education and communication. Because the economic situations of each European state were similar, they did not feel that their own development was *insulting* (94) the others. A century after the evolution and growth of globalization on the back of the colonized countries, the situation for the emerging new post-independence nations is entirely new, and different. These countries are underdeveloped within the post-war world economic system. European opulence and well-being, which was founded on slaves' labour and blood, still depends on keeping the Third World underdeveloped.

Third Worldism is therefore a key element in Fanon's analysis of how the new independent countries are treated in the international context of the 1950s and 1960s – and, postcolonial theorists would argue, ever since. For him it was important to understand how liberation from the colonizer set the liberated people a new challenge. It would be difficult but essential for the new nations to become economically, culturally, socially and politically liberated from the order enforced by the superpowers, and therefore to obtain a voice. 'The battle line against hunger, against ignorance, against poverty, and against unawareness ought to be ever present in the muscles and the intelligences of men and women' (203). Third Worldism was then both the acknowledgement of this new challenge and an awareness of these difficulties as well as the creation of a union to stand up to the developed countries. It took an active international stand through the shape of the UN's charter in 1945 with its fifty-one founding members – of which thirty-two were from the 'undeveloped' countries; the establishment of the Universal Declaration of Human Rights in 1948; and the 1955 Bandung Conference in Indonesia, which resulted in the formation of the Non-Aligned Movement. It was important to find a new direction, rather than having to choose between the capitalist and socialist systems (98–9). Fanon was against tribalism and nationalistic inventions. He favoured a true independent neocolonialist–capitalist-free internationalism, with the highlights being Fidel Castro's action in Cuba, the négritude movement, pan-Africanism and the awakening of Islam – although these movements had also to continue evolving in order to avoid falling into a Manichean view of their own identity and the world around. He wanted something different from that which the West (Europe and the United States) had created. In short, Third Worldism was to be encouraged, a bourgeoisie nationalism avoided and a national culture embraced.

*The Wretched of the Earth* attests to the lasting imprint of both anti-colonial and postcolonial ideologies, and is still instructive in relation to contemporary postcolonial wars and conflicts. Fanon has been described as an idealist, a term that has now gained a negative connotation. Yes, he was indeed an idealist but one with a clear understanding of the world and what was at stake, not only in colonial terms but also within the Cold War context. He foresaw the different scenarios that occurred in the following decades. He sought to inform, recruit and fight. His hope was that the masses would take control of their nation and identity. Throughout his career Fanon witnessed the suffering of the colonized. It was thus important for the Third World to move towards humanization with a human consciousness that was at the centre of the anti-colonial national movements. He was a true internationalist. 'After the conflict there is not only the disappearance of colonialism but also the disappearance of the colonized man' (246). *The Wretched of the Earth* constituted the last words of an anti-colonial activist.

> When I search for Man in the technique and the style of Europe, I see only a succession of negations of man, and an avalanche of murders. ...
>
> Let us decide not to imitate Europe; let us combine our muscles and our brains in a new direction. Let us try to create the whole man, whom Europe has been incapable of bringing to triumphant birth. ...
>
> For Europe, for ourselves, and for humanity, comrades, we must turn over a new leaf, we must work out new concepts, and try to set afoot a new man. (312–16)

## Further Reading

Gibson, Nigel C. (ed.), *Living Fanon: Global Perspectives* (Basingstoke: Palgrave Macmillan, 2011).
Gordon, Lewis, Denean Sharpley-Whiting, and Renee White, *Fanon: A Critical Reader* (London: Blackwell, 1996).
Macey, David, *Frantz Fanon: A Life* (London: Granta Books, 2000).
Renault, Matthieu, *Frantz Fanon: De l'Anticolonialisme à la Critique Postcoloniale* (Paris: Editions Amsterdam, 2011).

# 21

# Social Imperialism and Mao's Three Worlds: Deng Xiaoping's Speech at the UN General Assembly, 1974

Jennifer Altehenger

*At present, the international situation is most favourable to the developing countries and the peoples of the world. More and more, the old order based on colonialism, imperialism and hegemonism is being undermined and shaken to its foundations. International relations are changing drastically. The whole world is in turbulence and unrest. The situation is one of 'great disorder under heaven,' as we Chinese put it. This 'disorder' is a manifestation of the sharpening of all the basic contradictions in the contemporary world. It is accelerating the disintegration and decline of the decadent reactionary forces and stimulating the awakening and growth of the new emerging forces of the people.*

*In this situation of 'great disorder under heaven,' all the political forces in the world have undergone drastic division and realignment through prolonged trials of strength and struggle. A large number of Asian, African and Latin American countries have achieved independence one after another and they are playing an ever greater role in international affairs. As a result of the emergence of social-imperialism, the socialist camp which existed for a time after World War II is no longer in existence. Owing to the law of the uneven development of capitalism, the Western imperialist bloc, too, is disintegrating. Judging from the changes in international relations, the world today actually consists of three parts, or three worlds, that are both interconnected and in contradiction to one another. The United States and the Soviet Union make up the First World. The developing countries in Asia, Africa, Latin America and other regions make up the Third World. The developed countries between the two make up the Second World.*

On 10 April 1974, Deng Xiaoping, vice-premier of the People's Republic of China (PRC) State Council, presented a carefully drafted speech to the United Nations General Assembly.[1] The assembly had convened for its sixth special session since the founding of the United Nations in 1945. Requested by the Algerian delegation, the session lasted from 9 April to 2 May 1974 and focused on the two themes of raw materials and development. The protracted Algerian War and the oil price shock of 1973 had exposed the fragility of the existing world economic system, and so-called Third-World countries in Asia, Africa and Latin America pressed the urgency of developing a more just and equal economic order. At the end of the session, the delegates agreed on two resolutions: a 'Declaration on the Establishment of a New International Economic Order' (NIEO) and a 'Programme of Action on the Establishment of a New International Economic Order'.[2] Transformative in scope, this economic order was never brought into existence. It nonetheless signalled the presence and voice of Third-World countries.[3] Deng's speech was only one component on the session's agenda, yet it outlined socialist China's approach to international relations, political ideology and economic dependencies and contributed a markedly Chinese interpretation to conceptualizations of the 'Third World'.

Deng was the first Chinese leader to speak at a UN General Assembly since the PRC had taken over China's UN seat from the Republic of China in October 1971. Because of this, and because Deng would several years later lead the PRC into the era of 'reform and opening' and a momentous social and economic transformation, this speech has been associated closely with his person. Yet, his appointment as chairman of the Chinese delegation was rushed and not as carefully planned as later interpretations of his speech might suggest. A couple of weeks before the delegation was to travel from Beijing to New York, Mao Zedong had ensured that the Ministry of Foreign Affairs would select Deng to represent China at the UN. At short notice, the responsibility for drafting the speech was transferred from the Ministry of Trade to the Ministry of Foreign Affairs and it was decided that Deng would speak. Deng, with his international experience of living in France during the early 1920s, seemed a good replacement for premier Zhou Enlai who was battling cancer. With this shift to the Ministry of Foreign Affairs, the man responsible for drafting the speech, Qiao Guanhua, then vice-minister and soon-to-be minister of Foreign Affairs, infused a strongly political and ideological component into the text, outlining not merely an economic policy but also an international and developmental vision along the line of Mao's 'Three Worlds Theory'.[4]

The speech is not a classic example of one man's revolutionary thought, delivered to an audience and later canonized in his works. It is not a classic revolutionary text. It is instead an example of a revolutionary concept conceived by one man, Mao Zedong; a text written by another man, Qiao Guanhua; and a speech presented by yet another, Deng Xiaoping. It gained fame by its association with the venue, the United Nations, and by its association with a crucial moment in time, 1974, the last years of the Great Proletarian Cultural Revolution and an age of profound global realignments as part of the late Cold War, decolonization, national liberation movements and popular protests of 1968 and after. An interpretation of the speech, I argue, must account for the impromptu historical decisions that led Deng to travel to New York, for the setting in which the speech was presented, for the domestic Chinese context in which Mao thought up the Three Worlds Theory and for the international context which this theory was supposed to explain and influence. Because the ideas Deng presented at the special session were Mao Zedong's, Deng was merely a messenger. But the significance of the speech lay both in its content and in its historical symbolism as an event, in 1974 and for years after. Here Deng became China's international representative and, though it was far too early to call in 1974, positioned himself as China's future leader. As Deng's power grew following Mao's death in 1976, he eventually sought to disassociate himself from much of the content of his UN speech, while at the same time trying to profit from the symbolic status it had provided. Whereas the images of Deng at the speaker's podium below the United Nations insignia proliferated decades later, the actual speech was less frequently mentioned after the early 1980s and not included in Deng's *Selected Works*.[5]

How, then, might we interpret the above section of the speech, which formed the second and third paragraphs of a twenty-two-page manuscript? The two paragraphs outline the core components of the Three Worlds Theory and pave the way for a longer deliberation on world economic relations and development. Several points are noteworthy: strong emphasis is placed on the role of 'developing countries' and the agency of 'peoples of the world'. Deng refers to the 'old order' composed of 'colonialism', 'imperialism' and 'hegemonism', thus underlining the anti-imperialist legacy of socialist revolutionary thought. Mao's concept of a 'continuous revolution' reverberates in the mentions of 'turbulence', 'unrest', 'struggle' and the 'sharpening of basic contradictions' and these are summarized in one of the most common Chinese slogans: 'great disorder under heaven'. The 'decadent reactionary forces' are pitted against the 'emerging forces of the people' and the socialist camp is pronounced dead as 'a result of the emergence of social-imperialism'.

This was one of the key novelties in the speech. The Three Worlds Theory departed from established divisions because it no longer placed the Soviet

Union in the Second World and instead held that the Soviet Union was a 'social-imperialist' force exceeding in threat and viciousness its superpower counterpart, the United States. Rather than being bound by 'international class struggle' or by socialist allegiances, China's Third World was linked by a common stage of economic development that rendered it by comparison 'backward' and 'underdeveloped'.[6] On this basis, 'revolution', so the speech continued, 'is the main trend in the world today' (6). Accusations that the Soviet Union promoted social-imperialism were thus an ideological response to the Sino-Soviet split of 1961–2 and the military confrontations that had occurred along the Sino-Soviet border in Manchuria in 1969.

The Chinese communist approach to revolutions and the Third World built both on foreign as well as Chinese paradigms. Harry Truman included mention of 'underdeveloped' parts of the world in his inaugural address in 1949. A few years later, French demographer and economist Alfred Sauvy coined the term Third World – 'le tiers monde' – and it gained currency as a scientific paradigm in 1956. It described those countries that were underdeveloped, overpopulated and disadvantaged by comparison to the United States and the 'western' world, mostly Europe, which made up the First World, and the socialist bloc, which made up the Second World. At the same time, many of the newly labelled Third-World countries met at the Asian-African Conference in Bandung, Indonesia, in 1955. Though the term 'Third World' was not used in the final communiqué of the conference, the understanding was that the countries present at Bandung would each need to negotiate an identity and position between the Cold War superpowers. Increasingly, the term referred to countries that not only were economically less developed, but also did not profess allegiance to either superpower.[7] The Third World, however, soon denoted many different things: it could be spatial, territorial, social, political or economic.[8]

Mao's concept of three different worlds was marked not by ideological differences between capitalism and communism, but by levels of economic development and imperialist might and the popular revolutionary responses these engendered. It was an extension of his previous models for international relations: the Intermediate Zone and the Two Intermediate Zones. The thesis of the Intermediate Zone developed in the aftermath of the second World War and held that the expanse of Asia, Africa and Europe stood between the two superpowers and would prevent violent encroachment of US imperialist forces. During the mid-1950s, as part of the Chinese involvement in the Bandung conference, the Chinese Communist Party promoted the so-called 'Five Principles of Peaceful Co-existence'. These consisted of: mutual respect for territorial integrity and sovereignty, mutual non-aggression, non-interference in internal affairs, equality and mutual benefit, and peaceful coexistence.⁹ Several years later, during the early 1960s, Mao began to advocate an amended version of this thesis, delineating two intermediate zones instead of one. The first was now composed of Asia, Africa and Latin America, while European countries made up the second zone. The two zones were representative of Chinese alienation from its former Soviet 'big brother' following the introduction of policies of de-Stalinization. Although the Chinese government had promoted peaceful coexistence among African, Asian and Latin American countries, the Soviet decision to seek détente with the United States was unacceptable. Peaceful coexistence was not to apply to coexistence with the imperialist enemy. The two intermediate zones, moreover, were also a reflection of the Chinese party-state's attempt to position Chinese socialism as the vanguard of world revolutions and to promote a distinctly Chinese vision of socialist revolution, manifested most fervently in the Great Leap Forward.

Two intermediate zones, with one zone sharing in common the people's struggle against imperialism and for national liberation, led easily into the Three Worlds, as Deng delineated them in New York. In the aftermath of Sino-US rapprochement the Soviet Union had become the PRC's number one adversary. Social imperialism, a concept central to the Chinese Three Worlds Theory, provided a convenient threat to explain why countries of Mao's Third World ought to rally together. Fear of social imperialism and calls for political and economic independence were to bind together Asian, African and Latin American countries.

Unity among countries of the Third World was important not merely for China's international relations, but also for its social and political development. China's first major speech to the UN General Assembly came at a crucial moment domestically. The late Cultural Revolution was a time of heightened uncertainty following the excesses of its first years between 1966 and 1969. Mao was the ailing elder statesman, still pulling the reigns but also heavily influenced by his closest advisors (who in turn often did not agree with each other). Although he had consented to the rapprochement with the United States two years earlier, the Three Worlds Theory continued to portray the United States as an imperialist aggressor. This, in fact, would be one of the reasons why Deng distanced himself from the Three Worlds thesis during the early 1980s.

Solidarity with the Third World had been a rallying call of the Cultural Revolution. It had been popular in publications of the Red Guards and frequently included in articles of the *Peking Review*, a propaganda magazine published fortnightly in English, French, Spanish, Japanese and German. Propaganda posters featured Mao and the Chinese people walking hand-in-hand with their

Asian, African and Latin American comrades. The Cultural Revolution, in turn, had played a significant role in global popular protest movements of the late 1960s. Mao's *Little Red Book* symbolized continuous revolution and solidarity with the Third World. As the *Peking Review* commented in its special coverage of Deng's departure from Beijing airport on 6 April 1974, it was 'an atmosphere of unity in struggle'. 'Countries', so the coverage continued, 'want independence, nations want liberation, and the people want revolution'.[10] This quotation had also appeared in the first speech by the Chinese ambassador to the UN, Qiao Guanhua, in November 1971.[11] Although Deng was going to speak on development and economic independence, to the *Peking Review* his trip was all about uniting the people in revolution, with Cultural Revolution China at the forefront.

Chinese competition with the Soviet Union for leadership of the Third World marked the 1970s. Deng's speech was a climax in ongoing Chinese efforts to support national liberation movements across the globe in the name of anti-imperialism. Eventually, the Soviets won out, mainly because the Chinese government chose to back what they believed were Third-World 'struggles' of all kinds, regardless of whether these were driven by socialist ideology. Citing principles of peaceful coexistence and non-interference, the Chinese government had not ceased its support for Chile even after the coup against Allende in 1973. During the Angolan Civil War of 1975, they had supported the same groups that eventually also received military support from the South African apartheid regime, thus greatly harming the PRC's image as a true proponent of Third-World liberation. In the quest against social-imperialism, Chinese foreign policy decisions were focused on fighting Soviet dominance first; the domestic concerns of the various struggles of Third-World countries came second. The above abstract from Deng's speech is therefore as indicative of professed solidarity with the Third World, revolution and national liberation as it is of the firm intent first and foremost to counter social imperialism.

Deng's UN speech could therefore be read in many different ways: as an attempt to rally with the Third World; as an expression of Sino-Soviet rivalry; or as an opportunity to label the People's Republic of China a 'developing country'. This label would open new avenues for international co-operation but would also provide legitimacy for the profound domestic transformations that would follow in the late 1970s under Deng's aegis. Although Deng quietly disassociated himself from Mao's Three Worlds Theory during the early 1980s, he would continue to depict China as a developing country. Deng's speech has therefore served as one of many sources in popular and scholarly attempts to evaluate the late Cultural Revolution and 'understand China'. Was China genuinely supportive of the Third World? Or was the speech a succession of empty promises fulfilled only if it suited the PRC's own agenda? Was China a truly revolutionary leader and a committed anti-imperialist? Or had those Chinese leaders who would eventually steer the country towards 'reform and opening' already quietly moved to support economic reform and a shift away from revolutionary rhetoric?

The speech could be read as an expression of revolutionary goals or as a step towards a strategic developmental rhetoric that would mark the late 1970s and 1980s in China. Jeremy Friedman has argued that, though ultimately unsuccessful in gaining leadership of the Third World, the 'Chinese challenge changed the terms of the revolutionary conversation with the result that Moscow ultimately fought, and won, on Chinese terms'. For Chen Jian, the Three Worlds Theory 'further reduced the influence and power of the profoundly divided international Communist movement, creating another important condition for the Cold War to end with the collapse of the Soviet camp'.[12] Victories and defeats were temporary in the battle over revolutionary ideologies and terms, of which Deng's speech was one component. Revolution was part of a rhetorical strategy to participate in the international arena. But revolution could quickly give way to pragmatic policy needs, as later economic developments illustrate.

Discourses of development, linked with calls for equality, social justice, human rights and the ascendancy of the 'globalization' paradigm, soon shifted attention away from the Third World and its revolution. Yet, the idea of the Third World perseveres, partly because of habit and partly because it is closely linked to a modernization paradigm that shapes the way we think and talk about the world, even today.[13] Deng's performance at the UN and his trip to New York have been canonized as an event, not merely as a speech that eventually became enshrined in textual form. This is not least because any discussion of Deng's trip should always conclude with a mention of the 200 croissants which he purchased during a stopover in Paris on his return to Beijing and which reminded him of his time in France as a young revolutionary.

## Further Reading

Chen, Jian, 'China, the Third World, and the Cold War', in *The Cold War in the Third World*, ed. Robert J. McMahon (Oxford: Oxford University Press, 2013), pp. 85–100.

Cook, Alexander C., 'Third World Maoism', in *A Critical Introduction to Mao*, ed. Timothy Cheek (Cambridge: Cambridge University Press, 2010), pp. 288–312.

Dirlik, Arif, 'Spectres of the Third World: Global Modernity and the End of the Three Worlds', *Third World Quarterly* 25, no. 1 (2008): 131–48.

# Notes

## Introduction

1 T. Skocpol, *States and Social Revolutions: A Comparative Analysis of France, Russia, and China* (Cambridge: Cambridge University Press, 1979).
2 Ibid, pp. 5–6.
3 See, for example, David Parker, *Revolutions and the Revolutionary Tradition in the West, 1560-1991* (London and New York: Routledge, 2000); and Michael D. Richards, *Revolutions in World History* (London and New York: Routledge, 2004).
4 It has recently been suggested that Zhou Enlai actually misunderstood the question. See the blogpost by Dean Nicholas, dated 15 June 2011, on the *History Today* blog.

## Chapter 1

1 *An Agreement of the People for a Firme and Present Peace* (3 November 1647; British Library Thomason Tracts E412/21), pp. 2–4. Further references to this work will appear in parentheses in the text.
2 E. Vernon and P. Baker, 'Introduction: the History and Historiography of the *Agreements of the People*', in *The Agreements of the People, the Levellers and the Constitutional Crisis of the English Revolution*, ed. P. Baker and E. Vernon (Basingstoke: Palgrave Macmillan, 2012), pp. 11–17.
3 E. Vernon, '"A Firme and Present Peace; Upon Grounds of Common Right and Freedome": The Debate on the *Agreements of the People* and the Crisis of the Constitution, 1647-59', in *The Agreements of the People*, ed. P. Baker and E. Vernon (Basingstoke: Palgrave Macmillan, 2012), pp. 195–217.
4 M. Kishlansky, 'The Army and the Levellers: The Roads to Putney', *Historical Journal* 22 (1979): 795–824; I. Gentles, *The New Model Army in England, Ireland and Scotland, 1645-1653* (Oxford: Blackwell, 1992); A. Woolrych, 'Putney Revisited: Political Debate in the New Model Army in 1647', in *Politics and People in Revolutionary England*, ed. C. Jones, M. Newitt, and S. Roberts (Oxford: Blackwell, 1996); J. Morrill and P. Baker, 'The Case of the Armie Truly Re-Stated', in *The Putney Debates of 1647*, ed. M. Mendle (Cambridge: Cambridge University Press, 2001), pp. 103–24; E. Vernon and P. Baker, 'What Was the First Agreement

of the People?', *Historical Journal* 53 (2010): 39–60; and R. Foxley, *The Levellers: Radical Political Thought in the English Revolution* (Manchester: Manchester University Press, 2013), chapter 5.
5 *An Agreement of the People of England and the Places therewith Incorporated* (1649), broadside.
6 C. H. Firth (ed.), *The Clarke Papers* (London: Royal Historical Society, 1992 reprint edition), vol. 1, p. 301.
7 J. Lilburne, *The Free-mans Freedom Vindicated* (1646), p. 11.
8 I. Hampsher-Monk, 'The Political Theory of the Levellers: Putney, Property and Professor Macpherson', *Political Studies* 24 (1976): 397–422.
9 A. Orr, 'Constitutionalism: Ancient, Modern and Early Modern in the *Agreements of the People*', in Baker and Vernon, *The Agreements of the People*, pp. 76–96.
10 J. Lilburne, W. Walwyn, R. Overton, and T. Prince, *An Agreement of the Free People of England* (1649; the 'Third Agreement'), p. 7.

# Chapter 2

1 James Harrington, *The Commonwealth of Oceana*, ed. J. G. A. Pocock (Cambridge: Cambridge University Press, 1992), p. 11. Hereafter all references for this text will appear in parentheses.
2 Z. S. Fink, *The Classical Republicans: An Essay in the Recovery of a Pattern of Thought in Seventeenth-Century England* (Evanston, IL: Northwestern University Press, 1945); J. G. A. Pocock, *The Machiavellian Moment: Florentine Political Thought and the Atlantic Republican Tradition* (Princeton: Princeton University Press, 1975); *The Political Works of James Harrington*, ed. J. G. A. Pocock (Cambridge: Cambridge University Press, 1977).
3 John Milton's *The Readie and Easie Way* is an obvious exception here, but it was a last-ditch attempt at saving the republic (rather than a detailed reflection of Milton's considered views) and it was to some extent a response to Harrington. On the emphasis of English republicans on moral philosophy rather than constitution-building see J. Scott, *Commonwealth Principles* (Cambridge: Cambridge University Press, 2004).
4 W. Moyle, *An Essay Upon the Constitution of the Roman Government*, in *The Works of Walter Moyle Esq* (London: Darby &c., 1726), pp. 71–3.
5 See B. Worden, 'Republicanism, Regicide and Republic: The English Experience', in *Republicanism: A Shared European Heritage. Volume I: Republicanism and Constitutionalism in Early Modern Europe*, ed. M. Van Gelderen and Q. Skinner (Cambridge: Cambridge University Press, 2002), pp. 307–27. This notion has also been reinforced by recent work on the development of republican exclusivism.

See David Wootton, 'The True Origins of Republicanism: The Disciples of Baron and the Counter-Example of Venturi', in *Il Repubblicanismo Moderno: L'Idea di Republicca nella Riflessione Storica di Franco Venturi*, ed. Manuela Albertone (Naples: Bibliopolis, 2006), pp. 271–304; James Hankins, 'Exclusivist Republicanism and the Non-Monarchical Republic', *Political Theory* 38 (2010): 452–82.

6  John Aubrey, *Aubrey's Brief Lives*, ed. O. L. Dick (Harmondsworth: Penguin, 1949), p. 283. See also John Toland, 'Life of Harrington', in J. Harrington, *Oceana and Other Works of James Harrington*, ed. J. Toland (London, 1737), p. xvii.

7  *The Political Works of James Harrington*, ed. Pocock, p. 574.

8  Harrington's positive use and redefinition of the term 'democracy' has been noted by David Wootton in *Divine Right and Democracy: An Anthology of Political Writing in Stuart England* (Harmondsworth: Penguin, 1986), pp. 39–40. Jason Maloy has demonstrated that the term was also starting to be positively adopted in certain American colonies during the seventeenth century, but for the most part this was extremely unusual at the time. J. Maloy, *The Colonial American Origins of Modern Democratic Thought* (Cambridge: Cambridge University Press, 2008).

9  *The Political Works of James Harrington*, ed. Pocock, p. 777.

10 R. Hammersley, 'Rethinking the Political Thought of James Harrington: Royalism, Republicanism and Democracy', *History of European Ideas* 39, no. 3 (2013): 354–70.

11 While Derek Hirst's detailed study emphasized the inconsistency of franchises (both in theory and in practice) in seventeenth-century England and the lack of reliable country-wide figures, it would appear that Harrington was advocating fewer restrictions and a wider franchise than was typical of the time. D. Hirst, *The Representative of the People? Voters and Voting in England under the Early Stuarts* (Cambridge: Cambridge University Press, 1975), especially 1–105.

12 Though they have been the focus of this chapter, these were not the only terms that Harrington redefined in *The Commonwealth of Oceana*. J. C. Davis has written brilliantly on Harrington's inversion of the conventional understanding of 'equality' and Jonathan Scott has also talked more generally about Harrington's innovative attitude towards contemporary languages of politics. J. C. Davis, 'Equality in an unequal commonwealth: James Harrington's republicanism and the meaning of equality', in *Soldiers, Writers and Statesmen of the English Revolution*, ed. I. Gentles, J. Morrill and B. Worden (Cambridge: Cambridge University Press, 1998), pp. 229–42; J. Scott, 'The Rapture of Motion: James Harrington's republicanism', in *Political Discourse in Early Modern England*, ed. N. Phillipson and Q. Skinner (Cambridge: Cambridge University Press, 1993), pp. 139–63; and Scott, *Commonwealth Principles*.

13 For the recent debate over a 'classical' republican tradition in early modern England and Harrington's place within it see, in particular, P. A. Rahe, *Republics Ancient and Modern: Classical Republicanism and the American Revolution* (Chapel

Hill, NC: University of North Carolina Press, 1992); P. A. Rahe, *Against Throne and Altar: Machiavelli and Political Theory under the English Republic* (Cambridge: Cambridge University Press, 2008); and Scott, *Commonwealth Principles*.

## Chapter 3

1 Henry Sacheverell, *The Perils of False Brethren both in church, and state: set forth in a sermon preach'd before the Right Honourable, the Lord Mayor, aldermen, and citizens of London, at the Cathedral-Church of St Paul, on 5 November 1709* (2nd edn), p. 11.
2 Steve Pincus, *1688: The First Modern Revolution* (New Haven: Yale University Press, 2009).
3 Tony Claydon, *Europe and the Making of England, 1660-1760* (New York: Cambridge University Press, 2007).
4 Pincus, *1688*.
5 Lawrence Klein, 'The political significance of "politeness" in early eighteenth-century Britain', in *Politics, politeness and patriotism : Papers presented at the Folger Institute Seminar, 'Politics and Politeness : British Political Thought in the Age of Walpole'; directed by N.T. Phillipson (Proceedings of the Folger Institute Center for the History of British Political Thought, 5)*, ed. Gordon Schochet (Washington, DC: Folger Inst., 1993), 73–108.
6 Jurgen Habermas, *The Structural Transformation of the Public Sphere: An Inquiry into a Category of Bourgeois Society*, trans. Thomas Burger with the assistance of Frederick Lawrence (Cambridge, MA: MIT Press, 1989).
7 Hannah Smith, 'English "feminist" writings and Judith Drake's An Essay in defence of the female sex (1696)', *Historical Journal* 44, no. 3 (2001): 727–47.
8 Faramerz Dabhoiwala, 'Lust and Liberty', *Past & Present* 207 (2010): 89–179.

## Chapter 4

1 Gabriel Bonnot de Mably, *Des droits et des devoirs du citoyen, Collection complete des oeuvres de l'abbe de Mably*, vol. 11 (Paris: Guillaume Arnoux, 1794-5), pp. 285, 300–1, 437–8, 440–1. Further references to this work will appear in parentheses in the text.
2 Franco Venturi, *Utopia and Reform in the Enlightenment* (Cambridge: Cambridge University Press, 1971), p. 73.
3 Rachel Hammersley, *The English Republican Tradition and Eighteenth-Century France: Between the Ancients and the Moderns* (Manchester: Manchester University Press, 2010), especially pp. 86–98.

4 For a convincing analysis of the relations between republicanism and natural rights theory in Mably's thought, in a special issue of the journal *Corpus* devoted to 'natural rights', see Marc Belissa, 'La place du droit naturel chez Mably: éléments de débat', *Corpus: Revue de philosophie*, no. 64 (2013): 111–28.
5 For Mably's relation to Babeuf, we now have what is the most important work on the latter in a generation, in the outstanding study by Stéphanie Roza, 'Comment l'utopie est devenue un programme politique: Morelly, Mably, Babeuf, un débat avec Rousseau', Doctoral thesis, Université Paris I – Panthéon-Sorbonne, October 2013.
6 Michael Sonenscher, *Sans-Culottes: An Eighteenth-Century Emblem in the French Revolution* (Princeton: Princeton University Press, 2008), especially pp. 372–408.

# Chapter 5

1 Jean-Jacques Rousseau, *The Social Contract and Other Later Political Writings*, ed. and trans. Victor Gourevitch (Cambridge: Cambridge University Press, 1997), p. 41. Later references to this work will be indicated in parentheses in the text.
2 Étienne Dumont to Samuel Romilly, Friday, 22 May 1789 in Rousseau, *Correspondance complète de Jean Jacques Rousseau*, ed. R. A. Leigh (Oxford: Institut et Musée Voltaire, 1967–88), vol. 46, pp. 37–8.
3 Voltaire to Rousseau, 30 August 1755, Rousseau, *Correspondance complète de Jean Jacques Rousseau*, vol. 3, p. 259.
4 J. L. Talmon, *The Origins of Totalitarian Democracy* (London: Secker & Warburg, 1960); Joan McDonald, *Rousseau and the French Revolution, 1762-1791* (London: Bloomsbury Academic, 1965); and Holger Ross Lauritsen and Mikkel Thorup (eds), *Rousseau and Revolution* (London: Continuum, 2011).
5 David Hume, 'Of Civil Liberty', in *Political Essays*, ed. K. Haakonssen (Cambridge: Cambridge University Press, 1994), p. 55.
6 Bernard Mandeville, *The Fable of the Bees or Private Vices, Publick Benefits*, 2 vols. With a Commentary Critical, Historical, and Explanatory by F. B. Kaye (Indianapolis: Liberty Fund, 1988), Remark F, vol. 1, p. 85.
7 G. Vallette, *Jean-Jacques Rousseau Genevois* (Paris: Plon-Nourrit, 1911), pp. 239 and 294–326; H. Lüthy, 'Rousseau the Genevan', in *From Calvin to Rousseau* (New York: Basic Books, 1970), pp. 251–69; R. A. Leigh, 'Le *Contrat Social* Œuvre Genevoise?', *Annales de la Société Jean-Jacques Rousseau* 39 (1972–7): 93–111; P. Mason, 'The Genevan republican background to Rousseau's Social Contract', *History of Political Thought* 14 (1992): 547–72; G. Silvestrini, *Alle Radici del Pensiero di Rousseau* (Milan: Franco Angeli, 1993); and H. Rosenblatt, *Rousseau and Geneva: From the First Discourse to the Social Contract, 1749-1762* (Cambridge: Cambridge University Press, 1997).

## Chapter 6

1. The Jefferson Papers project collated and organized the different versions of the Declaration, from first drafts through to the final, approved text. See Julian P. Boyd (ed.), *Papers of Thomas Jefferson* (Princeton: Princeton University Press, 1950), vol. 1, pp. 413–32.
2. Most major works (listed at the end of this essay under further reading) examining the Declaration have analysed either the political and social principles that influenced Jefferson (Carl Becker and Garry Wills) or the converse: how the Declaration shaped political experience in the modern world (David Armitage). Pauline Maier's 1997 book, which seeks to contextualize every part of the Declaration, from the popular call from the American people to write one to its construction and dissemination, is the most complete treatment. Yet, even Maier largely missed the significance of the final grievance and how it gave shape to the amorphous body ('the American people') who were doing the declaring in the first place.
3. John Richard Alden, 'John Stuart Accuses William Bull', *William and Mary Quarterly* 3rd series, 2 (July 1945): 320.
4. For much more about these stories and their publication histories see my *The Common Cause: The Foundations of Race and Nation in the American Revolution* (Chapel Hill: University of North Carolina Press, 2016).
5. Thomas Jefferson to Henry Lee, 8 May 1825, in *Jefferson: Writings*, ed. Merrill Peterson (New York, 1984), p. 1501.
6. John Adams to Abigail Adams, Philadelphia, 3 July 1776, in *Letters of Delegates to Congress, 1774-1789*, ed. Paul H. Smith (Washington, DC, 1976), vol. 4, p. 375.
7. John Adams to Benjamin Rush, Quincy, 30 September 1805, in *The Spur of Fame: Dialogues of John Adams and Benjamin Rush, 1805-1813*, ed. John A. Schutz and Douglass Adair (San Marino, CA, 1966), p. 43.
8. *New York Journal* 8 August 1776. See also Peter Force (ed.), *American Archives* (Washington, DC: Government Printing Office, 1839), 5th series, vol. 1, p. 543.

## Chapter 7

1. Alexander Hamilton, 'Federalist, No 1', in James Madison, Alexander Hamilton, and John Jay, *The Federalist Papers*, ed. Isaac Kramnick (London: Penguin, 1987), pp. 88–9. Further references to this work will appear in parentheses in the text.
2. Pauline Maier, *Ratification: The People Debate the Constitution, 1787-1788* (New York: Simon & Schuster Paperbacks, 2011), pp. 84–5.

3  Isaac Kramnick, 'Editors Introduction', *The Federalist Papers*, p. 11.
4  Bernard Bailyn, 'The Central Themes of the American Revolution: An Interpretation', in *Essays on the American Revolution*, ed. Stephen G. Kurtz and James H. Hutson (Chapel Hill: University of North Carolina Press, 1973), pp. 3–10.
5  Thomas Paine, *Common Sense*, in *The Complete Works of Thomas Paine*, 2 vols, ed. Philip S. Foner (New York: Citadel Press, 1969), i, pp. 4–6.
6  Saul Cornell, *The Other Founders: Anti-Federalism and the Dissenting Tradition in America, 1788-1828* (Chapel Hill: published for the Omohundro Institute of Early American History and Culture by the University of North Carolina Press, 1999).
7  'Vices of the Political System of the United States, April 1787', Founders Online, National Archives (http://founders.archives.gov/documents/Madison/01-09-02-0187, ver. 2013-08-02). Source: *The Papers of James Madison*, vol. 9, *9 April 1786–24 May 1787 and supplement 1781–1784*, ed. Robert A. Rutland and William M. E. Rachal (Chicago: The University of Chicago Press, 1975), pp. 345–58.
8  A succinct account of the extensive debate over state versus federal authority is: Peter S. Onuf, 'State Sovereignty and the Making of the Constitution', in *Conceptual Change and the Constitution*, ed. Terence Ball and J. G. A. Pocock (Lawrence: University Press of Kansas, 1988), pp. 78–98.
9  On the importance of a 'usable past', see, Trevor Colbourn, *The Lamp of Experience: Whig History and the Intellectual Origins of the American Revolution* (Indianapolis: Liberty Fund, 1998; original 1965).
10  John Locke, 'The Second Treatise of Government', *Two Treatises of Government*, ed. Peter Laslett (Cambridge: Cambridge University Press, 1988), § 229, p. 415.

# Chapter 8

1  For this translation, see Emmanuel-Joseph Sieyès, *Political Writings*, ed. Michael Sonenscher (Indianapolis: Hackett, 2003), p. 94. References to further passages from this translation are indicated by entries in brackets in the text.
2  Jean-Jacques Rousseau, *Emile, ou de l'éducation* [1762], ed. Michel Launay (Paris: Garnier Flammarion, 1966), Bk. III, p. 252.
3  For a fuller account, see Michael Sonenscher, *Before the Deluge: Public Debt, Inequality, and the Intellectual Origins of the French Revolution* (Princeton: Princeton University Press, 2007).
4  This was the title used in the contemporary English translation of Sieyès's biography by his Prussian admirer Konrad Oelsner, *An Account of the Life of Sieyes* (London, 1795), p. 21. For a translation, see Sieyès, *Political Writings*, pp. 1–67.

## Chapter 9

1. A translation of the entire document can be found in Lynn Hunt, *The French Revolution and Human Rights: A Brief Documentary History* (Boston: Bedford Books of St. Martin's Press, 1996), pp. 77–9. When page numbers appear in parenthesis, they refer to documents found in this edition.
2. The most influential of the critics was the Anglo-Irish politician Edmund Burke, *Reflections on the Revolution in France: And on the Proceedings in Certain Societies in London Relative to That Event* (London: J. Dodsley, 1790). This work became one of the major sources of conservatism in the nineteenth and twentieth centuries.
3. The dictionaries of the French Academy can be consulted at http://artfl-project.uchicago.edu/content/dictionnaires-dautrefois.
4. For more on the question of origins, see Keith Michael Baker, 'The Idea of a Declaration of Rights,' in *The French Idea of Freedom: The Old Regime and the Declaration of Rights of 1789*, ed. Dale Van Kley (Stanford, CA: Stanford University Press, 1997), pp. 91–140.
5. Elise Marienstras and Naomi Wulf, 'French Translations and Reception of the Declaration of Independence,' *The Journal of American History* 85, no. 4 (1 March 1999): 1299–324.
6. The most influential of the defenders of the French Declaration was Thomas Paine. His *Rights of Man: Being an Answer to Mr. Burke's Attack on the French Revolution* (London: Jordan, 1791) appeared in multiple editions in Britain and the new United States and was translated many times, even into Yiddish in Amsterdam. The Spanish translations played an important role in justifying various independence movements in Latin America in the early nineteenth century. See, for example, John Keane, *Tom Paine: A Political Life* (London: Bloomsbury, 2003).
7. The Universal Declaration can be found in Lynn Hunt, *Inventing Human Rights: A History* (New York: W.W. Norton & Co, 2007), pp. 223–9.
8. This observation is based on a Google Ngram of 'rights of man' and 'human rights' from 1789 to 2000.
9. Massachusetts Anti-Slavery Society Board of Managers, *Annual Report of the Board of Managers of the Massachusetts Anti-Slavery Society, with Some Account of the Annual Meeting* (Boston: Isaac Knapp, 1836), p. 39.
10. The Declaration of Independence of the Democratic Republic of Vietnam can be found at http://chnm.gmu.edu/revolution/d/583/.

## Chapter 10

1. Thomas Paine, *Rights of Man*, ed. G. Claeys (Indianapolis: Hackett Publishing Co., 1992), pp. 37–8. Further references to this work will appear in parentheses in the text.

2. J. H. Burns, 'The Rights of Man Since the Reformation', in *An Introduction to the Study of Human Rights*, ed. Francis Vallat (London: Europa Publications, 1971), p. 25.
3. Thomas Hardy, *Memoir of Thomas Hardy* (London, 1832), p. 20; and Joseph Priestley, *Political Writings*, ed. Peter N. Miller (Cambridge: Cambridge University Press, 1993), pp. 24–5.
4. Jack Fruchtman Jr. uses the term 'secular millennialism' to describe Paine's views ('The Revolutionary Millennialism of Thomas Paine', *Studies in Eighteenth-Century Culture* 13 (1984): 66), and more generally Fruchtman, *Thomas Paine and the Religion of Nature* (Baltimore: Johns Hopkins University Press, 1993), p. 157 ff.
5. For example, the call to 'spread the knowledge of human rights', in *A Vindication of the Revolution Society, Against the Calumnies of Mr. Burke* (1792), reprinted in *Political Writings of the 1790s*, 8 vols, ed. G. Claeys (London: Pickering & Chatto, 1995), vol. 2, p. 409. The phrase 'rights of mankind' occurs as early as 1703 and is ten times as common as 'rights of man' between 1740 and 1760 and 'human rights', which emerges chiefly from the 1760s (Peter De Bolla, *The Architecture of Concepts* (New York: Fordham University Press, 2013), pp. 102, 113, 140).
6. James Griffin, *On Human Rights* (Oxford: Oxford University Press, 2008), p. 1. See further my 'Socialism and the Language of Rights', in *Revisiting the Origins of Human Rights: Genealogy of a European Idea*, ed. Miia Halme-Tuomisaari and Pamela Slotte (2015).
7. James Burgh, *The Dignity of Human Nature* (London, 1754).
8. Thus, Andrew Vincent writes of the idea of the individual as bearer of natural rights that 'Despite the apparent secularity of this theme, it was originally, particularly in the context of natural right arguments, configured in a predominantly Christian framework' (*The Politics of Human Rights,* Oxford: Oxford University Press, 2010, p. 74). But my point is to extend this idea to human rights as well. On 3 June 2013 Baroness Brinton noted in the House of Lords that the 'divine image' within us meant that 'we should all be treated equally' (*The Guardian*, 4 June 2013).
9. Thomas Paine, *The Complete Writings of Thomas Paine*, 2 vols, ed. Philip Foner (New York: Citadel Press, 1945), vol. 1, p. 10.
10. Edmund Burke, *The Collected Works of Edmund Burke*, 10 vols (London, 1899), vol. 3, pp. 279–80. For the wider context, see my *Thomas Paine: Social and Political Thought* (London: Unwin Hyman, 1989), and for the British debate, *Political Writings of the 1790s*.
11. Quoted in De Bolla, *The Architecture of Concepts*, pp. 158, 172.
12. Jonathan Israel, 'Philosophy, Religion and the Controversy about Basic Human Rights in 1789', in *Self-Evident Truths? Human Rights and the Enlightenment*, ed. Kate E. Tunstall (London: Bloomsbury, 2012), pp. 117–20, 125.
13. Alexis de Tocqueville, *On the State of Society in France Before the Revolution* (John Murray, 1856), pp. 19–22.

14  G. D. H. Cole, *Essays in Social Theory* (London: Macmillan, 1950), pp. 135–6.
15  Paine, *Complete Writings*, vol. 2, p. 274.
16  Mordecai Roshwald, 'The Concept of Human Rights', *Philosophy and Phenomenological Research*, 19 (1959): 375, 377.
17  De Bolla, *The Architecture of Concepts*, p. 208.
18  Paine, *Complete Writings*, vol. 1, p. 55.

# Chapter 11

1  'Sur les principes de morale politique qui doivent guider la Convention Nationale dans l'administration intérieur de la République', 17 Pluviôse (5 February 1794), in Maximilien Robespierre, *Oeuvres de Maximilien Robespierre*, eds Marc Bouloiseau, Albert Soboul et al, 11 vols (Paris: Société des études robespierristes, 1910–2007), vol. X, 356–7. Page references to this edition will be given in parentheses throughout the text of this essay.
2  For a recent analysis of debates around the Terror, see Marisa Linton, 'Terror and Politics' in *Oxford Handbook of the French Revolution*, ed. David Andress (Oxford: Oxford University Press, 2014). For a controversial new assessment of the Terror that focuses on its emotional dimensions, see Sophie Wahnich, *In Defence of the Terror: Liberty or Death in the French Revolution*, trans. David Fernbach (2003: this edition, London: Verso, 2012).
3  For a perceptive recent biography of Robespierre, see Peter McPhee, *Robespierre – a Revolutionary Life* (New Haven: Yale University Press, 2012).
4  Robespierre, 'Rapport sur les principes du gouvernement révolutionnaire', before the Convention, 5 Nivôse (25 December 1793), Robespierre, *Oeuvres*, vol. X, p. 274.
5  For more on the intellectual sources of Robespierre's ideas in this speech, see Marisa Linton, 'Robespierre's Political Principles', in *Robespierre*, ed. Colin Haydon and William Doyle (Cambridge: Cambridge University Press, 1990).
6  Charles-Louis de Secondat Montesquieu, (baron de), Foreword, *De L'Esprit des lois*, in *Oeuvres complètes*, ed. Roger Caillois, 2 vols (Paris, Bibliothèque de la Pléiade, 1949–51), vol. II. Robespierre's description of virtue as the mainspring of popular government paraphrases Montesquieu's formulation that virtue was the mainspring of republics: *De l'Esprit des lois*, Book III, p. 251.
7  Montesquieu, *De L'Esprit des lois*, Book IV, ch. 5, p. 267.
8  On the derivations and development of the eighteenth-century concept of virtue, see Marisa Linton, *The Politics of Virtue in Enlightenment France* (Houndmills: Palgrave, 2001).
9  Marisa Linton, 'Robespierre et l'authenticité révolutionnaire', *Annales Historiques de la Révolution Française*, 371 (janvier-mars 2013): 153–73. This is also forthcoming in an English version.

10  On the 'politicians' terror', see Marisa Linton, *Choosing Terror: Virtue, Friendship and Authenticity in the French Revolution* (Oxford: Oxford University Press, 2013).
11  Peter R. Campbell, Thomas E. Kaiser, and Marisa Linton (eds), *Conspiracy in the French Revolution* (Manchester: Manchester University Press, 2007).
12  For a detailed account of the process whereby Robespierre's attitude changed towards the Indulgents, see Linton, *Choosing Terror*, chs 7 and 8.
13  Georges Danton's speech calling for the establishment of the Revolutionary Tribunal, 10 March 1793, *Archives Parlementaires de 1787 à 1860*, ed. M. J. Madival et al, 127 vols (Paris: Librairie administrative de P. Dupont, 1862–), vol. LX, p. 162.
14  Jean-Clément Martin, *Violence et révolution: essais sur la naissance d'un mythe national* (Paris: Sueil, 2006); Annie Jourdan, 'Les discours de la terreur à l'époque révolutionnaire', *French Historical Studies* 36, 1 (December 2012): 52–81.
15  Robespierre, 'Contre les factions nouvelles et les députés corrompus', 8 Thermidor l'an II, 26 July 1794, *Oeuvres Complètes*, vol. X, p. 566.

# Chapter 12

1  See Jeremy Popkin's discussion on Leclerc's plans: *A Concise History of the Haitian Revolution* (Malden, MA: Wiley-Blackwell Publishing, 2012), pp. 118–20.
2  Jeremy Popkin, 'Jean-Jacques Dessalines, Norbert Thoret, and the Violent Aftermath of the Haitian Declaration of Independence', in *The Haitian Declaration of Independence*, ed. Julia Gaffield (Charlottesville, VA: University of Virginia Press, 2015).
3  Christopher Leslie Brown, *Moral Capital: Foundations of British Abolitionism* (Chapel Hill, NC: Published for the Omohundro Institute of Early American History and Culture, by the University of North Carolina Press, 2006), Chapter 2: 'The Politics of Slavery in the Years of Crisis'.
4  Julia Gaffield, 'Haiti and Jamaica in the re-making of the early nineteenth-century Atlantic World,' *William and Mary Quarterly* 69, no. 3 (2012): 583–614.
5  Deborah Jenson, *Beyond the Slave Narrative: Politics Sex, and Manuscripts in the Haitian Revolution* (Liverpool: Liverpool University Press, 2011), p. 145.
6  Julia Gaffield, '"Liberté, Indépendance": Haitian Antislavery and National Independence,' in *A Global History of Anti-Slavery Politics in the Nineteenth Century*, ed. William Mulligan and Maurice Bric (Basingstoke: Palgrave-Macmillan, 2013), p. 18.
7  Jean-Jacques Dessalines, 14 January 1804, quoted in Thomas Madiou, *Histoire D'Haïti, Vol 7*, (Port-au-Prince: H. Deschamps, 1987), p. 154; and Léo Elisabeth, "Les relations entre les Petites Antilles françaises et Haïti," *Outre-Mer* 90, no. 340–1 (2003): 179.

8  Eliga H. Gould, *Among the Powers of the Earth: The American Revolution and the Making of a New World Empire* (Cambridge, MA: Harvard University Press, 2012), p. 2.
9  David Armitage, *The Declaration of Independence: A Global History* (Cambridge, MA: Harvard University Press, 2007), p. 20.
10 Ada Ferrer, 'Haiti, Free Soil, and Antislavery in the Revolutionary Atlantic', *The American Historical Review* 117, no. 1 (2012): 43.
11 Doris L. Garraway, 'Empire of Freedom, Kingdom of Civilization: Henry Christophe, the Baron de Vastey, and the Paradoxes of Universalism in Postrevolutionary Haiti', *Small Axe* 16, no. 3 (2012): 6.
12 Doris Garraway, '"*Légitime Défense*": Universalism and Nationalism in the Discourse of the Haitian Revolution,' in *Tree of Liberty: Cultural Legacies of the Haitian Revolution in the Atlantic World*, ed. Dorris Garraway (Charlottesville, VA: University of Virginia Press, 2008), p. 79.

# Chapter 13

1  https://www.marxists.org/archive/marx/works/1848/communist-manifesto/ch02.htm.
2  Gareth Stedman Jones, 'Introduction', in *The Communist Manifesto*, ed. Karl Marx and Friedrich Engels (London: Penguin, 2002), p. 32.
3  https://www.marxists.org/archive/marx/works/1848/communist-manifesto/preface.htm.
4  Karl Marx, letter to J. Weydemeyer, 5th March 1852 in Karl Marx, Frederick Engels *Selected Works*, I (Moscow: Progress Publishers, 1977) p. 528.
5  Ibid., p. 129.
6  The French socialist leader Jean Jaurès took a line not unlike Proudhon's in his discussion of *The Communist Manifesto* in *Etudes socialistes*. This collection of essays was translated in 1906 and is available here: http://www.marxists.org/archive/jaures/1906/studies-socialism/ch05.htm.
7  Isaiah Berlin, *Karl Marx* (Oxford: Oxford University Press, 1939), pp. 111–20.
8  Ibid., p. 154.

# Chapter 14

1  *Du développement des idées révolutionnaires en Russie*, in A. I. Gertsen [Herzen], *Sobranie sochinenii v tridtsati tomakh* (Moscow: Izdatel'stvo Akademii nauk SSSR, 1954–65; hereafter *SS*), vol. 7, p. 125 (my translation). All subsequent page references to this work in the text of this chapter, which will appear in parentheses,

will be to this edition. The work was written in 1850, in Russian, and was first published in German translation and then in French (ibid., pp. 412–13). It is sometimes described as a pamphlet.
2  'La Russie', in Herzen, *SS*, vol. 6, pp. 150–86; 'Lettre d'un russe à Mazzini', ibid., pp. 224–30; 'Le peuple russe et le socialisme', ibid., vol. 7, pp. 271–306; 'La Russie et le vieux monde', ibid., vol. 12, pp. 134–66.
3  *Pis'ma iz Frantsii i Italii*, in Herzen, *SS*, vol. 5, pp. 7–224, and *S togo berega*, in vol. 6, pp. 7–142. The latter work has been translated into English, together with one of the essays in the other cycle I have mentioned: see the entry on Herzen in the further reading recommended at the end of the chapter.
4  I. Berlin, *Russian Thinkers*, ed. Henry Hardy and Aileen Kelly, 2nd edn (London: Penguin Books, 2008); and A. M. Kelly, *Views from the Other Shore: Essays on Herzen, Chekhov, and Bakhtin* (New Haven and London: Yale University Press, 1999).
5  This chapter, though, was little more than an extended quotation from his recently published collection of essays *From the Other Shore*.
6  That is, Peter the Great, sole ruler from 1696 to 1725.
7  Subsequent editions of Herzen's book are preceded by an introduction dated 1 August 1853. By that time Herzen had taken refuge in London, following the *coup d'état* of December 1851 by which Louis-Napoleon extended his rule in France and following, too, a series of personal catastrophes for Herzen.
8  Herzen, *SS*, vol. 5, pp. 154–5.
9  On the Petrashevskii circles, see especially J. H. Seddon, *The Petrashevtsy: A Study of the Russian Revolutionaries of 1848* (Manchester: Manchester University Press, 1985). On the young Dostoevskii's involvement in these circles, see Joseph Frank, *Dostoevsky: The Seeds of Revolt 1821–1849* (Princeton: Princeton University Press, 1976), pp. 239–91.
10  The view of Peter as a ruler who effected a cultural revolution is put forward by James Cracraft in his book *The Revolution of Peter the Great* (Cambridge, MA, and London: Harvard University Press, 2003).
11  Herzen, *SS*, vol. 6, pp. 31, 58, 137, 140–1.
12  See the work by Acton cited in the Further Reading section.

# Chapter 15

1  Introduction, *Socialism and Political Struggle* (1883). All Plekhanov's major texts can be found in the Marxists Internet Archive at http://www.marxists.org/archive/plekhanov/index.htm.
2  Introduction, *Socialism and Political Struggle*. Emphases added.
3  Ironically, the terrorist attempt did contribute eventually to the demise of tsarism. The repression that dominated autocratic political strategy after 1881 alienated

society, stood in the way of political reform and meant an inflexible state was trying to contain the pressures of an evolving, industrializing society.
4 As late as the 1970s and 1980s the slogan was used as a description of the Soviet Communist Party.
5 Stepan Razin was the Cossack leader of a very violent peasant rebellion in South Russia in 1670–1. Razin was captured and barbarically executed in Moscow.
6 Plekhanov's emphases.
7 In the words of one historian, Plekhanov 'denounced terrorism as a rash and impetuous movement, which would drain the energy of the revolutionists and provoke a government repression so severe as to make any agitation among the masses impossible'. L. Haimson, *The Russian Marxists and the Origins of Bolshevism* (Boston: Beacon Press, 1966), p. 37.
8 For example, the Rules of the First International, which Marx and others had drawn up, stated that 'the emancipation of the working classes must be conquered by the working classes themselves'. See: https://www.marxists.org/archive/marx/iwma/documents/1864/rules.htm. In his *Critique of the Gotha Programme* (1875) Marx misquoted the rules in a form which has become more familiar than the original, saying: 'The emancipation of the working class must be the act of the workers themselves.' https://www.marxists.org/archive/marx/works/1875/gotha/ch01.htm.
9 The terms narodnik and narodism are interchangeable with populist and populism, the latter two being used more widely today. However, the former versions are used by Plekhanov's translator and are closer to Plekhanov's own terminology so I have used them extensively here.
10 J. D. White in *Lenin* (London, 2001), pp. 44–5 discusses this intriguing possibility. There was also a conservative tendency in Russia, slavophilism, which also argued that Russia had its own path of development, unbeholden to other great powers. This idea still has resonance in Putin's Russia.
11 Marx died on 14 March 1883 and Plekhanov completed writing *Socialism and Political Struggle* on 25 October 1883.
12 For example, the definitive biography of Plekhanov in English, written by Samuel Baron, is entitled *Plekhanov: The Father of Russian Marxism* (London and Stanford: Stanford University Press,1963). Baron also edited *Plekhanov in Russian History and Soviet Historiography* (Pittsburgh: University of Pittsburgh Press, 1995). Relatively few other historians have focused on Plekhanov. Two significant exceptions are: L. Kolakowski, *Main Currents of Marxism*, Book 2, ch. xiv, pp. 620–39 (one volume edition) (New York and London: W. W. Norton and Company, 2005); and D. McLellan, *Marxism after Marx* 4th Rev. Edn (Basingstoke: Palgrave Macmillan, 2007).
13 The full quote is: 'But I know that recently in some rural assemblies the voices have been heard of people carried away by senseless daydreams of

the representatives of the *zemstvos* participating in the business of domestic administration. Let all be appraised that I, dedicating all My efforts to the well-being of the people, shall preserve the principle of autocracy as firmly and steadfastly, as it was preserved by My unforgettable late Parent.'

14  V. I. Lenin, 'What the "Friends of the People" Are and How They Fight the Social-Democrats: A Reply to Articles in *Russkoye Bogatstvo* Opposing the Marxists', in *Collected Works*, vol. 1, available at http://www.marxists.org/archive/lenin/works/1894/friends/index.htm and 'The Heritage We Renounce', ibid., vol. 2, http://www.marxists.org/archive/lenin/works/1897/dec/31c.htm.

15  For a discussion of *What Is to Be Done?* from this point of view see Christopher Read *Lenin: A Revolutionary Life* (London and New York: Routledge, 2005), pp. 51–9; and Neil Harding, *Lenin's Political Thought* (London: Macmillan, 1977), vol. 1, ch. 7, which is significantly entitled 'The Reaffirmation of Orthodoxy'.

# Chapter 16

1  Lars T. Lih, 'How a Founding Document was Found, or One Hundred Years of Lenin's *What Is to be Done?*', *Kritika* 4, no. 1 (Winter 2003): 1–45. For an extended critique of the standard 'worry about workers' interpretation, see Lih, *Lenin Rediscovered* (Chicago: Haymarket Books, 2009); this book contains a new translation of *What Is to Be Done?*, and the passage analysed here can be found on pp. 770–1.

2  Konstantin Dushenko, *Tsitaty iz russkoi istorii : spravochnik : 2200 tsitat ot prizvaniia variagov do nashikh dneĭ* (Moscow: EKSMO, 2006).

3  The phrase 'worry about workers' is taken from Reginald Zelnik, 'Worry about Workers: Concerns of the Russian Intelligentsia from the 1870s to *What Is to Be Done?*', in *Extending the Borders of Russian History*, ed. Marsha Seifert (Budapest: Central European University Press, 2003).

4  An excellent performance of Prokofiev's Cantata conducted by Gennady Rozhdestvensky can be found on Chandos CD 9095; performances of the Cantata can also be found on YouTube.

5  Lih, *Lenin Rediscovered*, p. 13.

6  For example, see Leopold Haimson, 'Lenin's Revolutionary Career Revisited', *Kritika* 5, no. 1 (Winter, 2004): 57–9.

7  In my translation of *What Is to Be Done?*, I avoided these difficulties by retaining the Russian word. In this shorter translation, I have used 'elemental' and 'elementality'. For a full discussion of the meaning of *stikhiinost*, see Lih, *Lenin Rediscovered*, pp. 616–28.

8  For example, in a Menshevik comment from April 1917, we read that Lenin is dangerous because 'he can recruit new supporters from among the revolution's

unconscious and spontaneous [*stikhiinye*] elements': Michael Hickey, *Competing Voices from the Russian Revolution* (Santa Barbara, CA: Greenwood, 2011), p. 115.
9  The word and its exalted overtones are used in an ironic way in one version of a well-known prison-camp song by Yuz Aleshkovsky: 'Tov. Stalin, vy bol'shoi uchenyi, V iazykoznanii prosto korifei' (Com. Stalin, you are a great scholar, a really great leader in linguistics). One of Stalin's last writings was *Marxism and Linguistics* (1950).
10  Lenin, PSS 38:215; CW 29:224–5 (March 1919).

## Chapter 17

1  Peter Kropotkin, 'Modern Science and Anarchism', in *Kropotkin's Revolutionary Pamphlets*, ed. Roger N. Baldwin [1901] (New York: Dover, 1970), pp. 150, 153, 157, 188. In-text references are to this edition.
2  General histories of anarchism include those by George Woodcock, *Anarchism: A History of Libertarian Ideas and Movements* (Harmondsworth: Penguin, 1975); James Joll, *The Anarchists*, 2nd edn (London: Methuen, 1979); and Peter Marshall, *Demanding the Impossible: A History of Anarchism* (London: Fontana, 1992).
3  The origin and meaning of this phrase is discussed by A. G. N. Flew, *Evolutionary Ethics* (London: Macmillan, 1967), pp. 13–15.
4  Peter Kropotkin, *Mutual Aid: A Factor of Evolution* [1902] (Harmondsworth, Penguin, 1939). See also Kropotkin, *Ethics: Origin and Development*, trans. Louis S. Friedland and Joseph R. Piroshnikoff [1924] (Dorchester: Prism, n.d.)
5  Kropotkin, *Mutual Aid*, p. 14.
6  Martin A. Miller, *Kropotkin* (Chicago and London: University of Chicago Press, 1976), pp. 149–50, 174–5.
7  See the idea of 'value pluralism' sketched, for example, by Isaiah Berlin, *Liberty*, ed. Henry Hardy (Oxford: Oxford University Press, 2002), pp. 212–17.
8  Stuart Hampshire, *Innocence and Experience* (Cambridge, MA: Harvard University Press, 1989), pp. 60–1.
9  John Locke, *Two Treatises of Government* [1689], ed. Peter Laslett (Cambridge: Cambridge University Press, 1970), Bk. II, ch. 2.

## Chapter 18

1  Liu Shao-chi, *How to Be a Good Communist* (Peking: Foreign Languages Press, 1951), pp. 8–9 and 12–13. Page numbers in parentheses hereafter.
2  Howard L. Boorman, 'How to be a Good Communist: The Political Ethics of Liu Shao-Ch'I', *Asian Survey* 3, no. 8 (1963): 374–6.

3   Lowell Dittmer, *Liu Shaoqi and the Chinese Cultural Revolution* (Armonk, NY and London: ME Sharpe, 1998), pp. 127–30 and 283–8.
4   Dittmer, *Liu Shaoqi*, pp. 8–18.
5   Mark Selden, *The Yenan way in Revolutionary China* (Cambridge, MA: Harvard University Press, 1971), pp. 188–200.
6   Communist Party of China, *Mao's China: Party Reform Documents, 1942-46*, trans. and intro. Boyd Compton (Seattle: University of Washington Press, 1952), pp. x, xlii and xxxviii–xxxiv.
7   David S. Nivison, 'Communist Ethics and Chinese Tradition,' *The Journal of Asian Studies* 16, no. 1 (1956): 58.
8   *Party Reform Documents*, pp. xvi–xxix.
9   Dittmer, *Liu Shaoqi*, p. 285; and *Party Reform Documents*, pp. xlv.
10  Gong Wenxiang, 'The legacy of Confucian culture in Maoist China,' *The Social Science Journal* 26, no. 4, (1989): 365–6; Cheng Yinghong, *Creating the 'New Man': From Enlightenment Ideals to Socialist Realities* (Honolulu: University of Hawaii Press, 2009), pp. 57–8; and David S. Nivison, *The Ways of Confucianism: investigations in Chinese philosophy* (Chicago: Open Court, 1996), pp. 252–3.
11  Teemu Ruskola, 'Law, Sexual Morality, and Gender Equality in Qing and Communist China,' *Yale Law Journal* 103 (1993): 2539–40.
12  Chen Weigang, *Confucian Marxism: A Reflection on Religion and Global Justice* (Leiden and Boston: Brill, 2014), pp. 187–9.
13  Norman Stockman, *Understanding Chinese Society* (Malden, MA: Polity Press, 2000), pp. 70–6, 81, 91 and 151.
14  Nivison, 'Communist Ethics', pp. 58–60.
15  Boorman, 'Good Communist', pp. 381–2.

# Chapter 19

1   The translation of the speech is taken from John K. Leung and Michael Y. M. Kau (eds), *The Writings of Mao Zedong, 1949-1976. Volume II, January 1956 – December 1957* (Armonk: M.E. Sharpe, 1992), pp. 43–66.
2   The document was circulated as Central Document (65) 751 on 27 December 1965, see Zhonggong zhongyang wenxian yanjiushi (ed.), *Jianguo yilai Mao Zedong wengao* [Mao Zedong's Post-1949 Manuscripts], vol. 11 (Beijing: Zhongyang wenxian chubanshe, 1996), p. 490. A reprint of page 1 from the Central Archives may be found in Zhongyang dang'an guan (ed.), *Zhongguo gongchandang bashi nian zhengui dang'an* [Precious archival materials from 80 years of Communist Party history], vol. 2 (Beijing: Zhongguo dang'an chubanshe, 2001), p. 1058.

3   Zhonggong zhongyang wenxian yanjiushi (ed.), *Jianguo yilai Mao Zedong wengao* [Mao Zedong's Post-1949 Manuscripts], vol. 6 (Beijing: Zhongyang wenxian chubanshe, 1992), p. 105.
4   For this argument see Stuart Schram, 'Chairman Hua edits Mao's Literary Heritage: "On the 10 Great Relationships"', *The China Quarterly* 69 (March 1977): 126–35.
5   The policy line of achieving 'greater, faster, better, and more economical results' was officially repudiated as part of the Great Leap policies in the early reform era.
6   See *Xuexi wenjian* [Study documents], 4 vols (n.p.: 1967), pp. 114–33.
7   The immediate context of the speech included mediating between two bureaucratic interest groups: see David Bachman, *Bureaucracy, economy, and leadership in China. The institutional origins of the Great Leap Forward* (Cambridge: Cambridge University Press 1991), p. 173f.
8   On the introduction of the term in Chinese discourse see Daniel Leese, "'Revolution'. Conceptualizing Political and Social Change in the Late Qing Dynasty", *Oriens Extremus* 51 (2012): 25–61.
9   Compare Cao Yingwang, 'Zhou Enlai yu Mao Zedong de "Lun shi da guanxi"' [The 'Ten Major Relationships' of Zhou Enlai and Mao Zedong], *Zhonggong dangshi yanjiu* 1 (1998): 54–60, which emphasizes Zhou Enlai's intellectual contributions to the speech.
10  This statement is taken from the 1981 resolution on party history, see 'Resolution on Certain Questions in the History of our Party since the Founding of the People's Republic of China', *Beijing Review* 27 (1981): 17.
11  On Jiang Zemin's twelve major relationships, see Jiang Zemin, "Zhengque chuli shehui zhuyi xiandaihua jianshe zhong de ruogan zhongda guanxi" [Correctly Deal With the Crucially Important Relations in the Construction of Socialist Modernization], in *Jiang Zemin wenxuan* [Jiang Zemin's Works], vol. 1 (Beijing: Renmin chubanshe, 2006), pp. 460–75.

# Chapter 20

1   Frantz Fanon, *The Wretched of the Earth*, trans. Constance Farrington with a preface by Jean-Paul Sartre (New York: Grove Press, 1963), pp. 245–6. Originally under the title *Les damnés de la terre* (Paris: François Maspero Ed., 1961). Page references to this edition will be given in parentheses throughout the text of this essay.
2   Michael Burawoy, 'Colonialism and Revolution, Fanon meets Bourdieu', http://burawoy.berkeley.edu/Bourdieu/5.Fanon.pdf (accessed 28 June 2014), p. 3.
3   See Alice Cherki, *Frantz Fanon: A portrait* (Paris: Seuil, 2000; Ithaca: Cornell University Press, 2006).

4  Zia Sardar, 'On Frantz Fanon', *Naked Punch Review*, 9 August 2011, http://www.nakedpunch.com/articles/47 (accessed 28 July 2014).
5  See Max Silverman, 'Frantz Fanon: Colonialism and Violence', in *Postcolonial Thought in the French-Speaking World*, ed. Charles Forsdick and David Murphy (Liverpool: Liverpool University Press, 2009), particularly pp. 86–9.
6  Matthieu Renault, *Frantz Fanon: De l'Anticolonialisme à la Critique Postcoloniale* (Paris: Editions Amsterdam, 2011), Introduction. It has been pointed out that postcolonial studies have put too much focus on using Fanon to understand current fights against inequalities, oppression and domination, at the risk of de-contextualizing the man and his writings. Here, Matthieu Renault has, rightly, highlighted that it is now necessary to go beyond the conflict of interpretations which presented a simple opposition between the 'anti-colonial Fanon' (historical) and the 'postcolonial-discourse Fanon', beyond a past and a future that deprive Fanon of any present.
7  See for instance, Albert Memmi, *The Colonizer and the Colonized* (translated from French *Portrait du Colonisé précédé du Portrait du Colonisateur*, Preface: Jean-Paul Sartre, Paris, 1957; London: Earthscan Ltd, 1990). Both Fanon's *Wretched* and Memmi's *Colonizer* original texts had a preface by Jean-Paul Sartre.
8  Pal Ahluwalia, *Out of Africa: Post-structuralism's Colonial Roots* (New York: Routledge, 2010), p. 54.
9  Grant Farred, 'Wretchedness', in *Living Fanon: Global Perspectives*, ed. Nigel C. Gibson (Basingstoke: Palgrave Macmillan, 2011), p. 160.
10  This last part is too often obliterated in scholars' commentaries, which focus perhaps too much on the first part of the process of Fanon's exploration of violence.

# Chapter 21

1  For an English translation, see: *Speech by the Chairman of the Delegation of the People's Republic of China, Teng Hsiao-ping, at the Special Session of the U.N. General Assembly (10 April 1974)* (Beijing: Foreign Language Press, 1974), pp. 2–3.
2  United Nations, General Assembly Official Records: Sixth Special Session Supplement No. 1 (A/9559), 3201 (S-VI) A/9556 and 3202 (S-VI) A/9556.
3  Mark Mazower, *Governing the World: The History of an Idea* (London: Allen Lane, 2012), pp. 244–72. On the New Economic Order see: Ibid., pp. 299–304.
4  Ezra F. Vogel, *Deng Xiaoping and the Transformation of China* (Cambridge, MA: The Belknap Press of Harvard University Press, 2011), pp. 83–7.
5  Ibid., p. 84.

6 Alexander C. Cook, 'Third World Maoism', in *A Critical Introduction to Mao*, ed. Timothy Cheek (Cambridge: Cambridge University Press, 2010), pp. 288–312, p. 297; Odd Arne Westad, 'Epilogue: The Cold War and the Third World', in *The Cold War in the Third World*, ed. Robert J. McMahon (Oxford: Oxford University Press, 2013), pp. 208–19, p. 216.

7 Christoph Kalter, 'A Shared Space of Imagination, Communication, and Action: Perspectives on the History of the "Third World"', in *The Third World in the Global 1960s*, ed. Samantha Christiansen and Zachary A. Scarlett (New York: Berghahn Books, 2013), pp. 23–38, 25.

8 Westad, 'Epilogue', pp. 208–19.

9 'Premier Chou Enlai's Main Speech at the Plenary Session of the Asian-African Conference, April 19, 1955', in *China Supports the Arab People's Struggle for National Independence: A Selection of Important Documents*, ed. Chinese People's Institute of Foreign Affairs (Beijing: Foreign Languages Press, 1958), pp. 9–19. On the Intermediate and Two Intermediate Zones see Chen Jian, 'China, the Third World, and the Cold War', in *The Cold War in the Third World*, ed. Robert J. McMahon (Oxford: Oxford University Press, 2013), pp. 85–100.

10 The first quotation is taken from the article 'Vice-premier Teng Hsiao-ping heads Chinese delegation to special session of U.N. General Assembly'; the second is taken from the article 'Resolute support for the Third World's just demands', both in *Peking Review* 17, no. 15 (12 April 1974): 5 and 8. Original documentary footage of the Chinese delegation at Beijing airport can be accessed at: http://mirc.sc.edu/islandora/object/usc%3A2089 [accessed 29 December 2013].

11 See Jeremy S. Friedman, 'Reviving Revolution: The Sino-Soviet Split, the "Third World", and the Fate of the Left', PhD-diss. Princeton, 2011, p. 287.

12 Friedman, 'Reviving the Revolution', p. 313; and Chen Jian, 'China, the Third World, and the Cold War', p. 86.

13 Arif Dirlik, 'Spectres of the Third World: Global Modernity and the End of the Three Worlds', *Third World Quarterly* 25, no. 1 (2008): 131–48.

# Index

Adams, John 57, 188n. 6
Addison, Joseph 34
*The Agreement of the People* 3–4, 7, 11–17, 183n. 1
Alexander II 126
Alexander III 126, 130
Algerian National Liberation Front (FLN) 168
American Declaration of Independence 6, 53–60, 61, 78, 79, 81
American Revolution of 1776 43, 60, 61, 69, 189n. 4
'amour de soi-même' 47
'amour propre', *see* egotism
anarchism 141, 142, 143–4, 145, 146, 148
Angolan Civil War of 1975 180
Archon, Lord (*Oceana*) 21, 23
aristocracy 20, 22, 24–5, 78, 80
Aristotle 20
  *Politics* 20
Astell, Mary 34
Aubrey, John 21, 185n. 6
Axelrod, Pavel 130, 135

Bakunin, Mikhail 122–3, 129
Bandung Conference 173, 178
Barthélémy, Jean-Jacques 43
  *Voyage du jeune Anacharsis en Grèce* 43
Berlin, Isaiah 114, 119, 194n. 7, 195n. 4
Black Power Movement 168
*bogatyr* 139
Bolsheviks 129, 130, 131, 137, 146–7, 154
Bonaparte, Napoléon 103
Boorman, Howard L. 155, 157, 199n. 15
Bourbon monarchy 38, 39, 40, 42, 120
bourgeoisie 33, 110, 113, 114, 119, 123, 170, 171, 172
Boyer, Jean-Pierre 105, 107

Burke, Edmund 28, 87, 89, 190n. 2, 191n. 10
  *Reflections on the Revolution in France* 87, 89

Cambridge School of political thought 3
capitalism 110, 115, 119, 123, 129, 142, 143, 171, 175, 178
Castro, Fidel 173
Césaire, Aimé 168
Chaadaev, Petr 122
Charles I 12, 14, 21, 31, 32
Charles II 30
China 7, 152, 153, 154–5, 157, 160, 161–2, 163, 164, 176, 177, 179, 180, 181
Chinese Civil War 152
Chinese Communist Party's (CCP's) 152, 154, 155, 157, 159, 160, 162, 163, 178
Christophe, Henry 107
civil war 12, 15, 31, 38, 40, 66, 67, 107
Claeys, Gregory 5, 85, 190n. 1
Coercive and Quebec Acts 55
Columbus, Christopher 107–8
*communauté des biens* 40, 43
*The Communist Manifesto* 5, 110, 194n. 4
  fascination of 112
  importance of 111–12
  purpose of 112
  as revolutionary text 115–16
  rhythm and intensity of 114
Confucius 151, 153, 155, 156, 157
  *Analects* 155
*Conjuration des Egaux* 43
Continental Congress 54, 63
Cordeliers 97
Cromwell, Oliver 20, 42
Crowder, George 6, 141
Cultural Revolution 33, 152, 153, 157, 160, 161, 165, 177, 179, 180

Danton, Georges   98, 99, 193n. 13
Darwin, Charles   144–5, 147, 148
Darwinism   141, 143, 144, 145
Decembrist Revolt of 1825   120
Declaration of Independence, *see* American Declaration of Independence; Haitian Declaration of Independence
Declaration of the Rights of Man and of the Citizen   5, 77–83, 87, 88, 89, 190n. 6
'Declaration on the Establishment of a New International Economic Order' (NIEO)   176
democracy   23, 24–5, 113, 123, 135, 138, 166, 185n. 8
Deng Xiaoping   2, 153, 161, 164–5, 175, 176, 177, 179, 180–1
*De officio hominis et civis* (*Les devoirs de l' homme et du citoyen*)   42
Desmoulins, Camille   97, 98
Dessalines, Jean-Jacques   102–3, 104–5, 106–7, 108, 193n. 7
Deutsch, Lev   130
Dickinson, John   87
Diderot, Denis   46
Dimitrov, Georgi   155
Drake, Judith   34, 186n. 7
Dumont, Etienne   46, 187n. 2
Dumouriez, Charles François   98

egotism   47
*Encyclopédie*   46
Engels, Friedrich   5, 6, 7, 8, 109, 110, 111–12, 113, 114, 119
English Revolution   2, 7, 19, 41
equality   3, 4, 16, 17, 60, 88, 89, 90, 96, 185n. 12
  political equality   16, 88
  principle of equality   16

Fabre d'Églantine, Philippe-François-Nazaire   98
Fanon, Frantz   6, 8, 167, 168, 169, 174, 200n. 1, 201n. 6
  *Black Skin, White Masks*   168
  on colonial domination   170, 172
  crucial themes of   170–1
  *A Dying Colonialism*   168
  on national struggle   170
  Third Worldism   172–3
  on tribalism   171, 173
  *The Wretched of the Earth*   167, 168, 169, 173–4, 200n. 1
Farred, Grant   172, 201n. 9
*Federalist Papers*   4, 61–2, 64, 65, 66, 67
Ferrer, Ada   107, 194n. 10
Fink, Zera   20
'Five Principles of Peaceful Co-existence'   178–9
Fourier, Charles   121
Fourierism   90
Foxley, Rachel   3, 5, 7
freedom of opinion   82–3
freedom of speech   28, 30
freedom of worship   28, 29–30, 34
French Declaration, *see* Declaration of the Rights of Man and of the Citizen
French National Convention   103
French Revolution   5, 6, 7, 9, 16, 28, 31, 39, 43, 45, 49, 69, 86, 87, 88, 93, 95, 98, 100, 120, 146, 171
Friedman, Jeremy   181, 202n. 12

Gaffield, Julia   3, 5, 7–8, 101, 193n. 6
Galilei, Galileo   142
Garraway, Doris   107, 108, 194n. 12
Geneva   46, 50, 69, 74
George III   54, 55, 56, 79
Glorious Revolution   28, 30, 33, 34, 40, 53
Godwin, William   146
Gogol, Nikolai   122
  *Dead Souls*   122
Gould, Eliga   106, 194n. 8
Granovskii, Timofei   123
Green Revolution   1
Grigorovich, Dmitrii   122
  *Anton the Unfortunate*   122
Guégan, Xavier   6, 167
Guizot, François   119
Guofeng, Hua   161

Habermas, Jürgen   33, 186n. 6
Haitian Declaration of Independence   101, 102, 103–4, 105, 107, 108
Haitian Revolution   102, 103, 107

Hamilton, Alexander   4, 61, 62, 64, 65, 66, 67, 188n. 1
Hammersley, Rachel   xiv, 42, 185n. 10, 186n. 3
  *The English Republican Tradition and Eighteenth-Century France: Between the Ancients and the Moderns*   42, 186n. 3
Hardy, Thomas   86, 191n. 3
Harrington, James   4, 19, 20–1, 22, 184n. 1, 185nn. 8, 12
  agrarian law   22–3
  *Aphorisms Political*   24
  *The Commonwealth of Oceana*   4, 19, 21, 22, 23, 24, 184n. 1, 185n. 12
  democracy   23–4
  *An Essay upon the Constitution of the Roman Government*   20, 184n. 4
  *A Model of a Democratical Government*   24
  *The Prerogative of Popular Government*   24
  revolutionary credentials   25
  treatment of aristocracy   22
Hegel, Georg Wilhelm Friedrich   144
Herzen, Alexander   3, 6, 7, 118–19, 120, 121, 122–4
  *From the Other Shore*   118, 121, 195n. 5
  'The Letter of a Russian to Mazzini'   118
  *Letters from France and Italy*   118, 120
  *On the Development of Revolutionary Ideas in Russia*   3, 117–24
  'Russia and the Old World'   118
  'The Russian People and Socialism'   118
  'Russian socialism'   118
Hobbes, Thomas   4, 14, 25, 30, 39, 48
Ho Chi Minh   80–1
Hogarth, William   34
  *The Harlot's Progress*   34
House of Commons   13–14, 66
Howlett, Jonathan J.   4, 6, 151
human rights   5, 16, 60, 80, 86–7, 91, 92, 191n. 5
Hume, David   49, 147, 187n. 5
  Hume's law   147
  'Of Civil Liberty'   49

Hungarian Revolt   118
Hunt, Lynn   4, 5, 7–8, 190n. 1
Hu Qiaomu   161

Ignatov, Vasili   130
Indulgents   97, 98, 99
Ireton, Henry   14
*Iskra*   135, 136
Israel, Jonathan   88, 191n. 12

Jacobin Committee of Public Safety   146
Jacobins   43, 97, 98, 99, 100, 120, 121, 123
James II   28, 34
Jay, John   4, 61, 62, 67
Jefferson, Thomas   53, 54–6, 57, 59, 60, 188n. 1
Jews, political rights to   81–2
Jian, Chen   181
Jiang Zemin   165–6, 200n. 11
Jones, Gareth Stedman   110, 194n. 2
Jourdan, Annie   99, 193n. 14

Kant, Immanuel   74–5
Kelly, Aileen   119, 195n. 4
Khrushchev, Nikita   160, 162
Knights, Mark   5, 27
Kol'tsov, Aleksei   122
*korifei*   138
Kropotkin, Peter   3, 6, 8, 142–4, 145, 146, 147, 148, 198n. 1
  *Modern Science and Anarchism*   3, 143, 145
*kustar*   138
*kustarnichestvo*   137–8

Lavrov, Peter   127
Leclerc, Victor Emmanuel   103
Leese, Daniel   6, 159, 200n. 8
Lenin, Vladimir   2, 3, 4, 5, 7, 130, 133–4, 135, 136, 137, 138–40, 157, 165
  *State and Revolution*   165
  *What Is to Be Done?*   2, 3, 130, 134–5, 136, 137, 139–40, 197nn. 1, 14
'le tiers monde', see Third World
Levellers   3, 4, 5, 7, 12, 13, 14, 15, 16
Lih, Lars   3, 4, 5, 7, 133
Lilburne, John   15, 184n. 7
Lincoln, Abraham   54, 59
Linton, Marisa   5, 93, 192n. 9

Liu Shaoqi 4, 8, 151, 152, 153–4, 155–6, 157, 160, 161, 164, 198n. 1
  *How to Be a Good Communist* 4, 151, 152, 153, 154, 157, 198n. 1
Locke, John 29, 87, 88, 148, 198n. 9
  *Two Treatises* of 1690 29
'Long March' 154
Louis XVI 70, 98
Louis-Philippe 119, 120
Louverture, Toussaint 103
Lu Xun 162
  *The True Story of Ah Q* 159, 162

Mably, Gabriel Bonnot de 4, 6, 8, 38, 39, 41, 42, 43, 186n. 1, 187n. 5
  *Des droits et des devoirs du citoyen* 37, 38, 39, 40, 42, 43, 186n. 1
  *Observations sur l' histoire de France* 38–9
  'On the principles of political morality' 95
Madison, James 4, 61, 62, 63, 65, 67
Mandeville, Bernard 49
  'The Fable of the Bees' 49, 187n. 6
Manley, Delarivier 34
Mao Zedong 8, 152, 153, 154, 157, 159, 160–6, 176, 177, 178, 179, 180
  *Little Red Book* 180
  'On the Ten Major Relationships' 159, 165–6
Martin, Jean-Clément 99, 193n. 4
Martynov, Aleksandr 136
Marx, Karl 1, 5, 6, 7, 8, 110, 112, 113–16, 119, 128, 129, 144, 194n. 4, 196n. 8
  *The German Ideology* 113
Marxism 1, 126, 127, 129, 130, 142, 144, 147, 152, 154, 156, 164, 196n. 12
Memmi, Albert 168, 172, 201n. 7
Mencius 151, 153, 154, 156
Menshevik 129, 130, 197n. 8
Miller, William 90
Ming, Wang 163
monarchy 20, 21, 22, 24–5, 38, 39, 70, 78, 80, 82, 94
Montesquieu, Charles-Louis de Secondat, baron de 96, 192n. 6

More, Thomas 43
Moyle, Walter 20, 184n. 4
Murav'ev, Nikita 120

narodism 128, 129, 130, 196n. 9
Narodnaya volya (The People's Will) 126
narodniks 127, 128, 129, 130, 131, 138, 196n. 9
National Convention 94, 103
natural law 87, 89, 148
natural right 4, 16, 43, 79, 86, 87, 89, 187n. 4, 191n. 8
Necker, Jacques 74
Neville, Henry 43
Nicholas I 118, 121
Nicholas II 130
Nivison, David S. 157, 199n. 7
Non-Aligned Movement 173

Occupy movements 1
Offord, Derek 6
Ogarev, Nikolai 121
Orange Revolution 1
Overton, Richard 15
Owenism 90

Paine, Thomas 5, 42, 62, 63, 85, 86, 87, 88–91, 92, 189n. 5, 190n. 1, 191n. 4
  *The Age of Reason* 91, 92
  *Agrarian Justice* 91
  *Common Sense* 42, 62, 63, 87, 189n. 5
  *Rights of Man* 5, 85, 86, 87, 89, 90, 91
Parisian revolution 120, 146
Parkinson, Robert 3, 4, 5, 7–8, 53
*Peking Review* 179, 180
*People's Daily* 152, 160, 161
People's Republic of China (PRC) State Council 152, 176, 180, 181
Pétion, Alexandre 107
Petrashevskii, Mikhail 121, 195n. 9
Pincus, Steve 28, 32, 186n. 2
Plekhanov, George 5, 7, 126–7, 128–9, 130, 131, 137, 138, 196nn. 7, 12
  *Our Differences* 126, 130
  *Socialism and Political Struggle* 126, 129, 195n. 1
Pobedonostsev, Konstantin 126

Pocock, J. G. A.   20, 184n. 1
Polevoi, Nikolai   122
political virtue   96, 100
Popish Plot   31
Popkin, Jeremy   103, 193n. 2
populists, *see* narodniks
*Praktiki*   136, 139, 140
Price, Richard   89, 90
  *Discourse on the Love of Our
    Country*   89
Priestley, Joseph   86, 90
'Programme of Action on the
    Establishment of a New
    International Economic
    Order'   176
Prokofiev, Sergei   134, 197n. 4
  *Cantata for the 20th Anniversary of the
    October Revolution*   134
*A Proposition in Order to the Proposing
    of a Commonwealth or
    Democracy*   24
Proudhon, Pierre-Joseph   112, 113, 114,
    115, 144
  'Philosophy of Misery'   113
Puritan Revolution   28
Pushkin, Aleksandr   122
Putney Debates   12, 14, 17

Qiao Guanhua   176, 177, 180

*Rabochee delo*   135, 136
Read, Christopher   5, 125, 158
Red Guard   161, 162–3
Republic of Virtue   96–7
revolution   1, 94, *see also* American
    Revolution of 1776; Cultural
    Revolution; English Revolution;
    French Revolution; Glorious
    Revolution; Green Revolution;
    Haitian Revolution; Orange
    Revolution; Parisian revolution;
    Puritan Revolution; Rose
    Revolution; Russian Revolution;
    Tulip Revolution; Xinhai
    Revolution
  as collective phenomenon   2
  history of   2, 7–8
  political   38

principles   27–35
textual approach perspective   3
revolutionary cultivation   151–7
*révolution ménagée*   37–43
Revolution of 1688, *see* Glorious
    Revolution
right of resistance   28, 29
Robespierre, Maximilian   5, 8, 93, 94–5,
    100, 192n. 4, 193n. 15
  attitude to violence and terror   98
  depiction of revolution   95–6
  fear of conspiracy   98–9
  on political virtue   96–7
  on terror   97, 99
Rodgers, Tom   4, 61
Rose Revolution   1
Rousseau, Jean-Jacques   2, 4, 7, 8, 17, 38,
    70, 73, 74, 75, 79, 89, 187n. 1,
    189n. 2
  argument on politics   48
  *Considerations on the Government of
    Poland*   75–6
  *Du contrat social*   42
  egotism   47
  *Emile*   48, 50, 70, 189n. 2
  *Second Discourse*   46–7, 50
  *Social Contract*   3, 4, 17, 45, 46, 47–8,
    49, 50, 51, 79, 187n. 7
  sovereignty and government,
    distinguishing between   49–50
  views on France   48–9
Ruskola, Teemu   155, 199n. 11
Russia   3, 7, 117, 118–20, 121–4, 126–9,
    131, 134, 139, 143, 196n. 10
Russian Revolution   1, 6, 127, 128, 138,
    139, 140
Russian Social Democracy   135, 137, 138
Ryleev, Kondratii   122

Sacheverell, Henry   5, 6, 28, 29, 30–5,
    186n. 1
Sartre, Jean-Paul   168, 169, 200n. 1
Sauvy, Alfred   178
Scott, Jonathan   20, 185n. 12
Shakerism   90
Shays's Rebellion   63
Sieyès, Emmanuel-Joseph   2, 4, 8, 69–76,
    189n. 1

*Vues sur les moyens d'exécution dont les représentants de la France pourront disposer en 1789*   72–4
*What Is the Third Estate?*   2, 69, 70, 71–2, 74–5, 76
'Sinification of Marxism'   154–5
Skocpol, Theda   2, 183n. 1
  *States and Social Revolutions*   2
Smith, Adam   143
social imperialism   175–81
sovereignty   13, 14, 15, 17, 49, 63, 65, 71, 73, 75, 78–9
*Spectator*   34
Spencer, Herbert   145, 147
Stanhope, Charles   39, 40
Stanhope, Philip Dormer   39, 40
*stikhiinost* and *stikhiinyi*   136, 137

terror   94, 97–9, 100, 120, 131
Test and Corporation Acts   30
Third World   173, 174, 176, 178, 179, 180, 181
'Three Worlds Theory'   2, 176, 177–8, 180, 181
Tocqueville, Alexis de   88, 191n. 13
Toleration Act   30
Treaty of Basel   105
Truman, Harry   178
Tulip Revolution   1
Turgenev, Ivan   122

Ulyanov, Aleksandr   138, 140
United Nations General Assembly   175, 176, 179, 201n. 2
Universal Declaration of Human Rights   80, 173

Valentinov, N.   134
Venturi, Franco   42, 186n. 2
  *Utopia and Reform in the Enlightenment*   42
virtue   93–100, 192n. 8, *see also* political virtue
Voltaire   38, 46, 47

Weigang, Chen   155, 199n. 12
  *Confucian Marxism*   155, 199n. 12
Weitling, Wilhelm   112, 113, 114
Whatmore, Richard   4, 7, 45
William of Orange   28
Williams, Abraham   87
Wright, Johnson Kent   4, 6, 7, 8, 37
Wright, Julian   5, 109

Xinhai Revolution   162

Zasulich, Vera   130, 135
Zeng Zi   156
Zhengfeng Campaign   152, 153, 154
Zhou Enlai   9, 164, 176, 183n. 4, 200n. 9

www.ingramcontent.com/pod-product-compliance
Lightning Source LLC
Chambersburg PA
CBHW052109300426
44116CB00010B/1600